WinFE
Windows Forensic Environment

Brett Shavers

ISBN:
9798398624267

DEDICATION

To those who find monsters, mad respect.

To my wife, Chikae, for everything is possible with you.

ACKNOWLEDGMENTS

Troy Larson came up with a really cool idea. WinFE is his baby.
I am just an evangelist for WinFE.

With that, creds for Troy, and all those who helped push WinFE to the tool that it is today through development, teaching, and its use.

Some of those named in the WinFE development club: Colin Ramsden , Misty, ChrisR, Royal Meier, B.G.Miller, Erwan.I, Peter Lerup, George M Garner Jr ,Nuno Brito, farad, TheHive, Wonko the Sane (Jaclaz), cdob, Atari800xi, alacran, steve6375, PTADEL0H0, and those many others who have beta tested, provided feedback, written scripts, and continue to help further the capabilities of WinFE.

CONTENTS

Introduction

As a quick introduction to the **Windows Forensics Environment** (WinFE); it is a bootable **forensic operating system** (FOS), based on the **Windows Pre-Installed Environment** (winpe), with a few registry modifications to prevent automounting of hard drives, much like a live Linux FOS.

> As winpe is fully documented by Microsoft, all technical information about winpe is referenced and recommended to you to review. WinFE's divergence from winpe consists simply (yet ingeniously) of registry changes. Windows PE (WinPE) https://docs.microsoft.com/en-us/windows-hardware/manufacture/desktop/winpe-intro

In the beginning....there was the MS DOS forensic floppy boot disk, imaging hard drives at the speed of DOS. An entire 1.44mb of storage space to be had storing all the forensic apps you could squeeze onto it. The life of imaging was wonderful. At least that's what I remember anyway.

Given the loss of floppy drives in computers coupled with the speed of imaging in Windows with hardware write blockers, it was only a short matter of time before DOS boot floppies went the way of the dinosaur. CDs/DVDs followed next. With the hardware imaging devices of advertised speeds over 7GB per minute, imaging through the Windows operating system may have also started down the road to being obsolete. Why would anyone want to image through Windows at 2-3GB/min when you can directly image at over 7GB per minute with a hardware device? You have to look a little closer at WinFE to get the answer.

Understanding the Neatness Factor of Windows Forensic Environment

So here comes WinFE, comparable to many of the forensic Linux operating systems (OS), with one important difference; it's not a Linux OS...it's Windows! This is not a small point because many of your everyday Windows forensics applications can be run on the WinFE FOS whereas with the Linux FOS, you must accept only those applications that run on Linux. Given the vast number of examiners being more proficient with Windows than Linux, the ease to which WinFE can be modified with drivers and software compared with a Linux FOS cannot be overstated. WinFE is easier because of familiarity with Windows.

If you have not yet built a WinFE, be prepared! You will not be able to wait after reading this guide! I stopped tracking the number of downloads of just one of the WinFE building platforms when the downloads broke 10,000. That was in 2015..

Just as important as to the number of downloads of WinFE, just who is using it? Let us start first with who is **teaching** WinFE to get a handle on who is using WinFE. Over the past years, particularly after an easy-to-build was developed using WinBuilder, WinFE has been taught at the Federal Law Enforcement Training Center (FLETC), SEARCH, the High Tech Crimes Investigators Association (HTCIA), the Computer Technology Investigators Network (CTIN), International Association of Chiefs of Police (IACP), the Internet Crimes Against Children Task Force (ICAC), military training programs, and too many colleges and universities to list.

That brings us to who **uses** WinFE. Given the training organizations listed, those trained in WinFE are working in law enforcement (federal, state, local), private forensic companies, electronic discovery firms, and military branches all over the world. WinFE has even been disclosed to be a tool used by US intelligence agencies. WinFE has gained so much traction as a solid forensic tool that it is difficult to find a digital forensics job listing that doesn't list it as desirable experience.

This guide is for you

This guide is intended to be an easy read, but at the same, give you everything you need to build a WinFE, use a WinFE, and defend your use of WinFE if ever needed. This is the *only* and the *most comprehensive* guide ever written on the Windows Forensic Environment. Ever.

Welcome to the WinFE club!

CHAPTER 1: Forensic Booting

Of all the factors involved to decide to forensically boot the evidence machine, the most important question is, 'Can the system **only** be booted to a FOS in order to acquire the electronic data?' If the only way to acquire a device is through a FOS, then your decision is easy: **boot to the FOS**.

However, if you have a choice, you have to make the decision as to which method is best. By "best", I mean *best* as **one reasonable** choice for the situation in front of you at the time. What is reasonable for one scenario may not be reasonable for another, so it is a judgement call based on the totality of the circumstances that you face when approaching any system to be seized.

The focus of this guide

This cheats guide is going to focus on one, and only one method of accessing an evidence media. Figure 1.1 shows the only two options on a computer approach when you need to access the evidence media. The system is either "on" or "off". Of course, it may be *turning* on or *turning* off if you happen upon either of those two states, but regardless, the system will be on or off in seconds if you happen upon one of those active states of activity.

The status of being on or off dictates your options. If the system is on, it may not make much sense to turn it off and then boot to a FOS (or it may, as this depends on the totality of your situation). This guide focuses on booting a system that is **off** to a FOS to either image, triage, or otherwise access the evidence media directly.

IMPORTANT: If you need volatile memory from a computer, the computer must be running (meaning, a forensic boot is inappropriate). If the computer that you need to collect data from is on (operating system is running), you need to decide whether to acquire the system "live" or shutdown the computer to acquire as a "dead box". Consideration factors include known and suspected encryption, as well as evidence that may reside only on a live system.

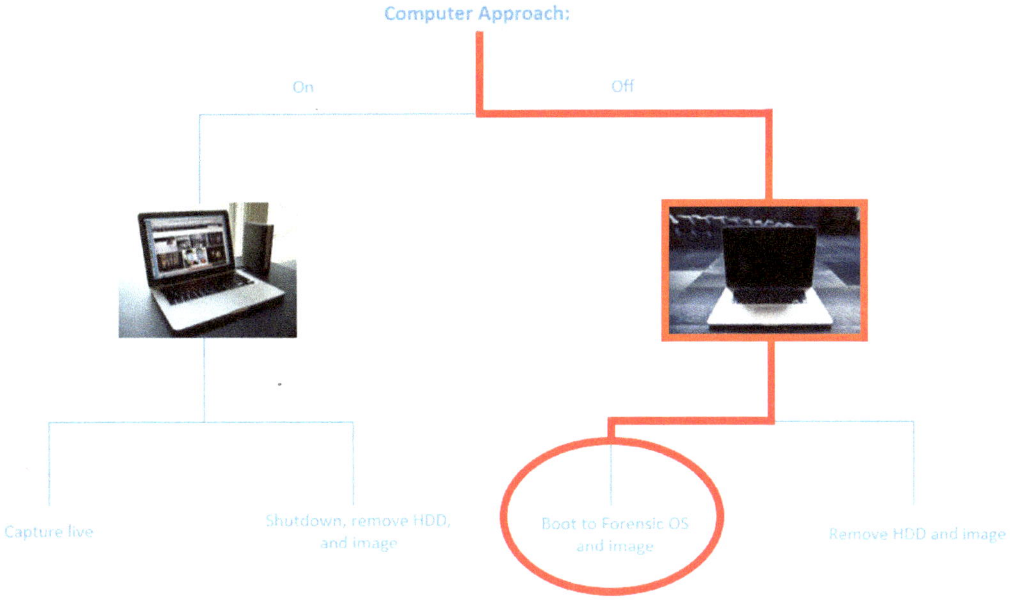

Figure 1.1 Accessing media

Given a computer system that is off, you still have decisions to make in accessing the media. Again, your situation today most likely will be different tomorrow and the next day. Every approach requires going through the same process of deciding how to access the media based on the totality of the circumstances of each machine to be accessed.

To help decide, Figure 1.2 shows an easy decision-making flowchart that you can use for practically any approach to accessing the media from any system that is turned off.

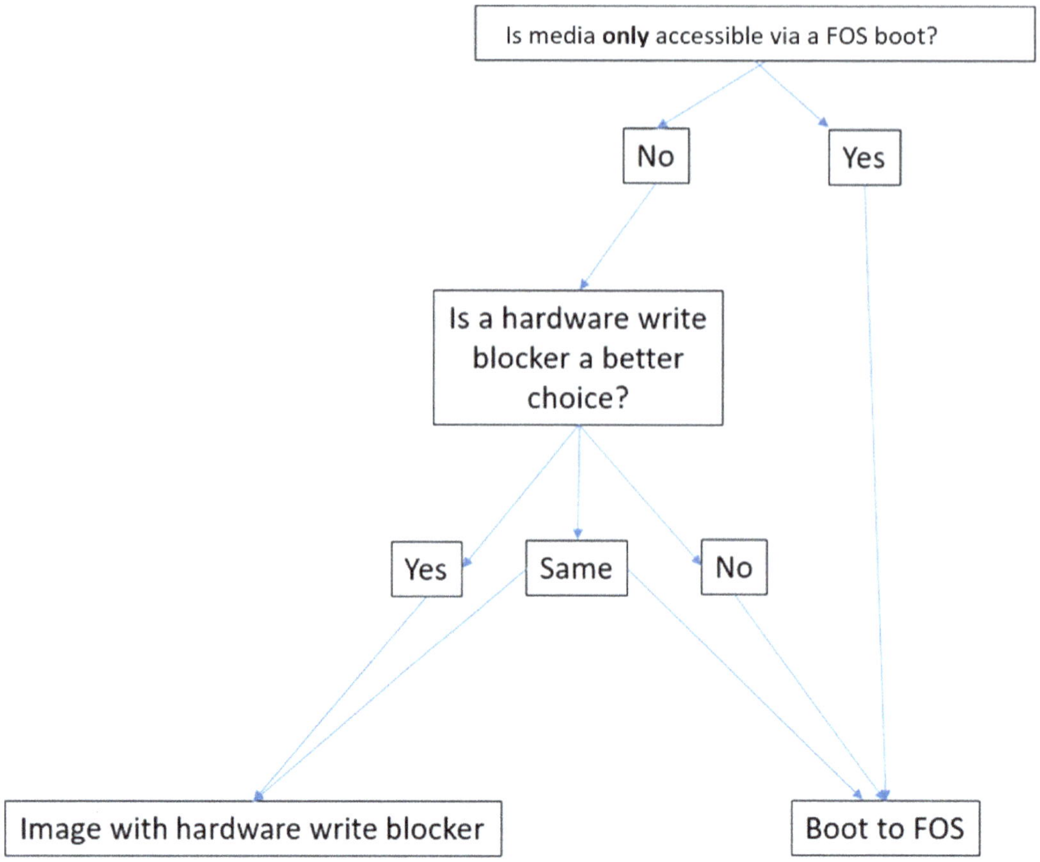

Figure 1.2 To boot or not boot to a FOS

When the system can be booted to a FOS or a hardware write blocker can be used, determining which method is "better" takes in other factors. For example, **time** may be a factor in that if you are short of time to acquire the data, it may be faster to boot to a FOS and immediately create an image rather than spend the time to disassemble the system, remove the hard drive, connect to a hardware write blocker, and use a forensic workstation/laptop to create an image. When multiple systems are involved, it may be faster booting all systems to a FOS with simultaneous imaging instead of one-by-one and sharing a limited supply of hardware write blockers.

Other decision-making factors include the number of personnel available to collect data, the availability of enough write-blocking hardware for all systems, available time, encryption, volatile memory, and personal preferences. Again, every computer system approach has its own factors to consider whether or not to boot to a FOS.

The boot process

Before the operating system runs, the computer goes through a boot (startup) process. The goal of a *forensic* boot is to divert (interrupt) the process before any changes are made to the storage media (hard drive) or the operating system. You should already have a good understanding of the boot process as a basic principle of computer systems, therefore, this is a high level overview rather than a description of all that goes into the booting process.

The intended goal of a computer boot process is to access the media (hard drive) in order to run the OS. Your goal is to interrupt the boot process by diverting it to your forensically sound, bootable media, and run the FOS that is on your media, while at the same time, *write-protecting the evidence media*. Figure 1.3 shows the diversion needed to prevent accessing the evidence media.

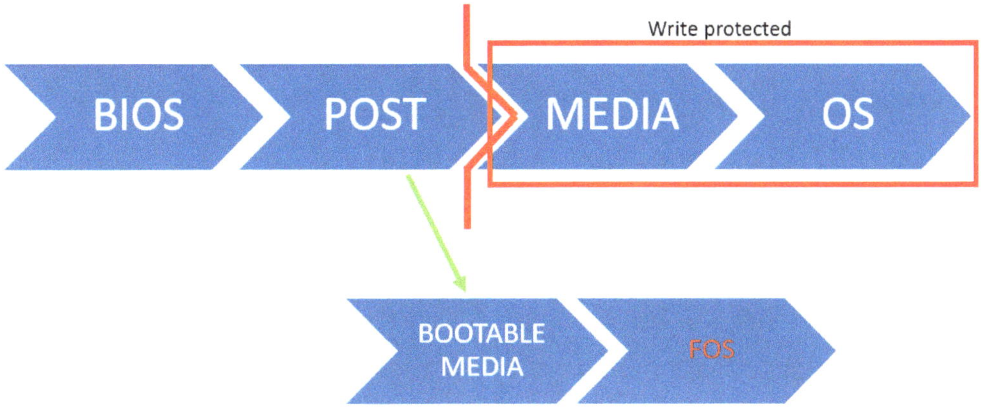

Figure 1.3 Interrupt the boot process!

The Mechanical Aspects

In order to boot a system to a FOS, it must be mechanically able to do so. The system must be able to allow external media connected to it, and be able to be configured to boot to the external media. External media can be anything that the system allows to be booted from, such as a CD, DVD, USB, or external drive.

Rather than guessing if external media is possible to boot the machine, you will need to access the BIOS (Figure 1.4) and ensure that the BIOS is already set to boot to external media or can be configured to do so.

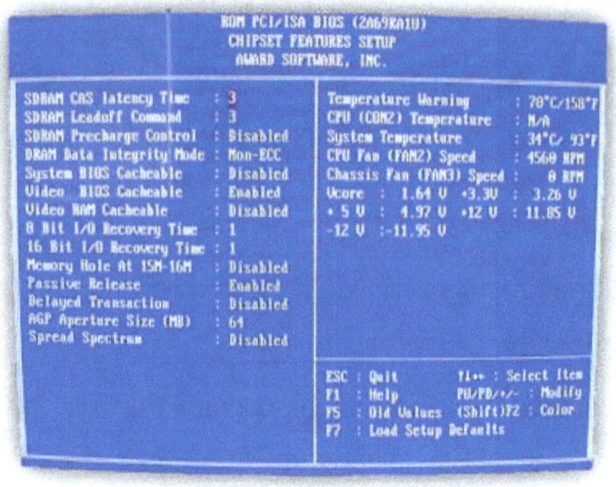

Figure 1.4 BIOS

As to entering the BIOS, this is another factor in which every computer approach will be different and needs focus to decide the correct steps. For example, entering the BIOS of a computer system generally requires pressing one or more keys to interrupt the boot process. There are too many combinations on too many systems to remember the BIOS interrupt keys.

Figure 1.5 shows a sampling of the keys typically used to interrupt the BIOS. Some of the interrupts require pressing one key, others require two. Some interrupts will interrupt to a booting selection screen and others will enter the BIOS settings. Check the keys each and every time on each and every computer you boot, no matter if you remember which key it was the last time on the same (SIMILAR!) machine.

Tip: Don't boot an evidence machine without checking which keys are required to enter the BIOS. Slapping the keyboard repeated in hopes of hitting the right key or combination of keys is a surefire way to boot directly into the evidence media.

It is possible and even likely that the same brand of computer will have different keys to enter the BIOS on different models within the same brand. As an example, there is one ASUS desktop uses F8 to enter the BIOS while another ASUS laptop uses Esc to enter the BIOS. The best method to find which keys are needed is to search the Internet for the keys needed for the exact make and model of the computer system you intend to boot to a FOS. *Apple is different too!*

Figure 1.5 Some of the possible BIOS interrupt keys

Another consideration is that of **which** external media is the computer system going to boot, even after you configure it to boot to your media. You may have WinFE on a USB flash drive, and the flash drive is correctly connected to the system, but it is possible that the boot process skips your USB flash drive. That means your evidence media will be accessed!

There could be any number of reasons that your FOS may be skipped in the boot process, but a solution to reduce the risk of accessing the evidence media is to use multiple FOS external media. If the evidence machine has more than one option for connecting external media, a good safety net is to connect a FOS in each of the media slots. That means potentially a CD/DVD, and multiple USB slots to fill. Older machines, such as seen in Figure 1.6, may have multiple options, while newer machines may have no option other than an extra USB port. If you have the option, use it and you may prevent booting to the evidence media.

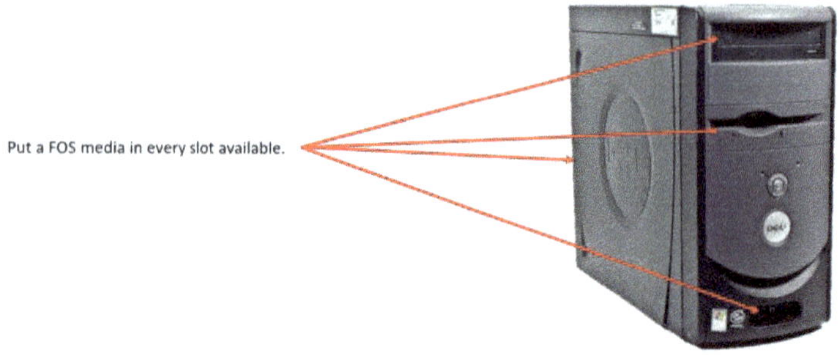

Figure 1.6 External media connections

You may also have to change the options within Windows by going to into Advanced Options as seen in Figure 1.7. This is another example of finding out how to boot a specific system before you start trying to boot that system. Know the keys. Know the system. Know how to configure the system to boot to your media.

1. Press Windows button and select **Settings**.
2. **Update & Security**.
3. **Recovery**.
4. **Restart Now** under Advanced startup.
5. **Troubleshoot**.
6. **Advanced** options.
7. Select **UEFI** Firmware Settings or other options.
8. **Restart**.

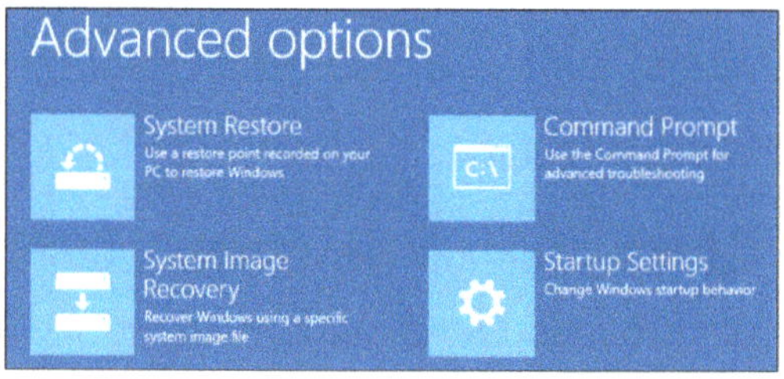

Figure 1.7 Advanced options

You did everything right, but it still booted to the evidence media!

This can happen. Maybe you overlooked something, such as not saving your changes in BIOS to change the boot media order. Or maybe the media you are using is not compatible with the system, or maybe you connected blank media instead of your FOS. The system could also have just skipped your media after you did everything correct. It can happen. Does that mean your evidence is tainted?

First thing if this happens is that you need to carry out your emergency plan that you prepared in this specific situation. Maybe you planned to pull the plug (from the back of the machine!) if this happened. Maybe you decided to create a live image rather than shut down and try again. Imaging live might be the best option in this scenario or maybe not. The point is to have the plan made **before** you boot the machine just in case, because time will be important either way. Do not forget to remove batteries from laptops before booting to a FOS, otherwise if you need to pull the plug, the machine will still be powered by the battery.

Back to fears of tainted evidence, relax. You are still fine with evidence access. Yes, there will be changes to the OS. Files will be accessed and modified. You will be the last user to boot the system. Those are the facts and you just need to document what happened. Write it up and move on to the task at hand. All the changes that you will see forensically will match that of the machine booting. Booting the machine is not going to delete user files, or create user files, or download files from the Internet if you take precautions, like not being connected to the Internet. Your evidence will still be there and you can expect uncomfortable questioning if having to testify to how the machine booted to the evidence media.

To alleviate some stress if this happens, review Figure 1.2 again. If the system could only be booted to a FOS, or booting to a FOS was a reasonable method, it was the totality of the situation that made the decision. How could booting to a FOS be unreasonable or not-the-best choice if it was the **only** choice?

Hard drives in some laptops can be removed with two screws and slide right out the side of the laptop to easily connect to a write blocker. Some desktops have such easy access to the hard drives that you don't even have to remove the hard drive in order to connect a hardware write blocker. None of these situations absolutely require using a hardware write blocker, but are considerations in making a decision.

But remember, it is the totality of the situation, not just the computer system that dictates your response. A lack of time, lack of resources, or other factors (such as being in a hostile environment) can turn any situation into a FOS booting situation regardless of how easy it appears to remove the evidence media.

CHAPTER 2: Write Blockers

It is important to be aware of differing opinions and capabilities between a hardware write blocker (HWB) and software write blocker (SWB) in order to make reasonable decisions and explain your decision when needed. For all practical purposes, both HWB and SWB will protect the evidence media from changes. Both are also susceptible to failures intentionally, unintentionally, and through defects.

The intended purpose of an HWB/SWB is to prevent **writes** to the media while at the same time, allowing **reads** of the media. Both have pros and cons in usage, again, based on the situation at hand. Both prevent writes and allows reads using different methods, where HWB uses hardware to control read/write, SWB uses software to control read/write. The visual difference, which comes into play for decision making, is seen in Figure 2.1. The HWB can be felt and seen, whereas a SWB is intangible as it is software.

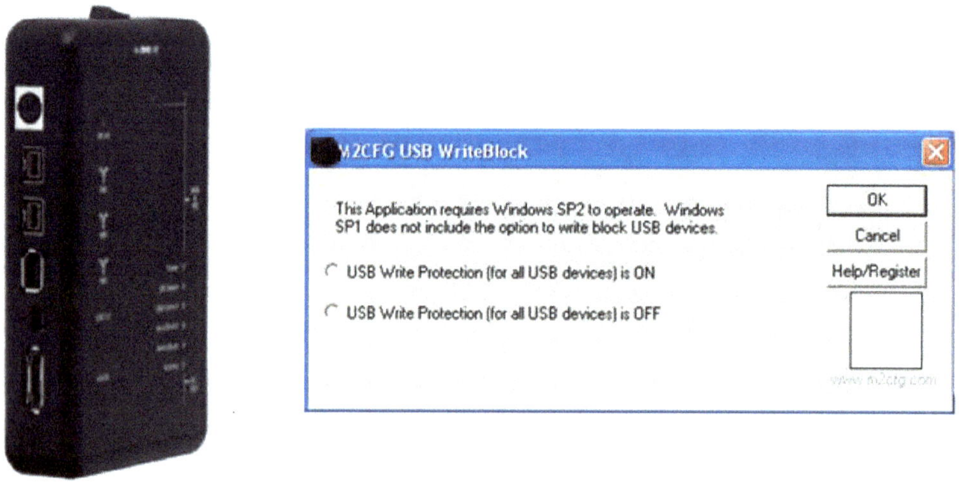

Figure 2.1 HWB and SWB

Back to making the choice of whether or not to boot to FOS, consider the pros and cons of each. Table 1 lists the pros (good points) of both the HWB and the SWB. These points are useful in making a decision on use and to justify your decision to use either the HWB or the SWB in both reports and testimony.

Hardware Write Blocker	Software Write Blocker
Visually simpler (can 'see' it)	Less hardware to rely on
Easier to explain to the layman	Simple to operate (push button)
Just need to connect to media	Any device that can be booted to FOS
Well-accepted in the community	Well-accepted in the community
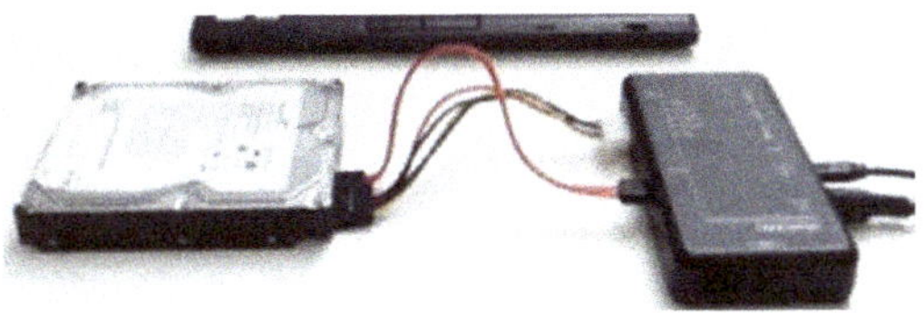	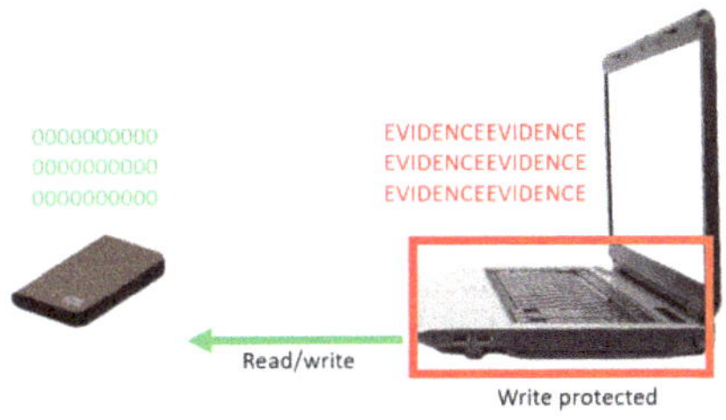

Table 1 Pros of HWB/SWB

As there are pros, there are also cons. Table 2 lists the cons of both the HWB and SWB. Again, these are points to help guide your decision making and justification of choice.

Hardware Write Blocker	Software Write Blocker
Extra gear to carry/use/maintain	Dependent upon OS
Firmware potential failure	Cannot "see" the write blocking
May slow the imaging process	Difficult to explain to layperson
Tied to one imaging device at a time	Only for systems able to boot to a FOS
	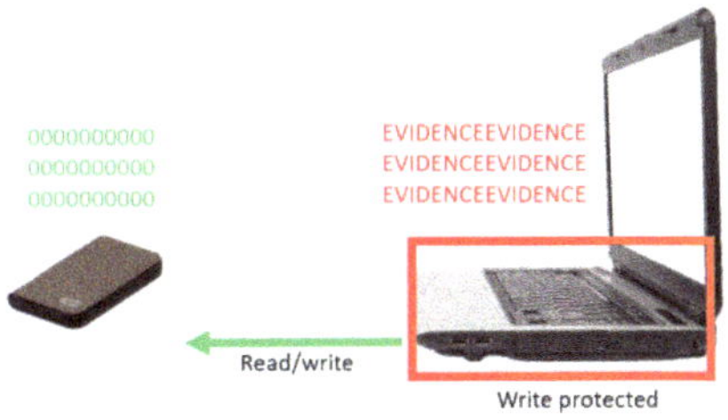

Table 2 Cons of HWB/SWB

More things to consider!

- Not every storage media can be protected with a HWB.
- Not every storage media can be protected with a SWB.
- Not every situation can have media protected by either a HWB or SWB

The point is that accessing evidence media (to collect data or otherwise access by searching or examining), involves a multitude of factors to make an informed decision. You must be diligent and make a reasonable decision based on what you know at the time for the situation that you have in front of you.

Fail proof?

As previously stated, both HWBs and SWBs can fail. They have failed. Not all and not all the time, and certainly it is not common. But the potential is there for either (or both) to fail. Past failures are important to know if nothing for the sake of justifying that one is not "better" than the other. Some notable HWB failures include:

> "...possible for the write-blocking feature of the product to be partially circumvented...it was possible for a "write" command..."
> https://tableau.guidancesoftware.com/index.php?pageid=support_notices

> "When this problem occurs, data read from the subject hard disk may be corrupted. In most situations, this makes the subject hard disk appear to be unpartitioned."
> https://tableau.guidancesoftware.com/index.php?pageid=support_notices

The SWB is also not immune to failure as documented in several sources, including in the KNOPPIX Bootable CD Validation Study for Live Forensic Preview of Suspects Computer by Earnest Baca:

> "It was quite startling to find that mounting EXT3 and reiserfs partitions read-only changed the state of the drive. I was very perplexed as to why the hash values changed."
> http://openstorage.gunadarma.ac.id/research/files/Forensics/OpenSource-Forensic/KNOPPIXValidation.pdf

Intentional breakage!

HWB/SWBs are developed and intended to prevent the modification of electronic media by preventing writes to the media. That is the pure intention of each. *However*, it is not only possible, but it is probable when intending to break the safety features, that you can. Software can be circumvented as can firmware. Nothing is 100% with anything, including write blockers, especially if someone intentionally wants to bypass the write protection features.

Since anything is possible, including being possible to intentionally bypass write protection in either HWBs or SWBs, your appropriate use makes all the difference. Use a HWB and SWB as intended to ensure that each works as developed. Much like a car can intentionally be driven off the road, a write blocker can be intentionally misused.

Unintentional circumventing can occur as well. With software write blockers, it is possible to run an application that will not be blocked by the software. In the WinFE chapters, we will discuss some of the applications where this can happen. The answer to whether or not HWB or SWB is infalliable is that they are not. They can be broken when used incorrectly or malicously. But you will use them correctly, so the only thing that can wrong will be beyond your control.

CHAPTER 3: Windows Forensic Environment History

This is the history of WinFE as far as I was involved. Troy Larson created it, shared it, and I only advocated its use while guiding improvements with the help of many others.

In 2008, at a Computer Technology Investigators Network (www.ctin.org) meeting near Seattle, Troy Larson asked me what I thought about a potential "Windows Forensic Operating System". I told him that I would buy it today! Unfortunately, he said something was coming, but not yet available. I had high hopes of what he meant as a Windows forensic operating system.

The next time that I saw Troy a month or so later, he gave me instructions on how to build this new "Windows Forensic Environment". Quite honestly, I was a little disappointed because the new forensic operating system was simply a winpe that only had two registry modifications. Although the registry modifications prevent Windows from auto-mounting the attached drives, that wasn't exactly what I expected as a forensic operating system from Microsoft...so I didn't put much effort to build one. Actually, I didn't even try for some time.

The hesitation I had in even thinking to get started creating a WinFE was the fear of how much time, effort, and testing to get it right, particularly since there are so many freely downloaded Linux Boot FOSs to download, test, and use. However, after a few failures with my favorite commercial Linux Boot FOS, I committed myself to try the WinFE.

My regret is not having done this sooner.

My suggestion is that if you are looking for a FOS that can do so much more than just image, then the time you spend making your own WinFE will not only be worth it, but you will wonder why you also hesitated so long as I did.

I followed Troy Larson's instructions of creating a bootable Windows Forensic Environment almost ten years ago. Granted, at the time, I was quite content with the then current system of using hardware write blockers, an occasional use of a hardware imaging tool, and the even fewer occasions of using a variety of forensic Linux boot FOSs. As neat as WinFE sounded and looked, I just didn't put a lot of effort into it as I didn't see the value of building the disk it at the time compared to what I was already using. But as usual, Troy was ahead of his time with his ideas and work and the rest of us play catch up.

With the number of computers that were being imaged onsite increasing, coupled with the problems of using Linux Boot FOSs that seem to be sporadically (if ever) updated or configured for what I needed onsite, WinFE has risen to the top of my first choices of imaging when forensic booting is used. With WinFE, I can quite easily add the specific drivers needed for most imaging work in seconds. Most impressive however, is the ability to use the forensic tools I use every day in a forensically sound Windows environment.

Such a simple thing to turn a win***P***e into a win***F***e, but some of the most ingenious ideas are simple, yet escape the vast majority of us. WinFE is one of those ingenious ideas and Troy gave it to me (and everyone else) to try out.

You will read all about WinFE in this guide, so I will hold off on spoiling the goodies that are coming up as you read through the pages. I will say that ever since that day in 2008, I have become the number one fan of WinFE, pushing its development well past that first build, and bringing more people into the overall development process over the years than I ever would have imagined.

I have taught WinFE to thousands of users both in classrooms and online courses, coordinated dozens of beta testers and software developers, and now WinFE is being taught at many governments training programs, including military forensic programs. WinFE has been referenced in journals and books, and you can even find forensic job requirements having WinFE as a desirable tool for experience. WinFE has come a long way, and the upcoming update, WinFE 10, being developed in 2019, will continue the trend of WinFE improvements!

Choosing a Forensic Operating System

WinFE has evolved over the years with different versions of building. You can choose the WinFE (or any FOS) that meets your needs for a given situation. Any FOS should be able to create a full disk image. That's easy enough. But others can give you more options in what you can do when running a FOS on the evidence machine.

Speaking only of Windows-based WinFEs that you can build, Figure 3.1 lists the versions that have been available over the past years. You'll notice that WinFE 10, is not listed in Figure 3.1, but is discussed later in this guide. WinFE 10 is an upgrade to WinFE Lite. The upgrade is not a minor upgrade and deserves its own conversation later. *Note: WinFE "10" is so named only due to being developed under Windows 10 but applies to Windows 11 as well.*

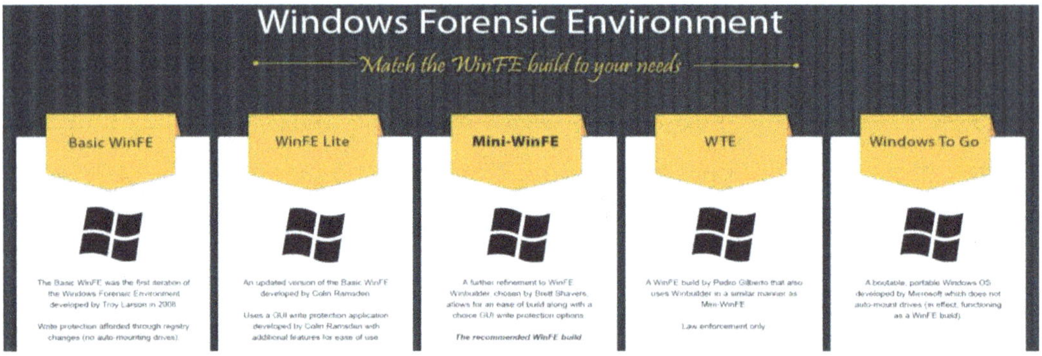

Figure 3.1 WinFE builds

As you read through this guide, you will be able to determine which build will be best in a given situation. Some are 'better' than others, but better only because of the specific task that you need to be done in a specific situation. There is a WinFE best for a full analysis, and another best for imaging speed, and so forth.

Linux FOSs are also covered in this guide as an overview, and nothing in this guide is meant to detract from the usefulness of a Linux OS. In fact, if you want to be as flexible and capable as you can, having WinFE and Linux FOSs in your toolbox is better than having only one FOS.

Additionally, having Mac/Apple specific collection FOS media is an important tool to also add to your collection. When it comes to collecting evidence from Apple systems, I recommend using a tool developed specifically for Apple/Mac.

The point of this section of choosing a FOS is that I do not want you to feel that one FOS is all you need, or that one FOS is able to do everything. Quite the opposite actually. I would not expect to ever see one FOS able to acquire all types of computers systems and operating systems. With that, have the tools at hand to handle the computer systems that you approach to acquire. Your FOS choice depends on each computer system you approach, and must likely will be different every time.

A brief overview of the WinFE build versions is below. Not listed are commercial versions which will be briefly mentioned in Chapter 11.

Version	Notes	32bit	64bit	ARM
Basic WinFE *Chapter 5*	Outdated, but you should know how this version functions as all others are based upon it.	√	√	
WinFE Lite *Chapter 9*	Outdated.	√		
WinBuilder WinFE *Chapter 8*	Not a practical build as can be overdone. Possible to incorrectly build a WinFE.	√	√	
Mini-WinFE *Chapter 9*	**Easiest build for majority of needs.**	√	√	
WinFE 10 *Chapter 10*	**Best build for most needs, also runs in ARM.**	√	√	√
WTE *Chapter 11*	No longer maintained. Based off of WinBuilder.	√	√	
Windows To Go *Chapter 11*	A full operating system useful for when specific applications are desired for use that do not run under WinFE.	√	√	

CHAPTER 4: DISKPART and Disk Toggling

We have to get through the core component of write protection in WinFE before building it. This is an important aspect to not only prevent writes to the evidence, but also to know how you can manage drives to do more with a FOS that you may have thought possible.

The underlying disk management in WinFE is "disk toggling", in that you can place drives offline, online, in a READONLY mode, and in a READ/WRITE mode. Depending upon how you toggle the drives, you may or may not be modifying the drive. Some modifications are normal, expected, and acceptable, especially if you need to perform a specific type of work on a system, such as triage using specific types of applications.

Here are the ways that disk toggling affects write protection in WinFE:

Drive Status	Read/Write Status
Placing drive ONLINE	Does **not** write to drive
Placing drive in READONLY	Does **not** write to drive
Taking a drive OFFLINE	Does **not** write to drive
Placing a volume ONLINE	Does **not** write to drive
Placing a volume in READONLY	**Does*** write to the disk (marks the disk)
Connecting a non-Windows drive	**Might*** write to the disk (a disk signature)
Placing a drive online in Windows to Go	Does **not** write to drive, but turns write protection **OFF**

*this may be acceptable and reasonable in a given situation and DOES NOT affect user-created data.

You can see that placing a drive ONLINE, READONLY, OFFLINE, and ONLINE doesn't affect the write protection nor modify the drive. Placing a **volume** READONLY does write to the disk, however, the write protection mark to the drive persists. The 'write' is a mark to the drive that denotes the volume was placed in READONLY. The mark will persist even after removing the volume from READONLY.

This is an important point because you may need to place a volume in READONLY to run certain software applications. For example, many live triage applications are not developed to run against a physical drive and can only see the logical (volumes) drives. Under WinFE where volumes are not able to be seen by these tools means that the tools won't be effective. So, place the volume in READONLY, WinFE makes a mark as such, and you can now use a triage tool that was designed to run on a live machine to now run under a FOS.

The incredible aspect of this is that when the tool had to be used on a running machine, trampling over some data while doing so, can now be run under WinFE and not trample over any data. WinFE in effect, turns a live-machine triage tool into a forensic triage tool by simply placing a write-protected volume as READONLY.

How about that disk signature "issue"? First off, it is not really an issue as the disk signature is well-documented. Figure 4.1 shows the disk signature that Windows will mark on non-Windows disk, such as a Linux disk. In personal tests, I have found that Windows (*WinFE*) will also **not** mark a non-Windows disk.

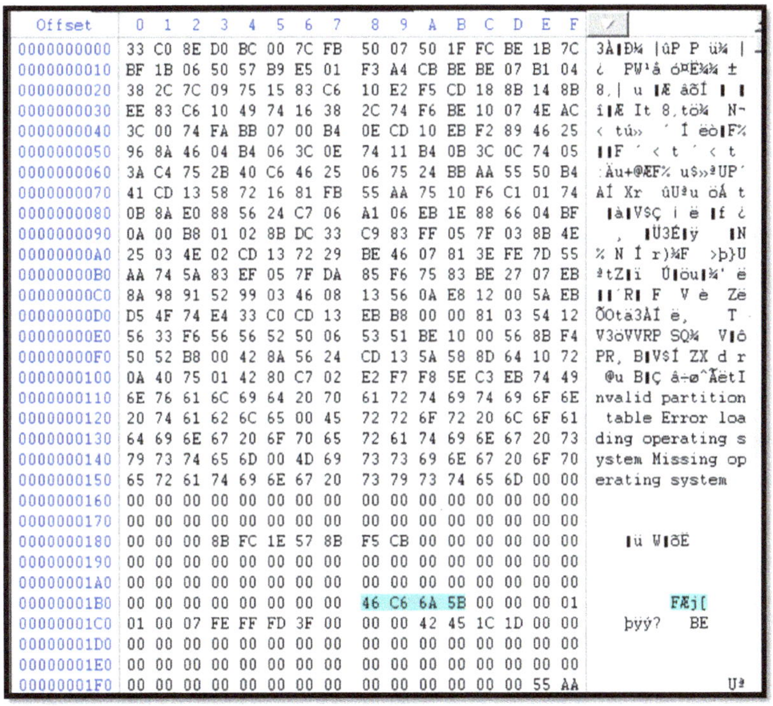

Figure 4.1 The Windows disk signature: offset 0x1B8

Troy Larson commented on this issue this more eloquently on the Grand Stream Blog with:

> "Windows FE will write a disk signature to a non-Windows disk. Windows FE writes a disk signature to any disk that doesn't have a disk signature. This is a well documented behavior of Windows, and, as such, is predictable. As predictable, the behavior can be expected and explained by the forensic investigator. Thus, one could use Windows FE on non-Windows disk, and have forensically sound findings--as long as the four bytes at the disk signature location are not at issue. I have seen nothing that indicates that Windows FE writes to any partitioned space--Windows or non-Windows.
>
> Windows FE may write a disk signature to a partitioned disk, if the disk does not already have a signature. The disk signature starts at 0x01B8. The partitioned space—volumes—are not written to.
>
> The read-only switch in DISKPART also writes a byte to the hard drive that makes that hard drive read-only to Windows.
>
> For these reasons the whole device hashing approach may result in differing hash values - however this behavior does not necessarily make the use of Windows FE forensically unsound."
> https://grandstreamdreams.blogspot.com/2009/02/windows-fe-details-teased-out-of-web.html#comment-8336733385232402953

The SAN (storage area network) policy for the registry settings are below (1-4). SAN policy 3 and SAN policy 4 turn a win***P***e into a win***F***e.

SAN policy	Description
1	Mounts all available storage devices.
2	Mounts all storage devices except those on a shared bus.
3	**Does not mount** storage devices.
4	Makes internal disks **offline**.

The key information for the registry keys are:

Key: HKLM\System\ControlSet001\Services\MountMgr
Name: NoAutoMount
Type: DWORD
Data: 1

Key: HKLM\System\ControlSet001\Services\partmgr\Parameters
Name: SanPolicy
Type: DWORD
Data: 3 or 4

You now know the limitations of write protection with WinFE, but also know that the markings to the drive do not impact the forensic analysis of electronic evidence, might not mark the drive at all, and when it must occur, is a thoroughly documented expectation of Windows.

Using DISKPART

The first step after booting to a Basic WinFE is prepping the hard drives attached to the system for data collection/imaging. For sake of clarity, the "evidence" drive will be the hard drive contained in your suspect/custodian machine. The "target" drive will be the external drive to which your image of the evidence drive will be stored.

`X:\windows\system32\DISKPART` is the first command to use to prep the drives. Once in DISKPART (Figure 4.2), you can now toggle the attached drives.

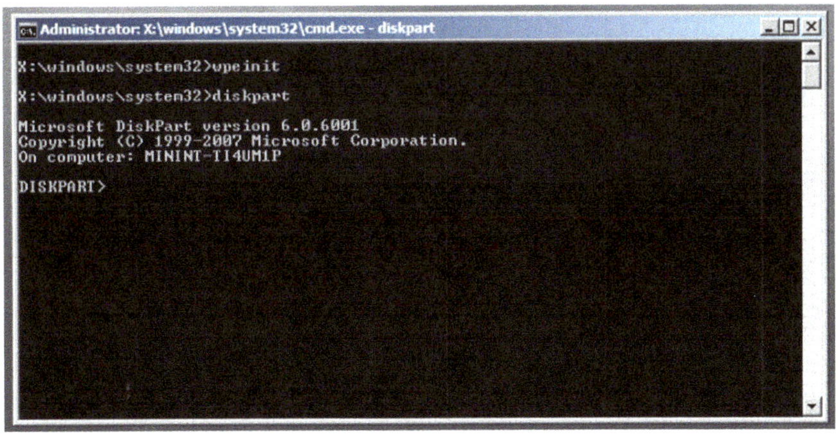

Figure 4.2 DISKPART

The Basic WinFE requires the use of DISKPART. Newer WinFE builds do not require, or recommend, the use of DISKPART as the write protect applications are easier and more effective. However, if needed, you can use DISKPART in any of the WinFE builds, and with that, it is a good idea to know what DISKPART can do.

The following page lists the DISKPART commands that are relevant to imaging a drive under WinFE (if not using a write protect GUI application). DISKPART has many more features and commands, but the following is the minimum and recommended commands to be aware. The list is in the order you need to place your target drive in a read/write mode.

`DISKPART> List Disks`
This command will list all drives connected to the system. You should be able to determine which your evidence drive is and which is your target drive

`DISKPART> Select Disk 1`
Select your target disk where you will store the image

`DISKPART> Detail Disk`
If you are unsure of the disk selected, this command will give you more information about it

`DISKPART> Online Disk`
If your target drive is not online already, this will put it online.
DISKPART may have problems with Dynamic Disks and USB drives (may have to reboot, unplug/plug)

`DISKPART> List Volume`
This command will list the volume(s) on your selected disk

`DISKPART> Select Volume 1`
Select the volume to where the image will be stored

`DISKPART> Attribute clear readonly`
This will set your target disk to read/write so that you can write an image

`DISKPART> Assign Letter=T`
This will assign a drive letter to your target drive.
**Use a letter that will help you recognize your target drive, in this example, T **

`DISKPART> Exit`

This will exit DISKPART, but keep the prompt open. You can now image to the "T" drive using your forensic software.

WARNING:

Be sure to correctly identify your disks.

It is possible to wipe your evidence with your empty target drive by mixing up your target drive with your evidence drive!

CHAPTER 5: Basic WinFE

This is the WinFE that started it all: The basic WinFE. Of course, it wasn't called the Basic WinFE (Figure 5.1) at the time as it was the only WinFE. Since then, different versions have come and gone and I respectfully refer to the first WinFE version as the Basic WinFE.

As a matter of foundation, I believe that if you want to know more about WinFE than simply using it, understanding how the basic WinFE is built is important, especially since all subsequent versions are built on top of the Basic WinFE.

I recommend that the Basic WinFE ***not*** be used as your primary WinFE system. The subsequent builds are better, more reliable, and easier to build/use. But even so, we need to dive a little into the Basic WinFE to understand what WinFE is all about in its foundation as this is where the write protection lives.

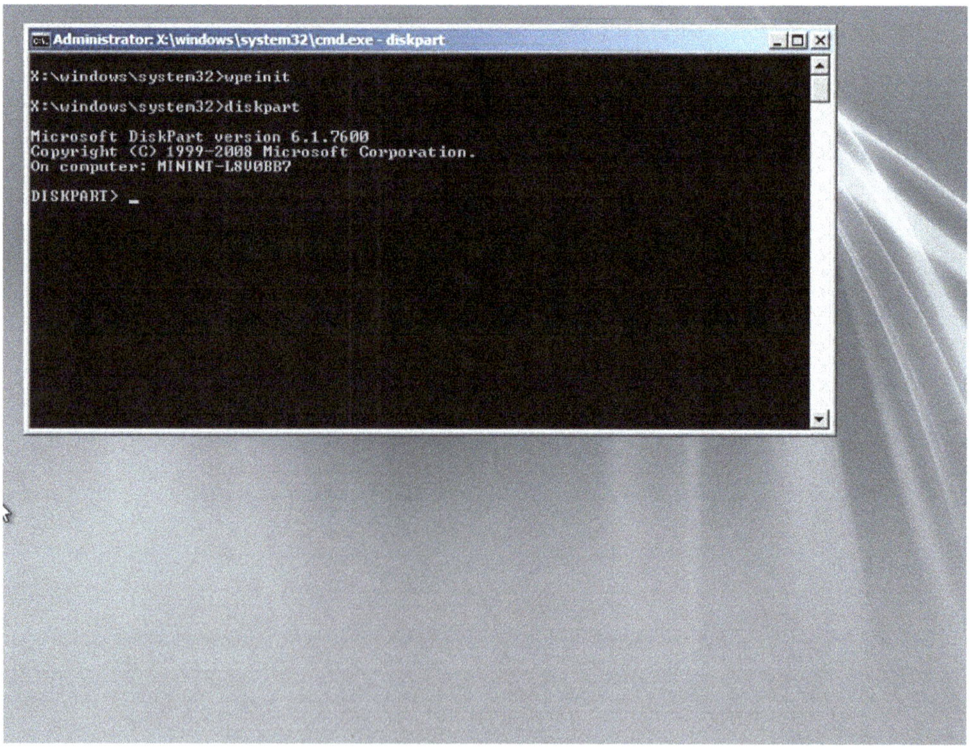

Figure 5.1 Basic WinFE

Building the Basic WinFE

One download, two registry changes, some copying of files, and burn your WinFE ISO to USB or CD. In many of the to be described steps, you can choose your own folder structure and names of the folders as to where to store your WinFE files, but for simplicity of explanations, you may want to use the structure set out in this guide at first. Building the Basic WinFE requires a series of steps to be followed exactly. I have seen demonstrations of building a Basic WinFE that were done incorrectly, and the demonstrations ended up being winpe building, not WinFE building.

Brief Review of Steps

Keep in mind that batch files can accomplish all the manual steps described in this chapter, and by using batch files, the chances of errors are virtually eliminated.

1. Copy Winpe files
2. Mount Winpe.wim
3. Add scripting package
4. Modify Registry
5. Install drivers
6. Create forensic tools folder and copy tools
7. Delete boot.fix
8. Unmount wimpe.wim and commit the changes
9. Create ISO
10. Test it.

Number 10 in this list is extremely important to ensure that the registry changes were done correctly. If not, you will have a winpe and will not know until after you find that your evidence media is found to have modifications during the imaging process.

Create a folder at the root of C:\ as below in Figure 5.2. The optional change to your boot screen is not recommended as it does not affect the functionality of WinFE, and is not discussed in this guide.

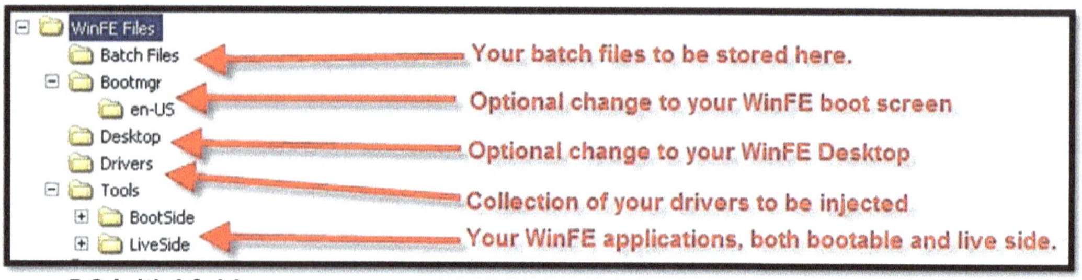

Figure 5.2 Initial folders

Keep in mind that the folders you created are separate from a folder structure that will be automatically created once your run the first command line (# 2 below).

1. Download and install Windows Automated Installation Kit (AIK) from www.microsoft.com
2. From the AIK command line (run as Administrator) copy the winpe files to your computer with the command:
   a. `copype.cmd x86 C:\WinFE`
   b. You may choose to replace the "x86" with either "amd64", or "ia64"

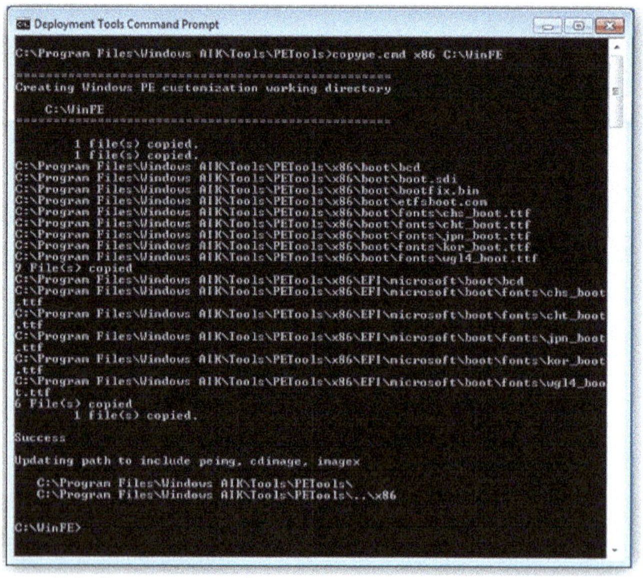

Figure 5.3 Copype.cmd

c. After completed, the directory structure on your C:\ drive will look like Figure 5.4:

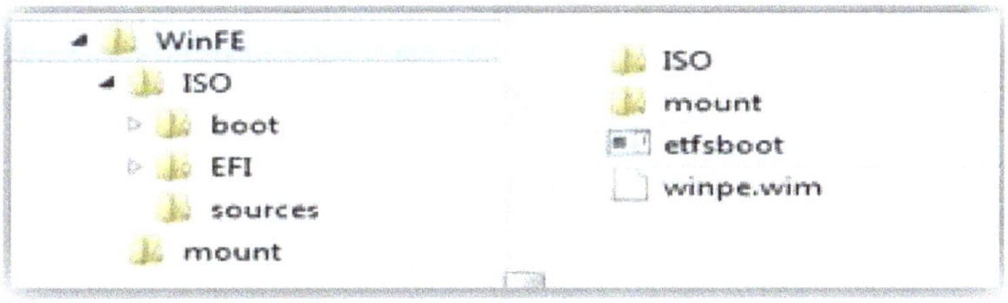

Figure 5.4 Build drive structure

3. The boot.wim image (Windows Imaging File Format)
   a. Instead of an ISO image, you will first be working with a .wim image. In order to modify this image and make it forensically sound, you need to mount it.
   b. There are two .wim images in the folder structure above.
      i. WinFE\ISO\sources\boot.wim
      ii. WinFE\winpe.wim
   c. The boot.wim will be used to create your final ISO. You can mount the winpe.wim or the boot.wim to install your tools. If you use the winpe.wim, simply delete the current boot.wim and move/rename winpe.wim to WinFE\ISO\sources (in order to replace the non-modified boot.wim).
   d. Mount the .wim image through the AIK command line (this will mount the image under the "mount" folder in order to make modifications and add your forensic applications) as seen in Figure 5.5.

```
imagex /mountrw C:\winFE\ISO\sources\boot.wim 1 C:\winFE\mount
```

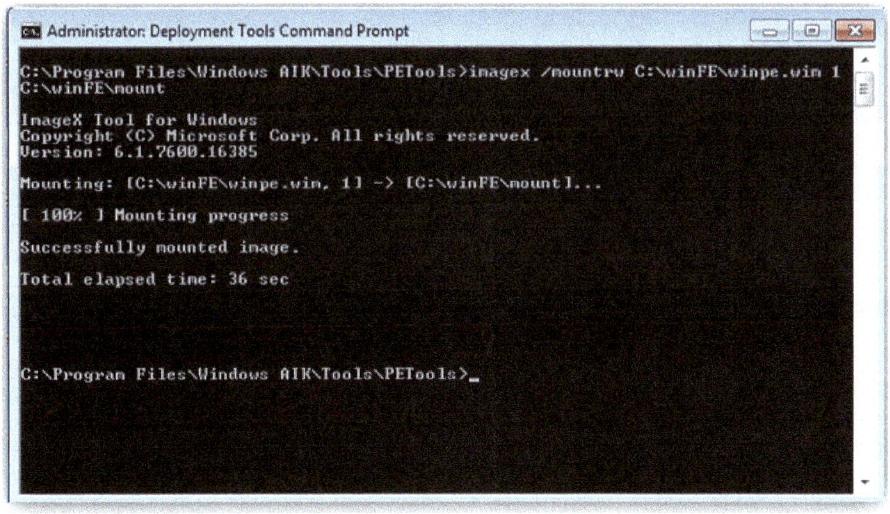

Figure 5.5 Mount .wim image

4. Modify the registry of the winpe mounted image
    a. Using Regedit, there are two registry modifications to be made for a forensically sound boot process.
    b. Load SYSTEM HIVE (Figure 5.6)
    c. In Regedit, Choose File – Load Hive
    d. Select the System file located at:

C:\WinFE\mount\Windows\System32\config

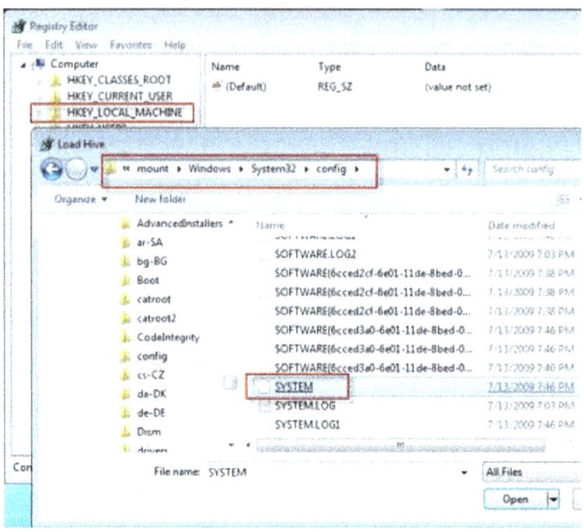

Figure 5.6 Load SYSTEM hive

    e. Name it WinFE (Figure 5.7)
    f. HKEY_LOCAL_MACHINE\WinFE\ControlSet001\services\mountmgr
    g. 1. Create a DWORD named NoAutoMount if it doesn't exist already by "right clicking" in Regedit and change the DWORD value to 1

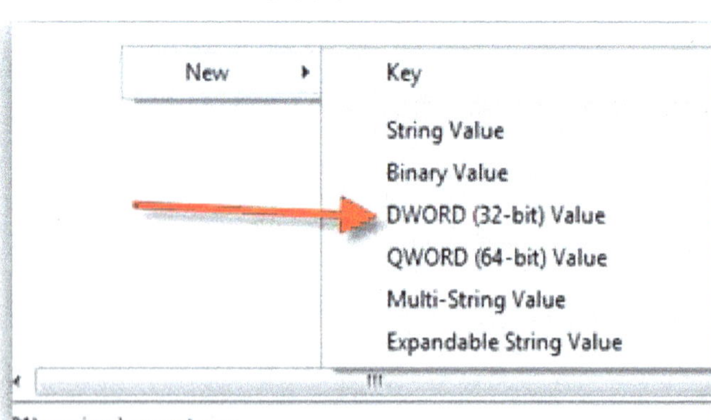

Figure 5.7 Create DWORD

h. HKEY_LOCAL_MACHINE\WinFE\ControlSet001\services\partmgr\Parameters
    i. Sans Policy -change the DWORD value to 3
i. Unload the WinFE SYSTEM HIVE
    i. Select the WinFE hive.
    ii. With Regedit, choose File – Unload Hive – "yes"

5. Options: Add your tools
    a. Create a WinFE folder in the mounted winpe image at the root of the mounted image. Copy your tools into this folder. Generally, only those programs that can run without installation can be successfully used with WinFE, such as most portable applications.

6. Options: Drivers
    a. Common or specific video drivers can be injected (aka..installed) into the mounted image through the AIK command line (AIK command line (where "drivers*.inf is the location of your drivers to be injected). As needed, drivers can be added just as easily, to include RAID drivers and other hardware specific drivers. WinRAR/7zip can be used to extract drivers (.inf) files from driver installation executables.

```
peimg.exe /inf=C:\drivers\*.inf C:\winFE\mount\Windows
```

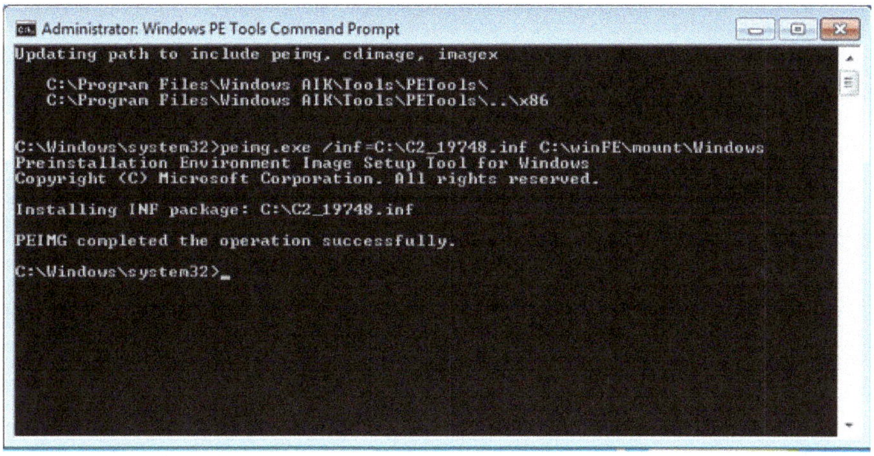

Figure 5.8 Inject drivers

7. Unmount your winpe.wim image (commit changes or you will have lost your work)

```
imagex.exe /unmount /commit C:\winFE\mount
```

8. Delete bootfix.bin located in C:\WinFE\ISO\boot (deleting this file will prevent the warning of "press any key to boot from cd")

9. Create ISO from the AIK command line (this command uses the

boot.wim image):

```
oscdimg -n -m -o -bC:\WinFE\etfsboot.com C:\WinFE\ISO C:\WinFE\WinFE.iso
```

10. Burn the ISO to a CD (or make USB bootable with WinFE) and test it.
11. Your forensic applications must be started from the command line (change directory to the application folder, run the executable via command line)

TIP: Batch files to do this work for you are part of the Windows Forensic Environment course at https://www.patreon.com/DFIRTraining. Subscribe to download all batch files with other WinFE downloads.

Before we leave the Basic WinFE, keep in mind that although this version works, it does not work as well as the current versions. You will find instructions for building a Basic WinFE online to this day, but the recommendation is to use a newer build version that includes Write Protect Tools (Chapter 6) rather than relying on DISKPART.

As a warning, I have seen Basic WinFE building instructions and videos online that were incorrectly building WinFEs and actually were not forensically sound (ie: winpe).

CHAPTER 6: Next Generation WinFE – *Write Protection Applications*

WinFE went to another level as soon as Colin Ramsden developed the first **WinFE Write Protect Tool** integrated in WinFE Lite (details in a later chapter on WinFE Lite). Colin's write protect tool resolved previous issues seen in WinFE in regards to mounting/dismounting drives, eliminated the need in using DISKPART, and creating an easy method to install drivers on the fly.

The first version of the WinFE Write Protect Tool is seen in Figure 6.1. Features include mounting/dismounting disks, rescan/detail disks, add drivers, and make Read/Only and Read/Write, all without having to use DISKPART. The write protect tool also eliminated issues with dynamic disks and problematic disks that the Basic WinFE/DISKPART could not toggle correctly. Just as important is the ease to identify all attached drives and the Read-Write/Online-Offline status of each drive. *The limitation of this version is that it is 32bit only.*

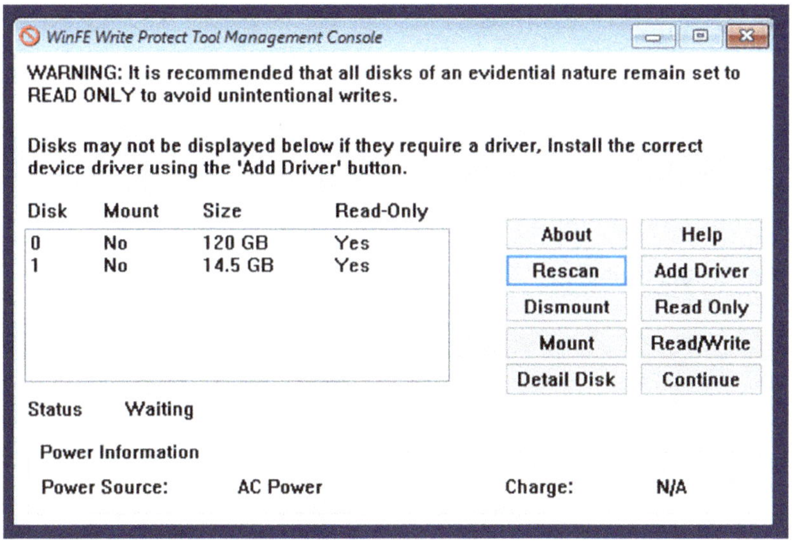

Figure 6.1 WinFE Write Protect Tool

The write protect tool has a banner warning (Figure 6.2) prior to use as a reminder of warnings for write protection. Specifically, a warning to be aware that DISKPART, Device Manager, and Disk Management tools can bypass write protection. The most important statement in the warning is to use "common sense" at all times.

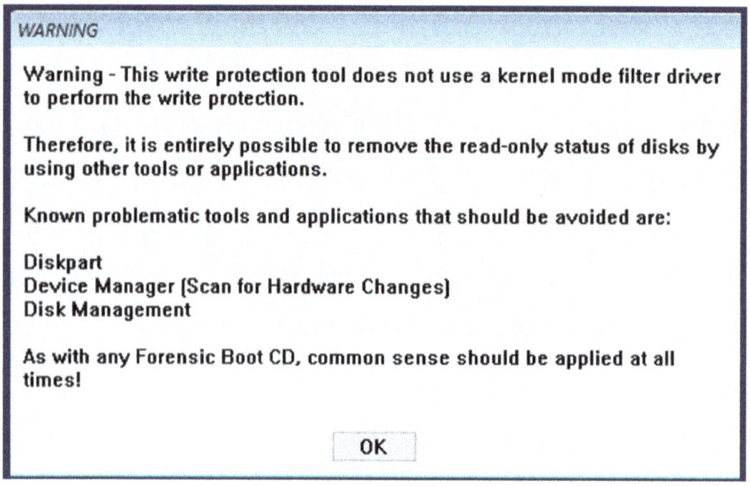

Figure 6.2 Write protect warning banner

This write protect tool was initially developed for WinFE Lite and later integrated into a Winbuilder write protect script. The Write Protect Tool has been updated in 2019 (Figure 6.3), with the ability to run in ARM and both 32bit and 64bit.

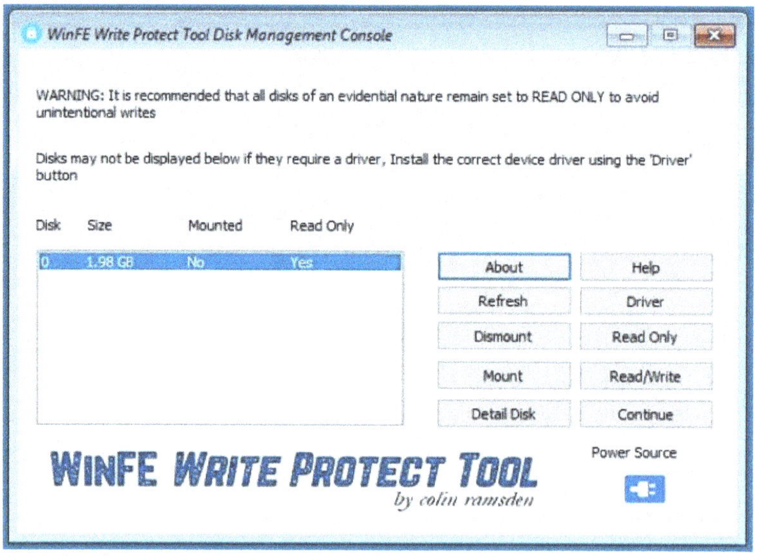

Figure 6.3 WinFE 10 Write Protect Tool

A second write protection application was developed for the WinBuilder versions of WinFE. The application, **Disk Mgr 0.9** as seen in Figure 6.4, does not denote 'forensics', however, the function is the same as Colin Ramsden's Write Protect Tool. Disks can be toggled in the same manner, however there are fewer features as compared to Colin Ramsden's Write Protect Tool. The Disk Mgr is also limited to use as a WinBuilder script unless it further develops for use outside of WinBuilder. The Disk Mgr is both a 32bit and 64bit application.

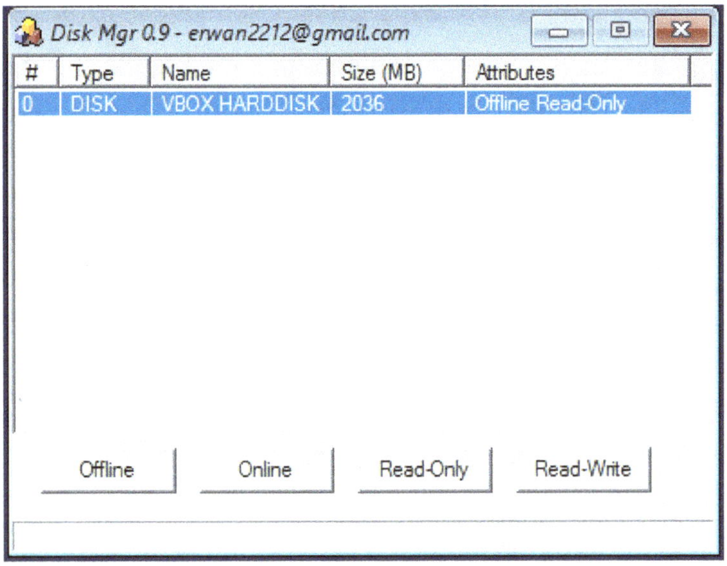

Figure 6.4 Disk Mgr 0.9

Each of these write protect applications are solid applications in forensic use. Besides the few differing features, personal preference may be the most important consideration in use in WinFE.

Write Protect Tool	32bit	64bit	ARM	WinBuilder (all versions)	WinFE Lite	WinFE 10
Colin Ramsden's WP (first version)	√			√	√	
Colin Ramsden's WP (current version)	√	√	√	√		√
Disk Mgr 0.9	√	√		√		

CHAPTER 7: WinBuilder WinFE

After years of building and using the Basic WinFE and WinFE Lite, I wanted an easier method of building WinFE. Mostly, I wanted to make customization easier in both building and usage. I also wanted the method to be freely available. With that, I came across several “winpe” GUI applications developed to build a winpe, and decided upon the WinBuilder application. With support from Nuno Brito of reboot.pro and others mentioned in this guide, a single WinFE script was written for WinBuilder that made building a WinFE nearly error-free and user-friendly. Plus, for the first time, WinFE actually *looked* like Windows (Figure 7.1).

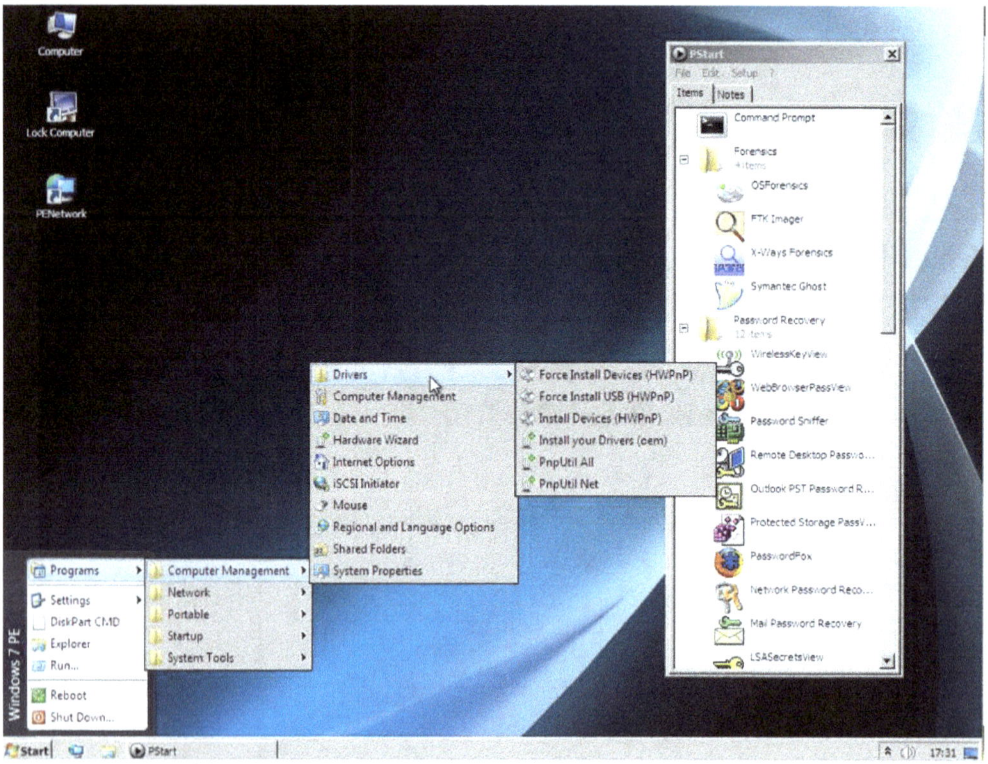

Figure 7.1 WinBuilder WinFE

WinBuilder

WinBuilder (http://www.reboot.pro) is a graphical user interface program that can be configured to build a customized winpe. The benefits to the WinBuilder (Figure 7.2) WinFE include:

- Support for more programs to run within WinFE
- Install drivers on the fly
- Better audio/video support
- Easy for first responders to use (looks like Windows; no command prompt use necessary)
- Easy and fast to build

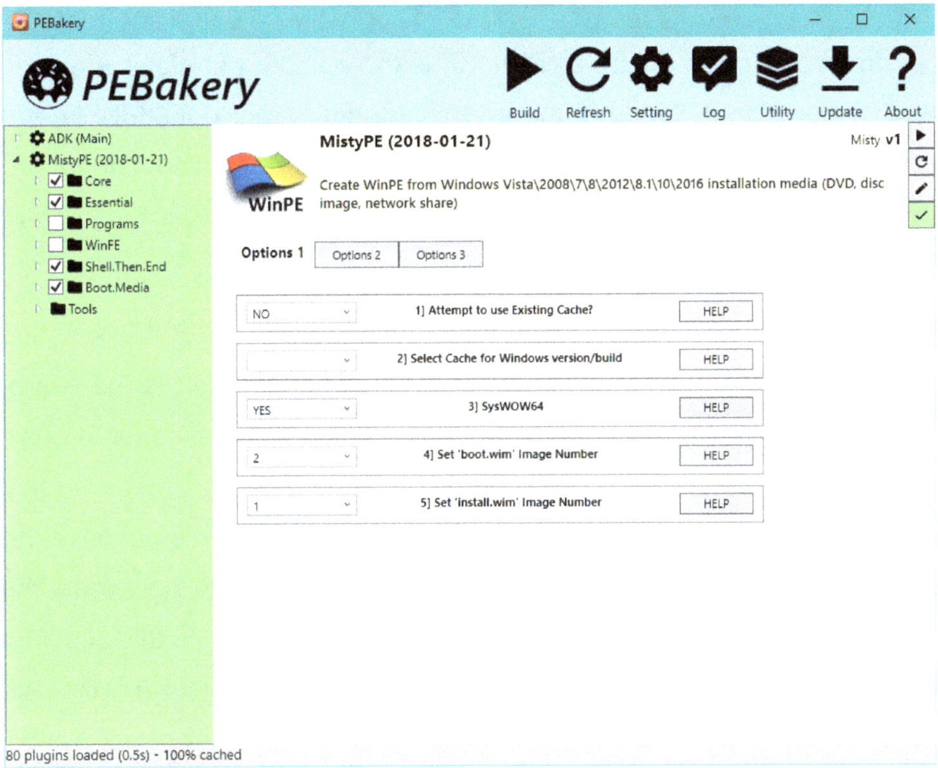

Figure 7.2 WinBuilder

WinBuilder does not require installation as it is a portable program. It can be extracted practically anywhere to run, but I recommend extracting to and running from the root of C:\. There are fewer issues with potentially long file paths and application issues when run from the root of your drive.

In the simplest description of WinBuilder, WinBuilder runs a series of scripts that you choose, and builds a winpe. This is comparable to the batch files process to build a Basic WinFE. Given that WinBuilder simply runs scripts that you choose to add, customizing WinFE is as easy as checking a box and clicking "Play". Batch files not needed!

The first version of the WinBuilder WinFE build did not have a write protect tool, but instead used DISKPART to toggle drives online/offline. In practice, the only difference between the Basic WinFE and the WinBuilder WinFE was that of appearance and additional components that can be added in the WinBuilder WinFE. The write protection was the same (registry modifications) as was the method of disk management. For that reason, *I recommend to **not** use the older write protect (DISKPART) script should you happen to find it online*.

Another drawback to the WinBuilder WinFE is the number of default scripts in the WinBuilder downloads. Many of the scripts are not 'forensic friendly' in that some, such as disk management scripts, will bypass write protection. Others are shareware or non-commercial use applications that are not suited for forensic (legal!) analysis.

In Chapter 9 and with more details in the appendix, Mini-WinFE is discussed as a custom WinBuilder configuration. The WinBuilder application is the same, but the chosen scripts, including the write protect tool, are best suited for forensic work. The build was named "Mini" since the goal was to have a minimal version of the full WinBuilder build. Additionally, since WinBuilder WinFE did not have the write protect script as a default added option, users needed to download the script separately and add it to the WinBuilder folder structure. Since this could be a failure point in building a WinFE, in which someone could build a winpe by mistake, Mini-WinFE was created to address building an error-free WinFE instead of inadvertently building a winpe.

Another common issue with the WinBuilder WinFE is that users commonly add unnecessary scripts to the build in order to be create a nearly full Windows OS. This method of building a WinBuilder WinFE results in the build process failing due to conflicts in scripts, or creating a WinFE that is bloated with unnecessary applications and useless visual effects.

We will see in Chapter 9 how to build a Mini-WinFE, which for all practical purposes is the same as a WinBuilder WinFE. By which, there is no need to duplicate the instructions in this chapter of a WinBuilder WinFE.

Important! WinBuilder Support

There is *no support* per se for WinBuilder for any errors you may encounter. WinBuilder is a free application, used by tens of thousands of people, and has an active community forum for which to search and ask for errors that you may encounter.

CHAPTER 8: Mini-WinFE

Mini-WinFE as seen in Figure 8.1, is the best recommendation out of all current WinFE builds as it covers the majority of uses, even beyond the latest version of WinFE 10. The major difference with WinFE 10 is that WinFE 10 adds support for Colin Ramsden's Write Protect Tool in 32bit, 64bit, and ARM architectures, along with an updated write protect tool. Both Mini-WinFE and WinFE 10 should be part of your set of FOSs, including your Linux and Mac FOSs, as each fills a specific need.

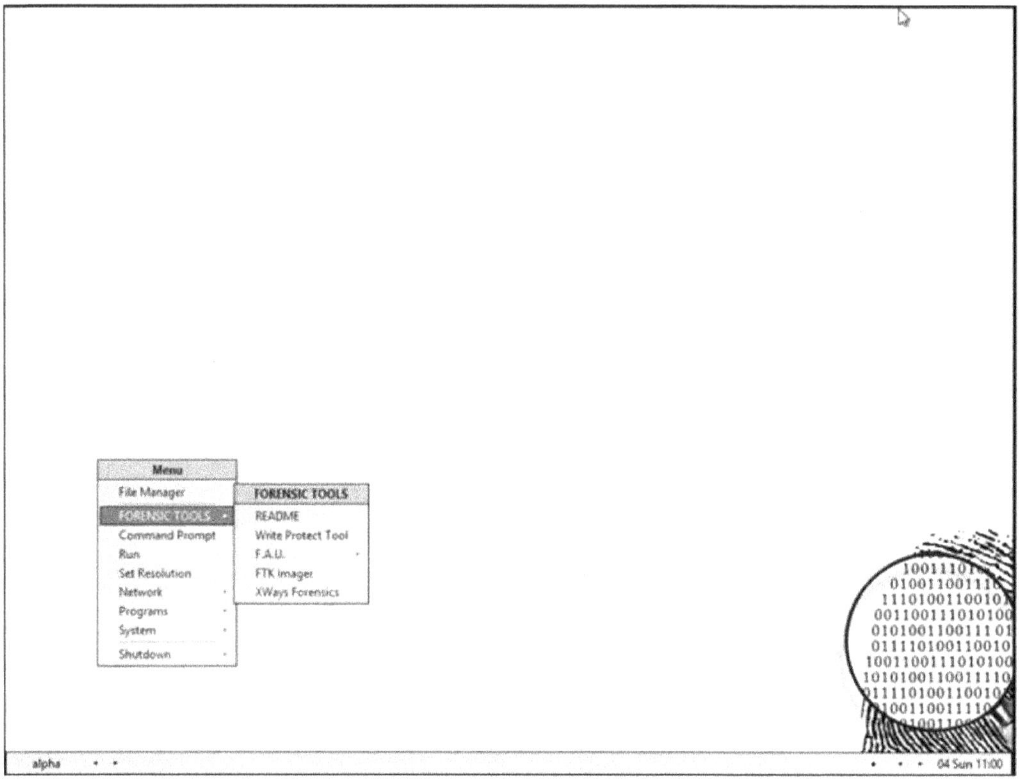

Figure 8.1 Mini-WinFE

You need three things to build a Mini-WinFE. Actually, you only need two things if you don't count adding your personal forensic applications. You need the files/folders seen in Figure 8.2: (1) WinBuilder Mini-WinFE, (2) a Windows OS installation media, and (3) your personal forensic applications.

Figure 8.2 Mini-WinFE required files

Mini-WinFE Project Downloads

You can find multiple versions of WinFE WinBuilder projects on the Internet. Some are no longer updated or maintained, but still available. Others are hosted on websites having nothing to do with WinFE or WinBuilder. The risk of randomly downloading what you think should be a WinFE builder is that you may download a build that has not been tested, may not correctly build a WinFE or worse yet, be malicious. On top of that, you can find pre-built WinFE ISO files online. There is no way that I can stress enough to **not download a pre-built WinFE**.

Besides violating the Microsoft EULA, there is no distribution of a downloadable WinFE that cannot be considered to not be malicious. In other words, unless the WinFE is a legitimate commercial version, at best, you are violating a Microsoft EULA and at worst, downloading a malicious build of WinFE.

One of the reasons that I have compiled WinFE materials and sources over the years is to ensure that valid build projects are being used, and to also prevent building WinFEs incorrectly to keep WinFE widely accepted as a community forensic tool.

I am not saying that any WinFE project not mentioned in this guide is invalid. As there are other winpe building applications online, both commercial and freeware, anyone can develop a different WinFE build using the same registry settings and perhaps a different write protect tool. However, that which is in this guide has been tested and used by thousands of users, worldwide.

Here is the breakdown of the legitimate and personally tested Mini-WinFE build sources:

Misty Projects http://mistyprojects.co.uk/mistype/mini-winfe.docs/readme.html

Colin Ramsden: https://www.winfe.net

As a side note, both of these listed builds are solid, verified, validated, and tested builds of WinFE. Each has a slight difference in the WinBuilder configurations and options, but the write protection validity is the same in each. Therefore, whichever build you choose, will be a good WinFE build.

Briefly, here are the differences:

Mini-WinFE.2014.07.03	Write protect tool only and hard-coded, no ADK
Mini-WinFE.2017.04.27	Write protect tool and forensic Disk Management tool both hard-coded, no ADK
MistyPE.2018.01.21	Write protect tool and forensic Disk Management tool both optional, with ADK
Mini-WinFE.2018.03.03	Write protect tool and forensic Disk Management tool both **hard-coded**, with **ADK**, and **only tools suited** for forensics per EULAs

The hard-coded write protect apps ensure that a winpe will not be built inadvertently, or even intentionally.

For a Mini-WinFE, the ADK is not necessary unless you want to further customize your build. Mostly, if you plan to add applications that require additional dependent files, you will need ADK. However, a Mini-WinFE is not the best choice to build out as a full OS for forensic analysis using resource intensive forensic applications. Check the Microsoft ADK website for details on ADK (https://www.microsoft.com/en-us/download/details.aspx?id=39982).

A hard-coded (locked) write protect script is also not necessary, although I believe it important to have in order to avoid incorrectly building a WinFE, especially when training first responders in WinFE use. The 2018+ versions of Mini-WinFE are updated as needed, and maintained whereas the older versions are not.

Building the Mini-WinFE (2018-01-21)

Instructions for the Mini-WinFE in this guide will be for the MistyPE.2018.01.21 build version (Figure 8.3). There are slight differences between the builds as described earlier, but for all practical purposes, the building of a Mini-WinFE is the same. The steps to build a Mini-WinFE are:

1) Run WinBuilder and select your Windows OS source media
2) Check the boxes for the scripts (applications) for your custom build
3) Press "Play"

That's it. As you can see, the Mini-WinFE build takes a lot of work out of building a WinFE! Even better, this entire process takes less than 5 minutes.

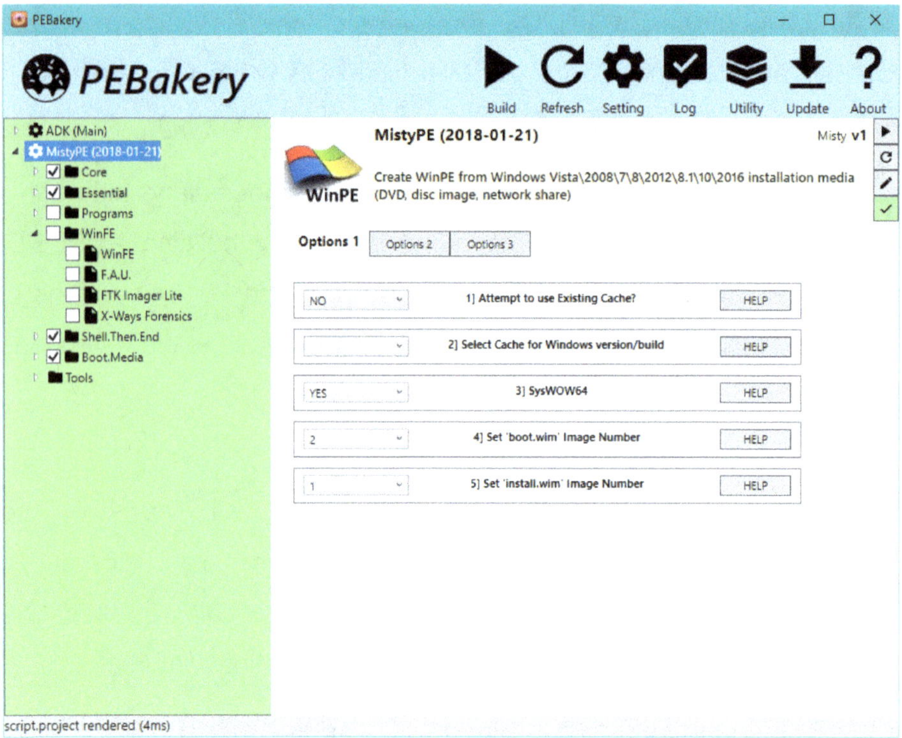

Figure 8.3 MistyPE (2018-01-21)

WinBuilder is extremely popular as a winpe builder because it is so easy to use. Simply extract MistyPE.2018.01.21.zip to the root of your C:\ to the folder structure seen in Figure 8.4. From here, "run" WinBuilder by executing Launcher.exe as administrator.

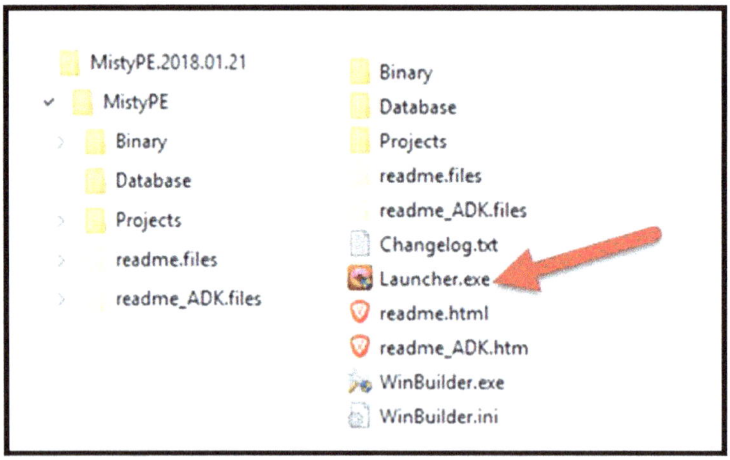

Figure 8.4 WinBuilder extracted

Your source!

WinBuilder cannot install Windows or create a winpe or WinFE by itself, otherwise, it would violate the Microsoft EULA. Therefore, it needs a Windows OS installation media to draw upon for creating the winpe/WinFE. This means you need to have access to a Windows OS. If you do not have your original installation media, either as an ISO file or DVD/USB, you can create the media via the Microsoft website here:

https://support.microsoft.com/en-us/help/15088/windows-10-create-installation-media

Once you have the installation source created, you need to point WinBuilder at it before you run WinBuilder. If you fail to point to the source, WinBuilder will fail and let you know that it needs a Windows source. If your source is an ISO file, you can mount the ISO as a drive letter and point WinBuilder to the drive letter, but I have found that WinBuilder will sometimes fail on a mounted ISO file, whereas if the ISO files are extracted to a folder, I've not encountered that issue. The majority of build errors are due to an incompatible Windows source. Not every source version has been tested, and if you come up with a source error, try a different Windows source media.

Figure 8.5 shows how to point to your Windows source installation folder. Choose Setting (#1), Projects (#2), and drill down to your source and select the folder (#3). Close the dialog and that's it. Now all you have to do is customize your build by checking boxes.

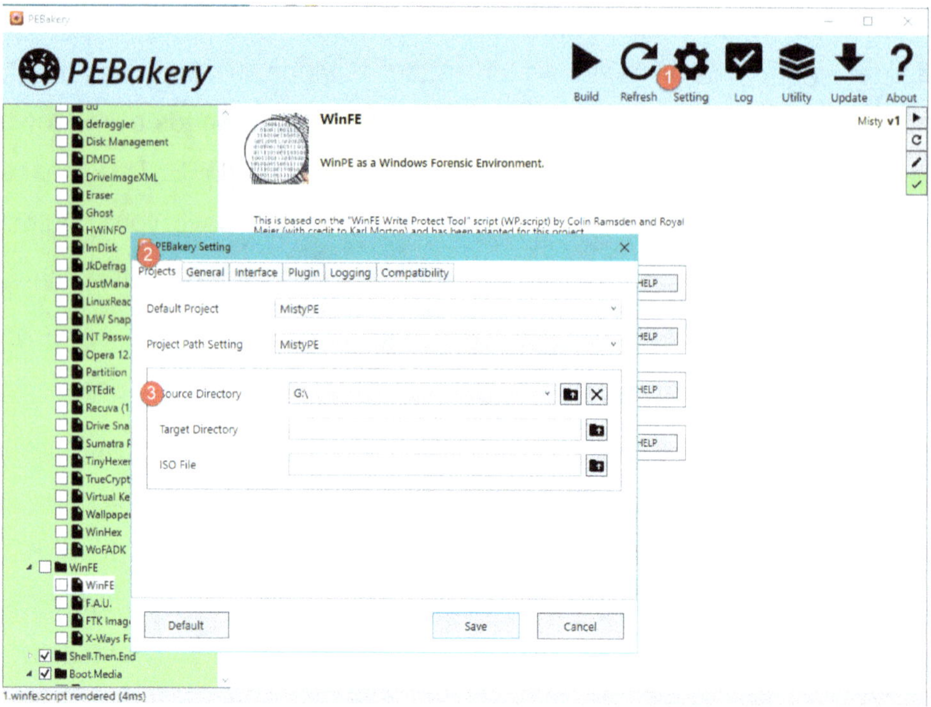

Figure 8.5 Windows source media

WinBuilder provides an intuitive method of checking boxes for the “scripts” that you want it to run (in the green section of the application). Let’s take one example of how the scripts work, or at least the minimum you need to know about the scripts. This is important to know as the scripts are the method of customizing your Mini-WinFE.

Figure 8.6 shows that 7-zip is selected in the WinBuilder interface. When WinBuilder runs to create the Mini-WinFE, it will process all the scripts you checked. In this case, the 7-zip script will be run and install the 7-zip application into the Mini-WinFE build.

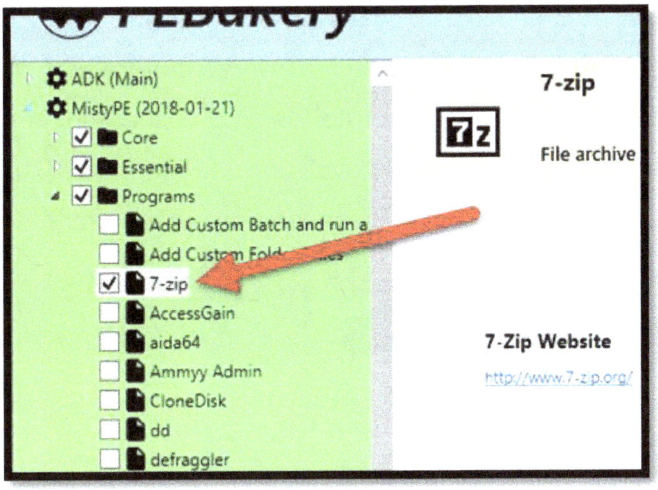

Figure 8.6 Example of 7-zip selected

The scripts are located in the WinBuilder folder structure (#1) with the file extension ".script" (#2) as seen in Figure 8.7. To remove a script from WinBuilder, delete the. script file directly from the folder structure, and then refresh WinBuilder with the "Refresh" button in the WinBuilder menu bar.

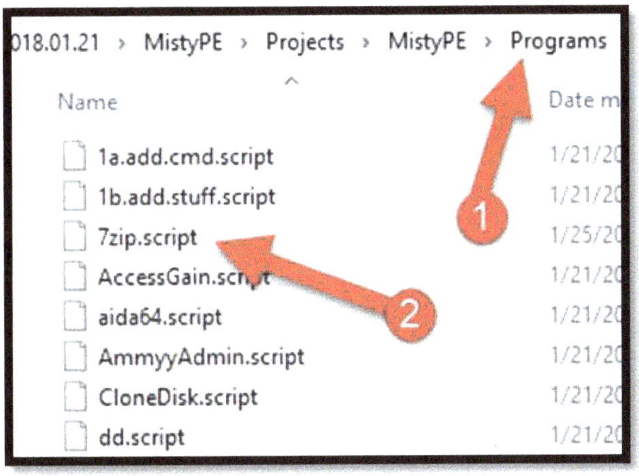

Figure 8.7 Scripts

Adding scripts to WinBuilder are as easy as it is to remove them. The reboot.pro website has hundreds of scripts that you can download and copy into the WinBuilder program folder as seen in Figure 8.8. There may be a script of interest that exists on the reboot.pro website that you can download and have injected into your Mini-WinFE with not more much effort than a download of a file.

If there is something Mini-WinFE doesn't do that you want it to do, and you cannot find a script for your needs, you can write your own scripts (reboot.pro has information on how to write scripts if you want to learn). For the scripts in your build, each script can be opened in Notepad, as seen in Figure 8.8. This may be of interest if you want to know what is happening with a script in WinBuilder when it builds your Mini-WinFE.

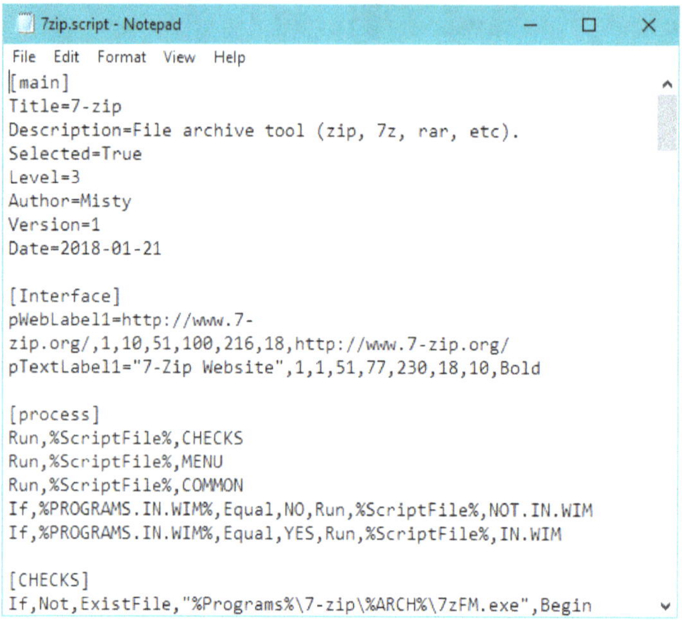


```
[main]
Title=7-zip
Description=File archive tool (zip, 7z, rar, etc).
Selected=True
Level=3
Author=Misty
Version=1
Date=2018-01-21

[Interface]
pWebLabel1=http://www.7-
zip.org/,1,10,51,100,216,18,http://www.7-zip.org/
pTextLabel1="7-Zip Website",1,1,51,77,230,18,10,Bold

[process]
Run,%ScriptFile%,CHECKS
Run,%ScriptFile%,MENU
Run,%ScriptFile%,COMMON
If,%PROGRAMS.IN.WIM%,Equal,NO,Run,%ScriptFile%,NOT.IN.WIM
If,%PROGRAMS.IN.WIM%,Equal,YES,Run,%ScriptFile%,IN.WIM

[CHECKS]
If,Not,ExistFile,"%Programs%\7-zip\%ARCH%\7zFM.exe",Begin
```

Figure 8.8 Script in Notepad

Customization of scripts inside WinBuilder

Many scripts have options for customization within WinBuilder. For example, in Figure 8.9, selecting FileManager (#1) brings up the script information (#2), that shows a choice of "Select File Manager" (#3), as well as opening the script in Notepad (#4) directly from within WinBuilder. You can select among the options that each script may offer, if there are options available.

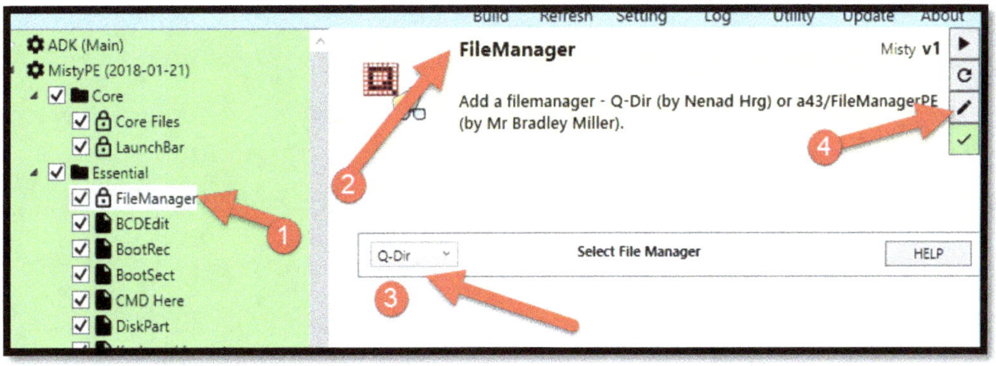

Figure 8.9 Customization of scripts

Optional versus mandatory scripts

Some scripts are mandatory in order to build a Mini-WinFE. Many of the mandatory scripts do not have options (File Manager is one exception). Figure 8.10 shows a hard-coded, mandatory script (#1) with a lock icon and an optional script (#2) with a file icon. It is possible to delete a mandatory script from the WinBuilder folder structure which will remove from WinBuilder, but most likely you will break the build process by removing a necessary script. Leave the locked scripts alone; WinBuilder needs them! Most of the pre-checked scripts are also necessary for your build, so best to leave them checked.

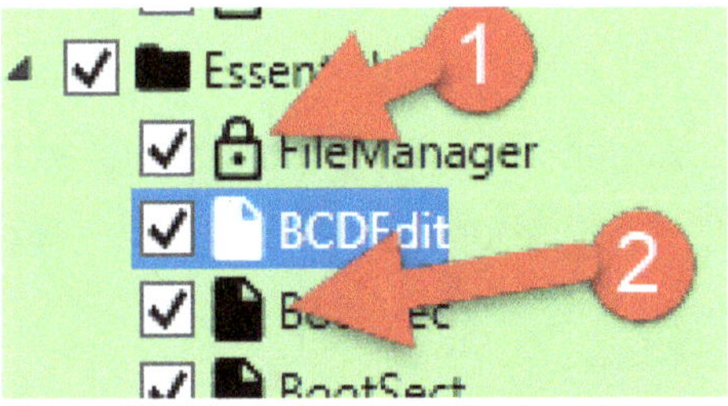

Figure 8.10 Mandatory vs Optional Scripts

So many default scripts…

Practically every WinBuilder project (including the Mini-WinFE projects), contains many scripts that are unnecessary in a FOS. Figure 8.11 shows a partial listing of the scripts included in the Mini-WinFE project used in this chapter.

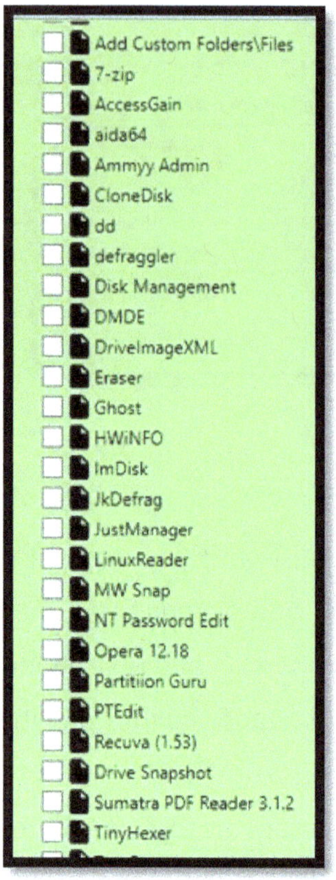

Figure 8.11 MANY SCRIPTS!

When building a Mini-WinFE, you can ignore the scripts that you do not need without affecting the build process. Actually, the build process will be quicker with fewer scripts having to be run. Because you can choose the scripts that you need and ignore the scripts you do not need, your Mini-WinFE can be customized exactly to your needs.

One of the concerns that I have with many scripts being in the projects by default is that each script is a program (7-zip as an example), and each program has its own EULA that needs to be checked for commercial use, or at least not restricted to demo or home use. On top of that, some scripts will bypass the write protection of any write protect application. With that, each script needs to be tested in a build to ensure none will bypass the write protection.

With WinBuilder and the available scripts, an entire office suite, photo editing software, video players, and more can be added to the build. The vast majority of these applications are not only unnecessary for a FOS, but place undue stress on the evidence machine that you need to access the media. Stress in the manner that when a FOS is running on an evidence machine, the machine is at work (the drive is spinning, the machine is generating heat, etc...). At any point, the drive could die, or the machine could stop due to end-of-life. Best is to use only the applications needed for the task at hand, whether it be imaging, targeted collection, or triage in order to complete your task as soon as possible. Extra work on the evidence machine such as writing reports with an office suite on Mini-WinFE should be done elsewhere.

Most all scripts in WinBuilder are self-explanatory, or have clearly described options. Even WinBuilder has scripts to create an ISO and bootable USB if you check the boxes for the scripts to run when the build is complete (Figure 8.12). Again, WinBuilder is very intuitive to use.

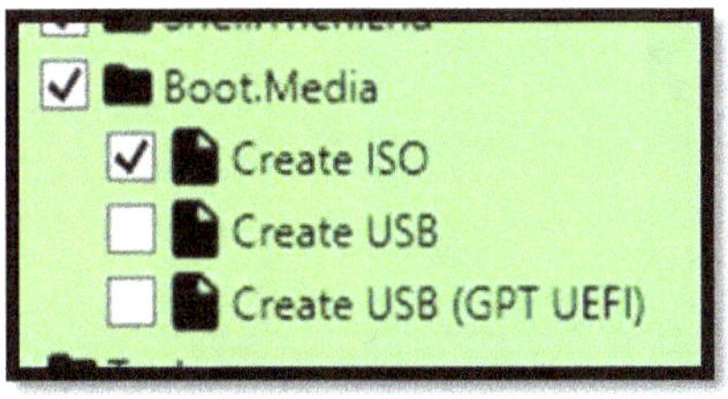

Figure 8.12 ISO and USB bootable

Forensic scripts

The WinFE projects generally contain a few forensic scripts to minimize time in injecting programs into the WinFE build (in addition to the write protect scripts). The most current scripts include those seen in Figure 8.13 (F.A.U., FTK Imager Lite, and X-Ways Forensics). In addition to scripts for these programs, there are scripts for WinHex, Encase, Field Search, and a few others that can be found online, or can be written by users. The three selected in Figure 8.13 have been found to run without issue, fully, and not require any dependent files other than what is in Mini-WinFE in the default build projects. Other forensic scripts have had issues in dependency files and running with errors under WinFE.

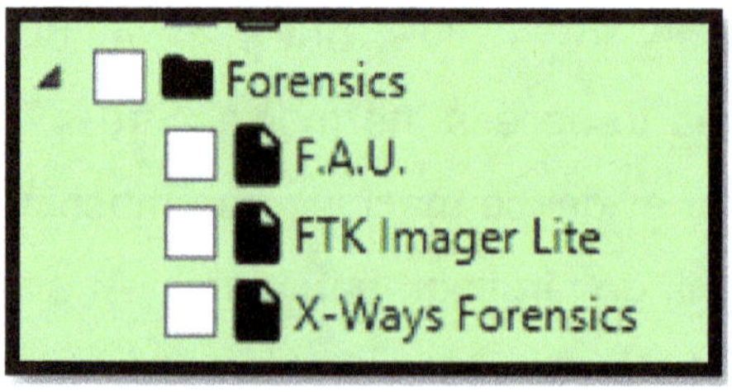

Figure 8.13 Forensic scripts

One of the ways of keeping Mini-WinFE in compliance with forensic program EULAs is that the scripts for commercial applications (Figure 8.14) are not downloaded by WinBuilder: they need to exist locally on your machine (#3) and WinBuilder will copy them into the build. This includes the free FTK Imager program, because even through Accessdata/Exterro provides FTK Imager freely, the user needs to download and accept the EULA before WinBuilder will copy it into the build.

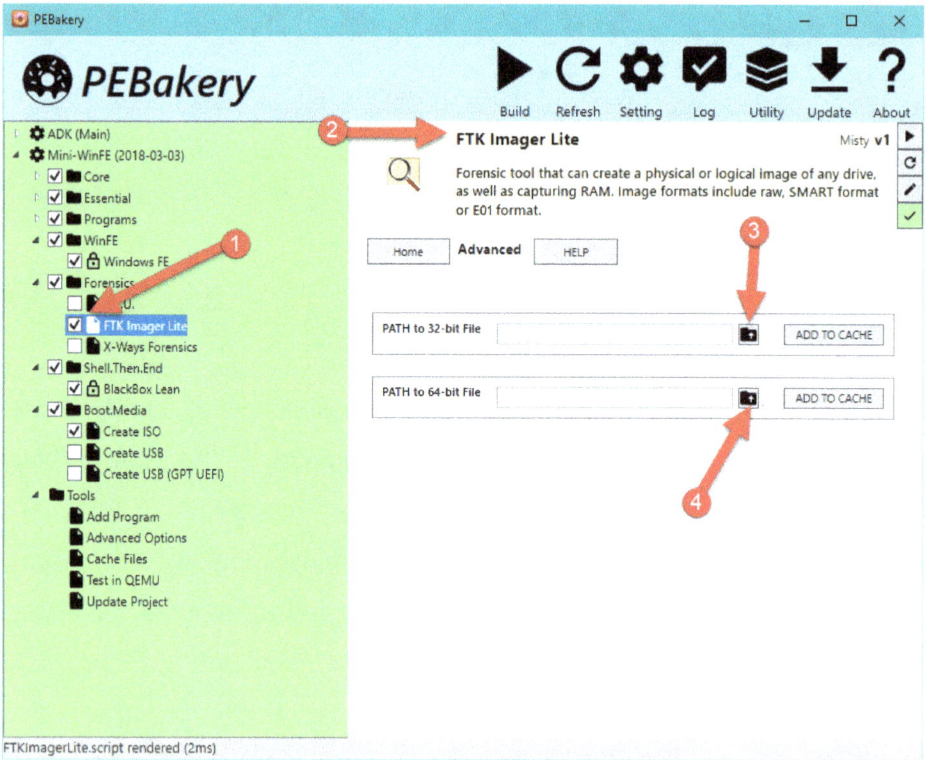

Figure 8.14 Adding forensic apps

A useful script in WinBuilder/Mini-WinFE is that of **Add Custom Folders\Files** as seen in Figure 8.15. If you have programs that you wish to use in WinFE and you don't want to write a script to inject the programs into the build, simply point this script to a folder on your computer that contains your programs. You will then have a folder of forensic tools in your WinFE build without having to spend the time writing and troubleshooting a script.

To run the programs, navigate to the directory in WinFE and run the executables. This is one of the most useful scripts as it eliminates writing scripts to automate the injection of the programs into WinFE.

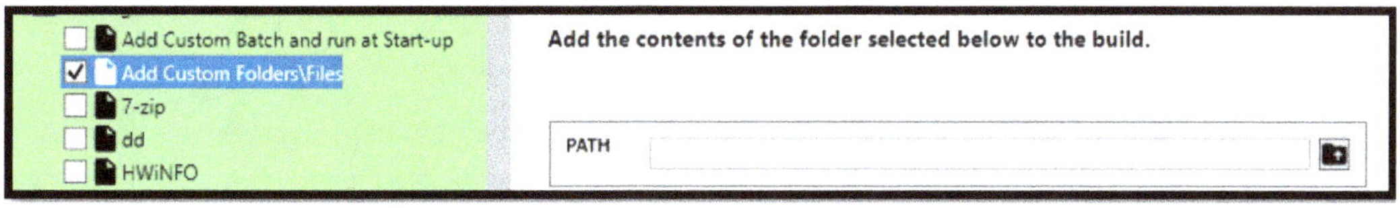

Figure 8.15 Custom folders\Files

The key point of Mini-WinFE

I saved the WinFE scripts section in this chapter last, because of their importance in order to understand the options of each. There are different WinFE scripts, with different options. The scripts for the WinBuilder builds include:

Write Protect Script/Application	Recommendation
DISKPART only	Avoid using it!
Write Protect Tool **optional**	Ok, but be careful, and limited to 32bit.
Write Protect Tool **hard-coded**	Use, but limited to 32bit.
Write Protect Tool and forensic Disk Management tool both **optional**	Ok, but be careful.
Write Protect Tool and forensic Disk Management tool both **hard-code**	Use. Great for both first responders and examiners.

The best option for Mini-WinFE is the script that contains **both** the Write Protect Tool and the Disk Management (forensic) tool **and** is hard-coded (locked). This gives the option of either a 32bit or 64bit build and prevents inadvertently building a winpe instead of a WinFE. I cannot stress the importance enough as I have seen a winpe being built instead of a WinFE, and this is something that can be easily prevented.

Determining the version of the write protect script that you have is simple. Check to see if the WinFE script is locked or not (Figure 8.16) in your WinBuilder application.

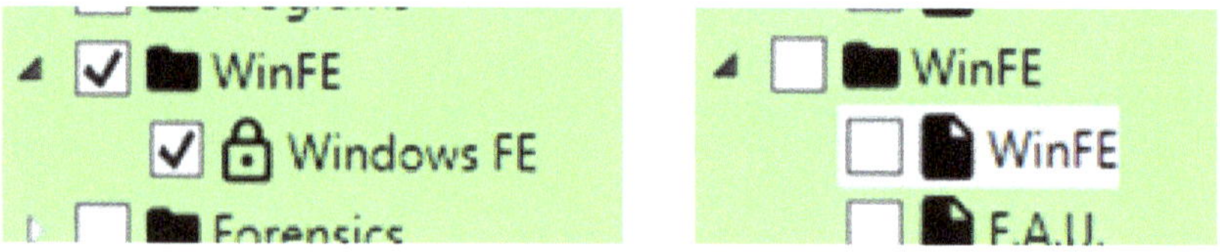

Figure 8.16 Locked WinFE and Unlocked (optional) WinFE

If you can uncheck the WinFE/Windows FE checkbox, you are not working with the hard-coded, error-free version of the write protect script. It will still work; however, you will need to be diligent to ensure that you build a WinFE and avoid building a winpe.

There are other important differences between the two WinFE scripts. One script (the unlocked version seen in Figure 8.17) provides an option for 'no automount' and an option to not run at startup. With this script, you could theoretically check the appropriate WinFE box, and potentially still not have a WinFE if you did not check the "NoAutoMount" option, and/or did not select to "Run at startup".

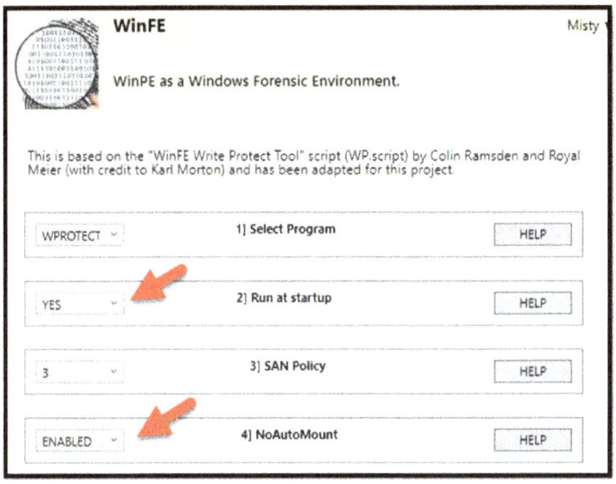

Figure 8.17 Unlocked WinFE Script

The locked version of the WinFE script (Figure 8.17) does not give any options to de-select the script, nor options to not run at startup, nor not automount drives. This is the **most secure way to build a Mini-WinFE** as it is impossible to inadvertently build a winpe. When teaching first responders, this is the best script to use. This is not to say that first responders would not be competent in using the unlocked script, but as a time savings function in teaching and for preventing errors, the locked script is better.

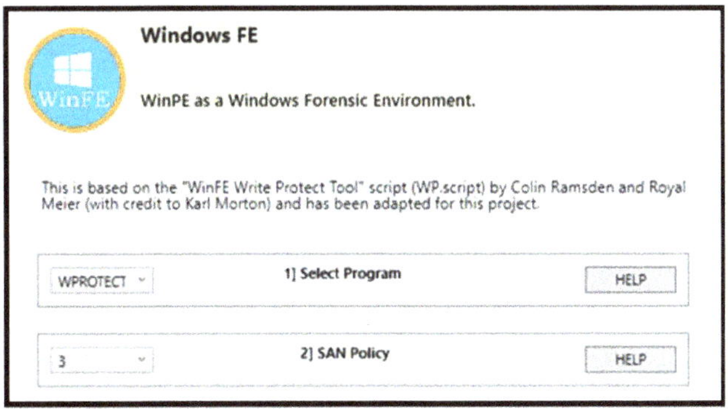

Figure 8.17 Locked version

Choosing the appropriate write protect tool

There are two options, with a help button (#1) for reminders of which tool you need. WPROTECT (#2) is the Colin Ramsden Write Protect tool and DISKMGR (#3) is Erwan's Disk Manager program. If you choose WPROTECT and build a 64bit version, the build will revert to Erwan's Disk Manager program as WPROTECT is only 32bit. Figure 8.18 shows the options in the selections.

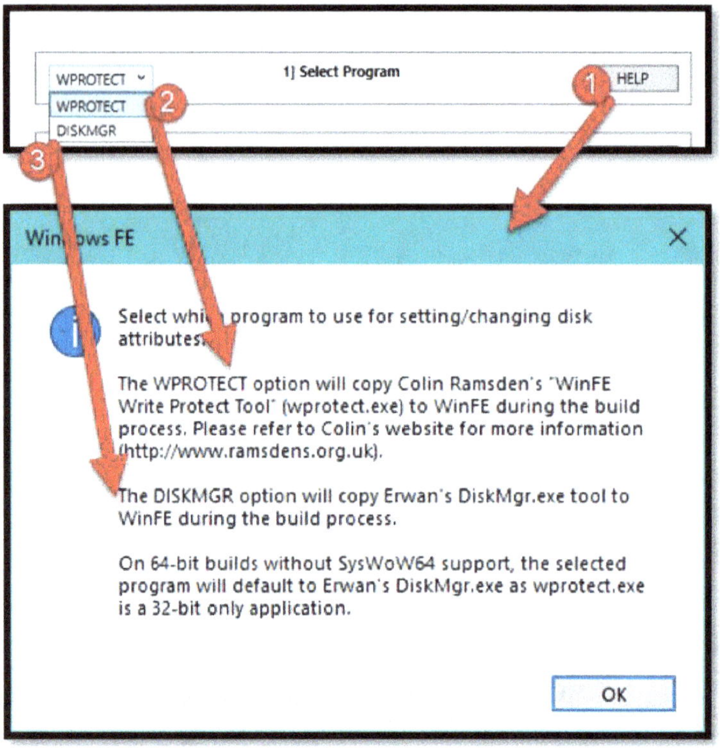

Figure 8.18 Selection of write protection program

SAN Policy

SAN Policy 3 and 4 are the latest upgrades to mounting drives in WinFE. The difference between the options can been seen in the help file (#1) in Figure 8.19. The only difference is that SAN Policy 3 (#2) keeps all drives OFFLINE when booted, whereas SAN Policy 4 (#4) only keeps the internal drives OFFLINE. SAN Policy 4 will save you a step of placing your target drive ONLINE and subsequently in READ/WRITE in order to write an image or save files to it.

For simplicity sake, in that knowing which drives are in which status, you can choose SAN Policy 3 and know that upon booting WinFE, all drives are OFFLINE, regardless if internal or external or boot. This may be the better option for first responders who may not be using WinFE with enough frequency to remember that some drives will be OFFLINE and some will be ONLINE upon booting, and just treat all drives the same from booting.

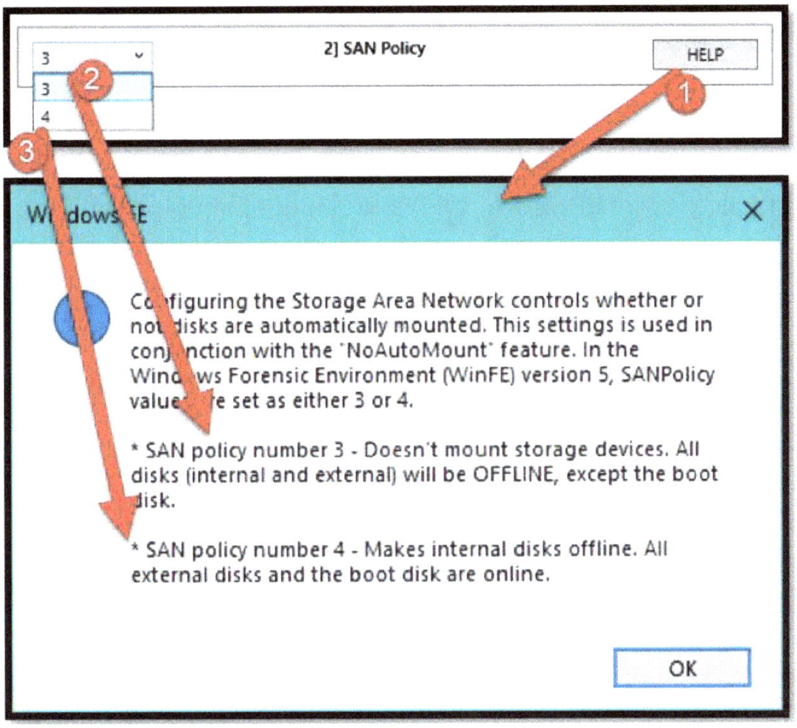

Figure 8.19 SAN policy selection

The Mini-WinFE Menu

The menu is accessed by right clicking anywhere on the desktop. If you elected to have WinBuilder inject X-Ways Forensics, FTK Imager, and/or F.A.U., you will see the menu items. Otherwise, any tools copied into the build or outside the build will be accessed via File Explorer. The Launch Bar command in the menu provides the same menu options, but in a Mac/Linux launch bar appearance.

Tips and Tricks, aka, news you can use

You have the information to build a Mini-WinFE, from where to download a legitimate project, choosing appropriate scripts, and running WinBuilder. There are some building tips that will be helpful to you based on my experience of building hundreds of WinFEs over the past decade. Some of these tips will save you hours of frustration.

- The Mini-WinFE is the best build to start with and end with.
- Use the scripts in the Mini-WinFE. They work as-is.
- Use the 'copy folder/file' script rather than write a script for tools.
- Accept that many programs won't run in Mini-WinFE.
- The time spent forcing a tool to work in WinFE is better spent elsewhere.
- Mini-WinFE is just a "**pe**", not a complete "OS".
- The more you add, the larger media you need to run Mini-WinFE.
- The more you add, the more RAM that may be need to run Mini-WinFE.
- The more you add, the more chance fewer machines it will work with.
- Change the desktop background so you know you are in WinFE, not the host.
- Use portable applications only.
- Use Windows To Go if you really need to run an application that doesn't run in Mini-WinFE.
- Realistically determine your Mini-WinFE purpose. 95% is probably imaging...build your Mini-WinFE to fit your realistic needs.
- Place your forensic apps outside the WinFE build (on a USB) as it is easier to update programs by copying onto the WinFE USB than it is to rebuild a WinFE.
- Store driver packs on the WinFE USB/CD in case you need a driver to install on the fly (driver packs are available on reboot.pro. Just search for driver packs on the website).

Forcing programs to work in WinFE

If there is a specific program that you want to work in Mini-WinFE, but you are getting errors like seen in Figure 8.20, you have a few choices. One, you can work through the errors by finding the dependent files and copying them into WinFE. Two, you can try another WinFE WinBuilder that may have the dependent files by default, such as a full WinBuilder project that is not WinFE.

You will need to copy the WinFE write protect script into the project. Or better yet, consider if you really want to make the program work in WinFE.

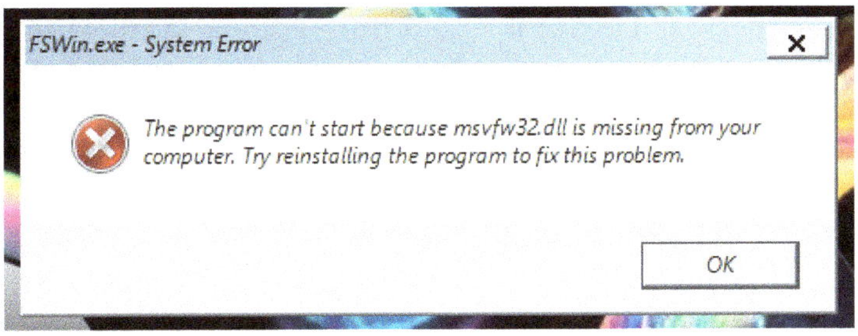

Figure 8.20 Program error

How much do you want the tool to run in WinFE?

We each have our 'favorite' tools, and with WinFE, we may want to be able to run that tool in WinFE. When the tools don't run without errors, the decision to make it work should be looked at on a slide scale of effort. If you are the developer of the tool, you more likely will be able to make it work under WinFE as you have the code and can modify the tool. If you are not the developer of the tool, you will have to modify WinFE as you cannot modify the tool. Any tool that I want to introduce into Mini-WinFE that does not work the first time is placed on a sliding scale as seen in Figure 8.21. Depending on the expected effort and chance of getting the tool to work in WinFE, I decide if the time will be worth the effort.

There are some tools that I can do without in WinFE and others that I may really want to work. I tend to stick with the "Simple to Depends" rule unless it is a tool that I wrote and can re-write it to work in WinFE. Otherwise, the better decision may be to not try to force it to work in WinFE and choose another FOS (Windows To Go, etc..).

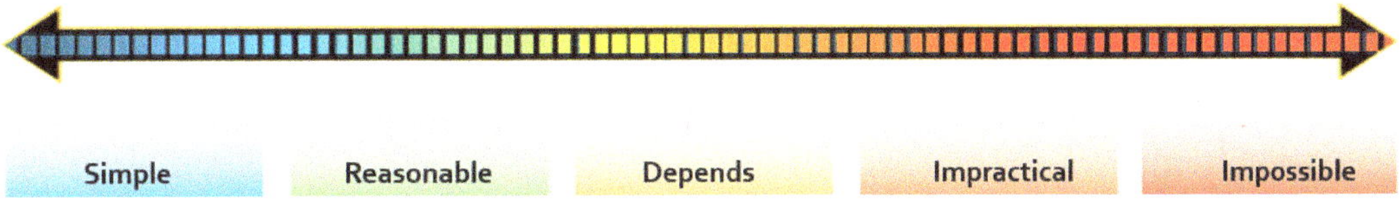

Figure 8.21 Sliding scale to get a tool to work

Errors but still works?

Some tools that you may want to add will show an error but will still function. To continue using a tool that gives constant errors but appears to function is a decision you need to make, as maybe the tool is functioning for what you need or maybe the errors directly affect the tasks that you need to be done.

If you are looking for a FOS that is packed with forensic applications, then the only choice will be one of the many Live Linux distros like CAINE or DEFT. But I refer you to the intended purpose of the FOS that you need. Do you need hundreds of applications or just a few? Do you really want to pack a WinFE full of applications that you know that you won't use?

As one who has done it, let me warn you that I know you will end up over-building a Mini-WinFE in an attempt to make it into a full-fledged Windows OS. I know that you will do this because WinFE is neat. My warning to you is that after you over-build a WinFE, realize that you overdid it, you will see that the Mini-WinFE as-is will fit almost all of your needs. An over-built WinFE is just too much for the time needed to build and test, and too much for the vast majority of what you need a FOS to accomplish.

CHAPTER 9: WinFE 10

We have now come to WinFE 10, released in 2020! Again, the biggest changes of WinFE come from Colin Ramsden, first with his write protect application and now with WinFE able to run in the **ARM architecture**!

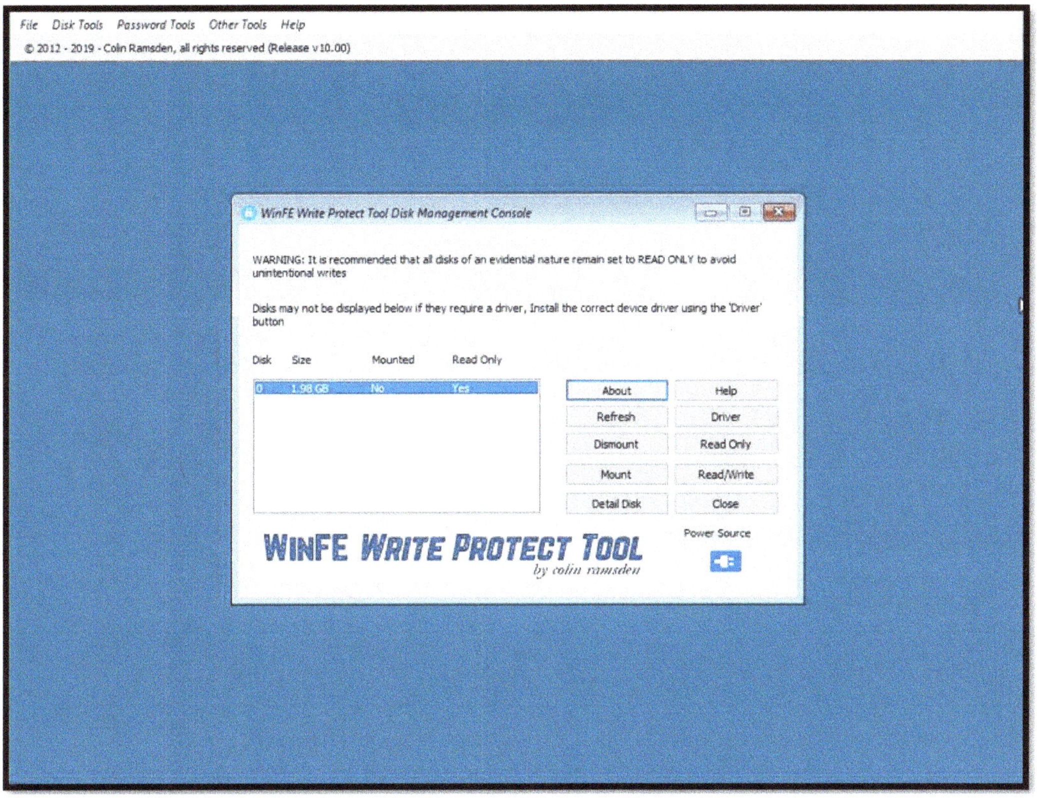

Figure 9.1 WinFE 10

With the Basic WinFE, we used the command line (batch files) to build the WinFE, then moved onto a GUI (WinBuilder) to build the Mini-WinFE, and now we are back to the command line to build WinFE 10. But do not be afraid of the command line. The build process is still fairly quick and painless.

Colin Ramsden's website, www.winfe.net, is the authoritative source on building WinFE 10. The following instructions are paraphrased in a slightly different manner to give an alternative in how to look at building WinFE 10. Figure 9.2 is a visual of the build steps of WinFE 10.

Through a series of commands and file/folder copying, the WinFE 10 build files are prepared first (file preparation, software installation, building the files). Once the WinFE files are prepped, then you can choose to build any or all of the build options seen below in Figure 9.2.

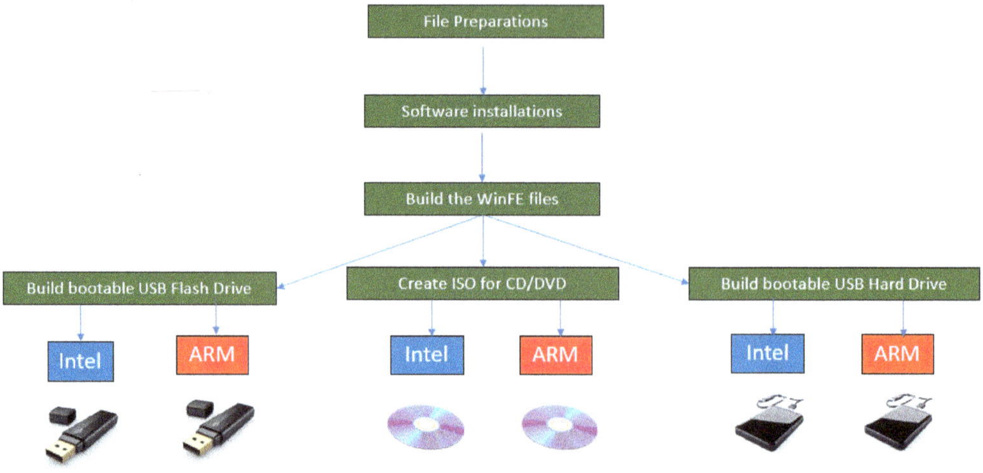

Figure 9.2 WinFE 10 Build Process

WinFE 10 build options.

The choices of WinFE 10 bootable media as seen in Figure 9.2 are:

- WinFE 10 bootable USB flash drive - **Intel** (**x86, x64**)
- WinFE 10 bootable USB flash drive - **ARM**
- WinFE 10 bootable CD/DVD - **Intel** (**x86, x64**)
- WinFE 10 bootable CD/DVD - **ARM**
- WinFE 10 bootable USB hard drive - **Intel** (**x86, x64**)
- WinFE 10 bootable USB hard drive - **ARM**

Much like you maintain your forensic gear ready-to-go, consider creating multiple WinFE 10 bootable media on-hand in the same ready-to-go manner. Building a WinFE 10 (or any WinFE!) under tight time constraints can result in frustrations in time to build, operator and build errors, and little time to test prior to use. Build and test at your leisure so that you can use immediately when needed.

Build Tips

- Use elevated command prompts (configure cmd.exe to run admin by default)
- Accept default installation file paths for applications.
- Download only from trusted websites (winfe.net, Microsoft.com, 7-zip.org, Accessdata.com, etc…).
- The bootable USB flash drive should not be greater than 32 Gigabytes (FAT32 size limitation).
- Recommended to use one drive to store your WinFE work, separate from your C:\ drive. This guide uses "W:\". You can build WinFE on your host (C:\) drive if desired.
- Building a WinFE within a virtual machine may be a timesaver when needing to revert to snapshots if errors in the build process.
- Make batch files for some commands to save time and reduce typos.
- Build a WinFE 10 before you need it so you can test it at your leisure.

Be sure to match the requirements at a minimum of build standards. Older versions of operating system, frameworks, or ADK can result in build failures. Be sure to download source files directly from their sources and do not rely on 3rd party sources, simply because if your build is not forensically sound, then nothing it touches will be either.

Requirements

1. **Windows 10 Pro**, build version of at least 1803 (at least this version)
2. **Windows 10 ADK**, version 1803*
   - https://docs.microsoft.com/en-us/windows-hardware/get-started/adk-install
3. **WinFE 10 Intel x86/x64 framework package (from www.winfe.net)**
   - Intel x86/x64 framework package
4. **WinFE 10 ARM framework package (from www.winfe.net)**
   - ARM framework package
5. **7-Zip**
   - https://www.7-zip.org/
6. **FTK Imager 3.4.0.1 (32-bit)**
   - https://accessdata.com/product-download#past-versions
7. **FTK Imager 4.2.0 (64-bit)**
   - https://accessdata.com/product-download#past-versions

*Regarding the Windows ADK requirement;

*"Starting with Windows 10, **version 1809**, Windows Preinstallation Environment (PE) is released separately from the Assessment and Deployment Kit (ADK). To add Windows PE to your ADK installation, download the Windows PE Addon and run the included installer after installing the ADK." https://docs.microsoft.com/en-us/windows-hardware/get-started/adk-install*

Either version (1803 which includes PE or later versions that do not) will build WinFE 10. The important point to remember is to know which version you are using because you need the PE addon component for the build process to complete successfully.

As with any WinFE build, not all forensic software will run fully or at all in WinFE 10. Try to add your tools of choice and test if workable. The best tools, and usually the most common to work, are portable applications; however, some applications that have not been developed to be portable may actually run as portable apps in WinFE. You won't know if you don't try!

Steps 1-3 are to prepare the WinFE files before building. Step 2 is an example of adding your tools to the build (ie: install 32bit, copy files, uninstall 32bit, install 64bit, copy files, uninstall 64bit).

Step 1 : Application and file preparation

1. Install 7-zip
2. Install Windows 10 ADK
3. Unzip ('Extract here') the Intel x86/x64 framework package to **`W:\`**
4. Unzip ('Extract here') the ARM framework package to **`W:\`**

Step 2 : Forensic software installations (*the WinFE 10 ARM* includes *an imager in the build*)

1. *Uninstall any FTK Imager applications.*
2. Install FTK Imager 3.4.0.1 (32-bit, accept default path).
3. Copy the entire contents of the FTK Imager folder '**`C:\Program Files(x86)\AccessData\`**'
4. Paste the 'FTK Imager' folder into **`'W:\IntelWinFE\USB\x86-x64\tools\x86'`**.
5. *Uninstall the 32-bit version of 'FTK Imager'.*
6. Install FTK Imager 4.2.0 (64-bit, accept default path).
7. Copy the entire FTK Imager folder at **`'C:\Program Files\AccessData\'`**
8. Paste the 'FTK Imager' folder into **`'W:\IntelWinFE\USB\x86-x64\tools\x64'`**.
9. *Uninstall the 64-bit version of 'FTK Imager'.*
10. Place additional tools in the appropriate build paths (...**`x86`** and ....**`x64`**)

Step 3 : WinFE Build Files Preparation

1. From a cmd.exe prompt, navigate into the **`'W:\IntelWinFE'`** folder.
2. Type **`'MakeWinFEx64-x86.bat'`**
3. Press enter.
4. The WinFE 10 'Intel' files have been created.
5. From a cmd.exe prompt, navigate into the **`'W:\ARMWinFE'`** folder.
6. Type **`'MakeWinFEARM.bat'`**
7. Press enter.
8. The WinFE 10 'ARM' files have been created.

The following are WinFE builds on various media in both ARM and Intel (**BLUE** – Intel, **RED**-ARM).

Step 4 Option 1: Build a WinFE 10 (*Intel*) bootable CD/DVD ISO

1. From a cmd.exe prompt, navigate into the **'W:\IntelWinFE'** folder.
2. Type **'Makex64-x86-CD.bat'**
3. Press enter.
4. Your ISO folder now contains a WinFE 10 'Intel' bootable CD/DVD ISO file

Step 4 Option 2: Build a WinFE 10 (*ARM*) bootable CD/DVD ISO

1. From a cmd.exe prompt, navigate into the **'W:\ARMWinFE'** folder.
2. Type **'MakeARM-CD.bat'**
3. Press enter.
4. Your ISO folder now contains a WinFE 10 'ARM bootable CD/DVD ISO file

Step 4 Option 3: Build a WinFE 10 (*Intel*) bootable USB flash drive (UFD)

1. Plug in the USB flash drive to be used for an *Intel* WinFE 10
2. At a cmd.exe prompt, type '**diskpart**' and press enter, then enter the following commands

```
DISKPART>
Type: List Disk <Enter>
Type: Select Disk X (X being your USB Flash Drive) <Enter>
Type: Clean <Enter>
Type: Create Partition Primary <Enter>
Type: Format FS=FAT32 Quick <Enter>
Type: Active <Enter>
Type: Assign <Enter>
Type: Exit <Enter>
```

3. Navigate to **'W:\IntelWinFE\USB\x86-x64\'**.
4. Copy all these folders (boot, efi, etc..) to the root of your newly prepared, bootable WinFE 10 USB flash drive.
5. Return to the cmd.exe prompt and type the following (do not include the trailing '\' as part of the drive letter).

```
bootsect.exe /nt60 <USB flash drive letter>: /force
/mbr
```

6. Safely eject the completed WinFE 10 (***Intel***) USB Flash Drive!

Step 4 Option 4: Build a WinFE 10 (*ARM*) bootable USB flash drive (UFD)

1. Plug in the USB flash drive to be used for an *ARM* WinFE 10
2. At a cmd.exe prompt, type '**diskpart**' and press enter, then enter the following commands

```
DISKPART>
Type: List Disk <Enter>
Type: Select Disk X (X being your USB Flash Drive) <Enter>
Type: Clean <Enter>
Type: Create Partition Primary <Enter>
Type: Format FS=FAT32 Quick <Enter>
Type: Active <Enter>
Type: Assign <Enter>
Type: Exit <Enter>
```

3. Navigate to '**W:\ARMWinFE\USB\ARM**'.
4. Copy all folders (boot, efi, etc..) to the root of your newly prepared, bootable WinFE 10 USB flash drive.
5. Return to the cmd.exe prompt and type the following (do not include the trailing '\' as part of the drive letter).

```
bootsect.exe /nt60 <USB flash drive letter>: /force /mbr
```

6. Safely eject the completed WinFE 10 (***ARM***) USB Flash Drive!

Step 4 Option 5: Build a WinFE 10 (*Intel*) bootable USB hard disk drive (UHD)

1. Plug in the USB hard disk drive to be used for an *Intel* WinFE 10
2. At a cmd.exe prompt, type '**diskpart**' and press enter, then enter the following commands

```
DISKPART>
Type: List Disk <Enter>
Type: Select Disk X (X being your USB Hard Disk Drive)
<Enter>
Type: Clean <Enter>
Type: Create Partition Primary Size = 8000 <Enter>
Type: Format FS=FAT32 Quick <Enter>
Type: Active <Enter>
Type: Assign <Enter>
Type: Create Partition Primary <Enter>
Type: Format FS=NTFS Quick <Enter>
Type: Assign <Enter>
Type: Exit <Enter>
```

3. Navigate to '**W:\IntelWinFE\USB\x86-x64**\'.
4. Copy all folders (boot, efi, sources, etc..) to the root of the WinFE 10 USB hard disk drive.
5. Return to the cmd.exe prompt and type the following (do not include the trailing '\' as part of the drive letter).

```
bootsect.exe /nt60 <FAT32 volume letter>: /force /mbr
```

6. Safely eject the completed WinFE 10 (***Intel***) USB Hard Disk Drive!

Step 4 Option 6: Build a WinFE 10 (*ARM*) bootable USB hard disk drive (UHD)

1. Plug in the USB hard disk drive to be used for an *Intel* WinFE 10
2. At a cmd.exe prompt, type '**diskpart**' and press enter, then enter the following commands

```
DISKPART>
Type: List Disk <Enter>
Type: Select Disk X (X being your USB Hard Disk Drive)
<Enter>
Type: Clean <Enter>
Type: Create Partition Primary Size = 8000 <Enter>
Type: Format FS=FAT32 Quick <Enter>
Type: Active <Enter>
Type: Assign <Enter>
Type: Create Partition Primary <Enter>
Type: Format FS=NTFS Quick <Enter>
Type: Assign <Enter>
Type: Exit <Enter>
```

3. Navigate to '**W:\ARMWinFE\USB\ARM**'.
4. Copy all folders (boot, efi, sources, etc..) to the root of the WinFE 10 USB hard disk drive.
5. Return to the cmd.exe prompt and type the following (do not include the trailing '\' as part of the drive letter).

```
bootsect.exe /nt60 <FAT32 volume letter>: /force /mbr
```

6. Safely eject the completed WinFE 10 (***ARM***) USB Hard Disk Drive!

WinFE 10 Features

WinFE 10 is a pre-configured WinFE build. The default features include the Write Protect Tool, a Basic Disk Imager, Password Tools, and standard Windows components (Notepad, Explorer, Windows Defender, Command Prompt, and Network Support). Each of these features are accessible through the menu bar. The Write Protect Tool previously discussed can be seen in Figure 9.3.

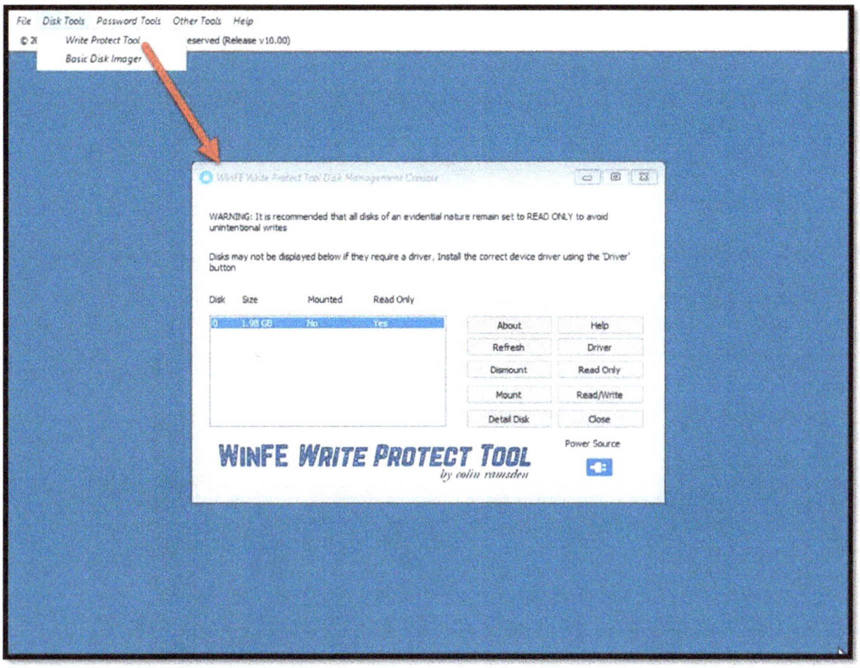

Figure 9.3 WinFE 10 Menu Bar

The default imaging program (Basic Disk Imager, Figure 9.4) was developed by Colin Ramsden and creates dd (flat) images of media. Although yet-another-dd-imager may not sound exciting, this imager is because **it runs in ARM**, which most Windows-based imaging programs do not.

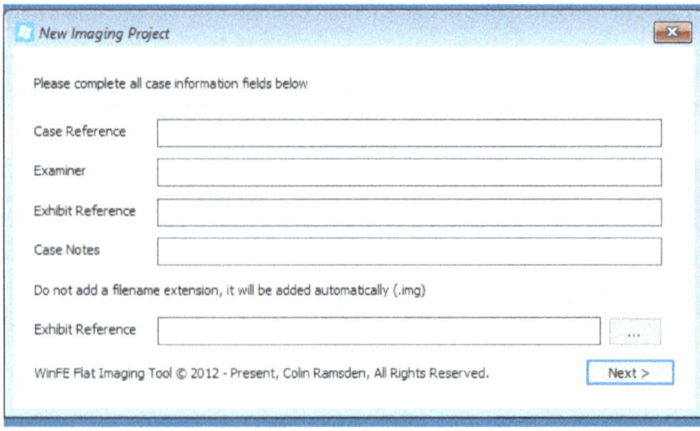

Figure 9.4 WinFE 10 Basic Disk Imager

The Password Tools include a Standard Reset and an Advanced Reset. The Advanced Reset is used for Active Directory client computers. The Password Tools require a license key (Figure 9.5) from www.WindowsPasswordTool.com. Once your key has been entered, the disk with the password to be reset must be READ/WRITE and MOUNTED in order to make changes.

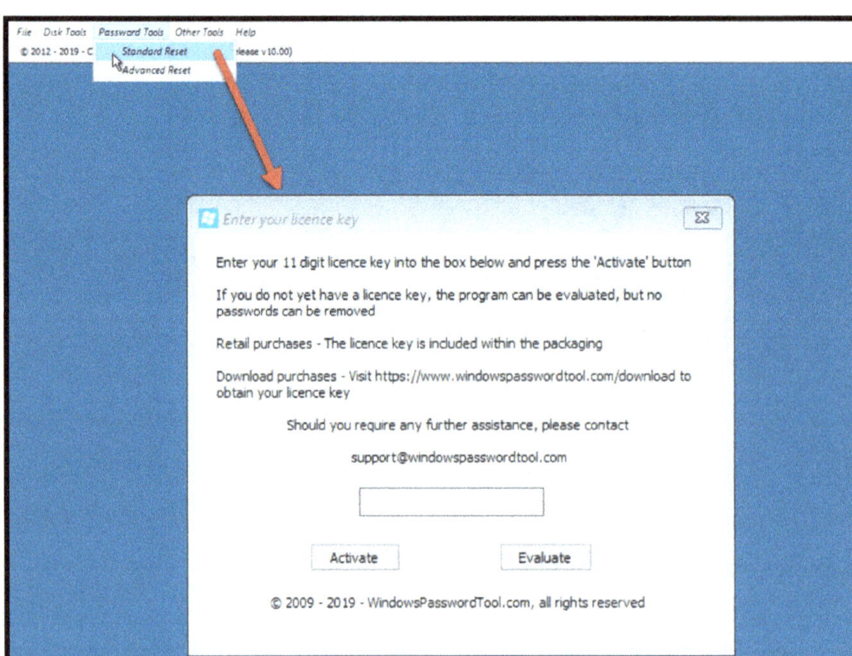

Figure 9.5 Enter license key

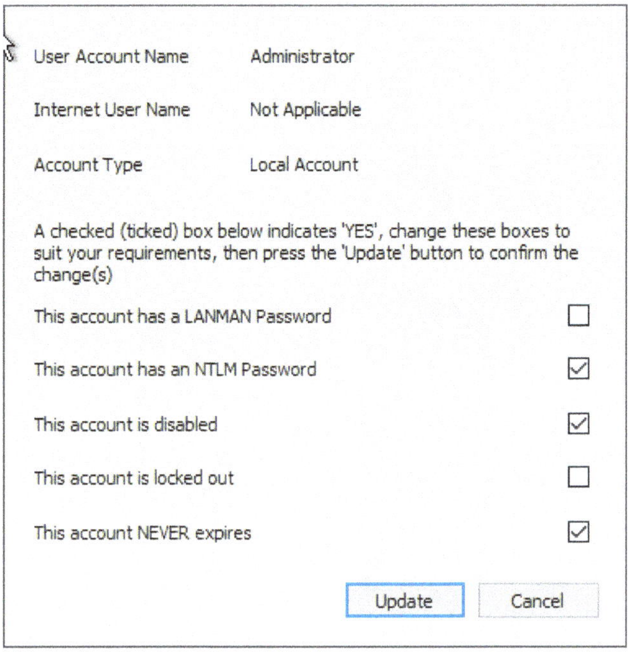

Figure 9.6 Update changes

Bitlocker Support

You can encrypt the WinFE NTFS partition with Bitlocker from the command line using Manage-Bde.exe. Using Manage-Bde.exe, you can also manage BitLocked drives on the evidence machines after booting into WinFE. For information on using Manage-Bde.exe, refer to Microsoft's documentation at https://docs.microsoft.com/en-us/windows-server/administration/windows-commands/manage-bde.

For example, WinFE can boot a BitLocked machine, and if the password is available, can unlock the machine via command line as seen below:

```
manage-bde -unlock E: -recoverypassword 111111-222222-333333-444444-555555-666666-777777-888888
```

Network Support

WinFE 10 can access a network via the PE Network Manager seen in Figure 9.7 (any WinFE can practically connect to a network as well). This may be useful in some situations to access the Internet to either remotely control a

WinFE booted machine and/or copy files from the WinFE booted machines across the network/Internet.

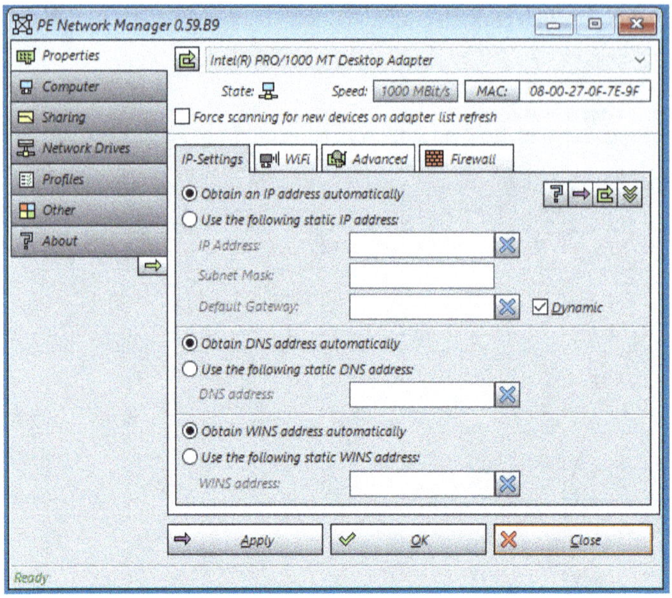

Figure 9.7 Network access

Windows Defender?

Windows Defender can be used in WinFE 10 if both the WinFE and hard drive to be scanned are online and in READ/WRITE mode. To update Windows Defender, download the latest updates from https://www.askvg.com/official-links-to-download-latest-virus-definition-updates-offline-installers-for-microsoft-security-essentials-mse/ and save to the root of the bootable WinFE USB device. Windows Defender actually takes effort and time to be able to get working in WinFE, and until an easier (less time consuming!) method is developed, you can ignore Windows Defender in WinFE 10.

Your forensic tools!

WinFE 10 does not provide a menu for the tools that you added during the build process like Mini-WinFE does. However, you can access them through File Explorer, under your CD Drive letter as seen in Figure 9.8. For tools that do not run in WinFE 10, be sure that you are running the matching architecture such as a 32bit tool in a 32bit WinFE 10.

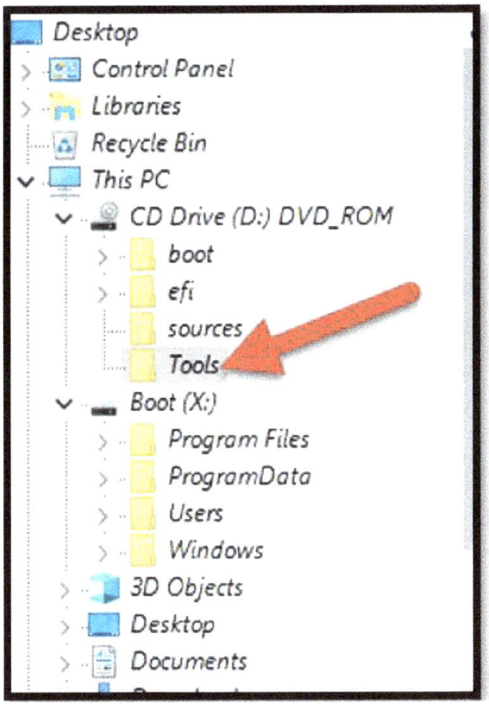

Figure 9.8 Tools location in WinFE 10

Another option of accessing forensic applications (or any application that you have for that matter), is through external media that you attach to the system. So, if you neglected to add a tool, or while onsite decide to use a tool that you didn't consider before, you do not need to rebuild WinFE. Simply plug in an external media, such as a flash drive that contains the tool you need and run the program from the external media. For USB flash drives and hard drives, you can copy programs to the device without having to rebuild WinFE as compared to WinFE 10 running from a CD or DVD.

CHAPTER 10: Other WinFE Builds

We have covered the most popular WinFE builds. There are other WinFE builds that you can find online, and certainly more to come. You will also find instructions on building a WinFE in numerous blogs and videos. For many of the online instructions, the build instructions are for a Basic WinFE. Even if the instructions are using the latest version of Windows, if DISKPART is the method for disk toggling, it is still a Basic WinFE.

Windows Triage Environment (WTE)

As WinBuilder is popular, there have been customized WinFEs available on different websites. One of the builds that looked promising was "WTE, Windows Triage Environment". The website, seen in Figure 10.1, is no longer online, and it appears that the content has been put on SourceForge.net, but I cannot vouch for the validity of WTE on SourceForge.net.

Figure 10.1 WTE webpage

I won't link to the original website URL as it now redirects to a non-forensic website. Some of the reasons that I found WTE to be promising was that it used WinBuilder, included Colin Ramsden's Write Protect Tool, and also included quite a few custom applications that are useful for triage (Figure 10.2). Unfortunately, this build seems no longer supported and I include it here as a reminder of not using 'just any WinFE' project that you find online unless it is current and maintained. The other reason this outdated build is listed is to show that you can also customize a WinFE to suit your needs and preferences.

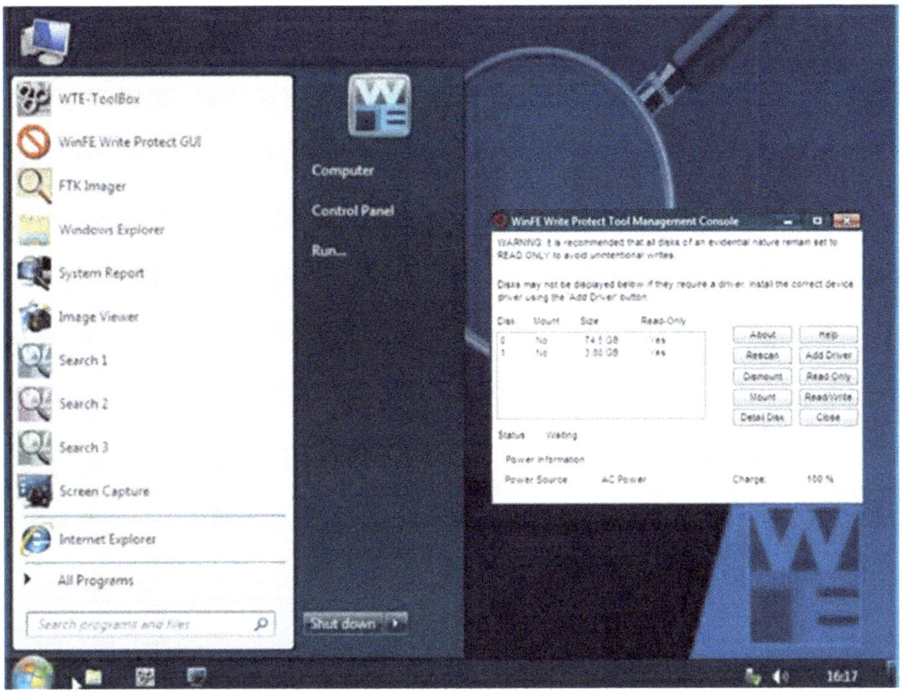

Figure 10.2 WTE Menu and Write Protect Tool

Torrents!

Over the years, I have received many requests of "*can you just send me the WinFE ISO*?" My common and repeated responses have always been that you have must build your own WinFE. My assumption is that some people are too busy to spend the time to learn how to build a WinFE and desperately need it, immediately. It is certainly best to prepare when you don't need a WinFE so that you can be ready when you do need a WinFE.

My other advice is **not downloading** a WinFE from anyone on the Internet. Downloading a pre-built WinFE from a website **most likely is going to violate**

the Microsoft EULA. But that is not the only serious issue. The WinFE ISO is probably infected with malicious software in the ISO file that you will never be able to remove, or even detect. Using such a WinFE will taint any evidence you collect. Don't do that.

Some links to download a WinFE ISO are plainly redirects to malicious Websites, such as shown in Figure 10.3 and others are actual ISO downloads that are most certainly infected with malware.

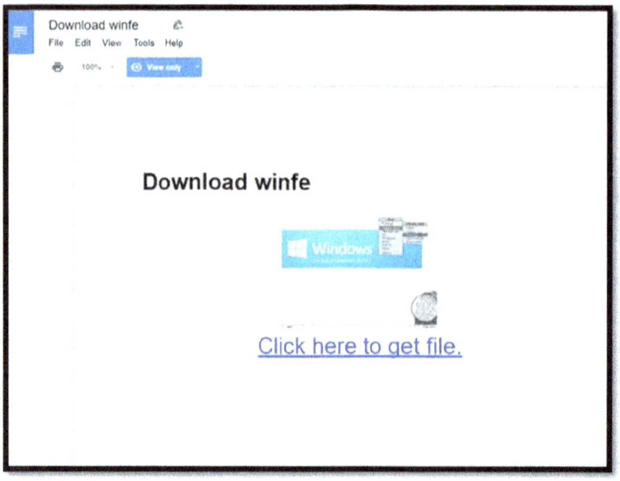

Figure 10.3 Malware link!

Windows to Go

We have covered all WinFEs including the maliciously infected WinFEs! The next build to discuss is Windows to Go (W2G or WTG) as seen in Figure 10.4. W2G is not a WinFE by definition since it is not built from a winpe. However, W2G is as close to a full Windows operating system as you can get!

Since W2G boots computers via external media, such as an external hard drive or USB flash drive, and puts the internal drives OFFLINE, for all intents and purposes, functions like a WinFE but with all the features of a full Windows OS. There are a few subtle, yet substantial differences that you need to be aware.

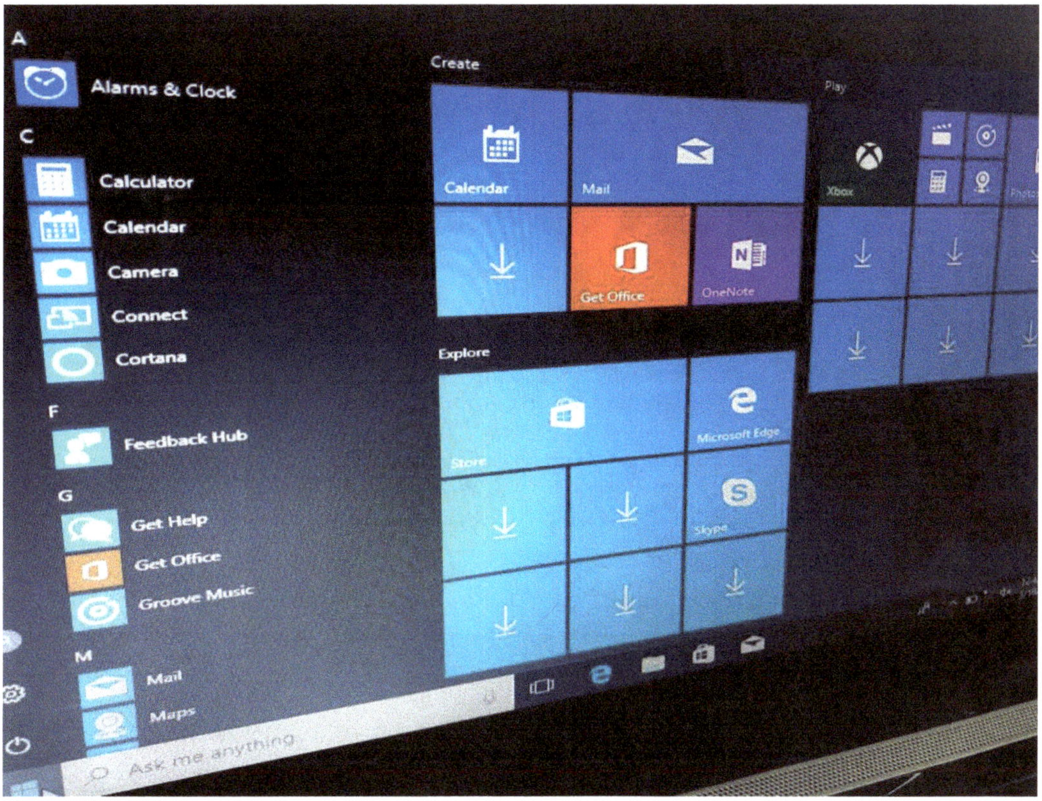

Figure 10.4 Windows To Go

First, the use of W2G needs little by way of instruction. It is quite simply, and literally, a Windows operating system that can run the tools that can run in Windows. This means that if a tool that you must have does not run in WinFE, it will almost without exception run in W2G as long as it runs in Windows.

Building a W2G is also very easy, as it is point-and-click from start to finish. Beginning from the Control Panel in Windows seen in Figure 10.5, click “Windows To Go”, and follow all prompts toward the building of your W2G media.

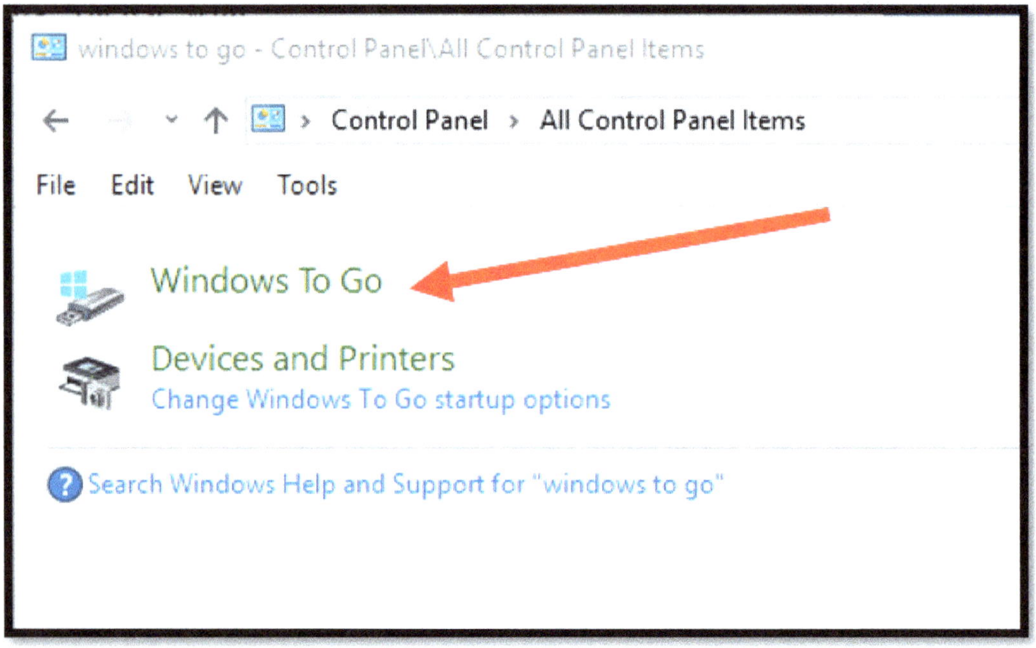

Figure 10.5 Windows To Go

The features of W2G as a FOS make for an effective method to image, triage, or preview data on an evidence machine. Not only can you use any forensic tool that normally runs in a non-W2G Windows OS, but also BitLocker is available in W2G. If the W2G media has enough available space (larger than the evidence media), the entire image can be saved within the W2G partition. With the option of BitLocker on the partition, an image can be securely created and transported within the BitLocked media. The imaging speeds may slow due to reading/writing on the same media, but if security is a concern, this would be an easy option.

Now for the bad news

The source for a W2G is the **Enterprise Edition** of Microsoft Windows, as W2G is an enterprise feature. This is an important aspect of W2G if you are not in an Enterprise environment or do not have access to an Enterprise license. It is possible to create a W2G with a non-Enterprise license, and even use a demo Enterprise license, but be aware that this may not be in alignment with the Microsoft EULA.

There are also online commercial vendors that sell W2G building applications, much like WinBuilder, but developed commercially to build a W2G. One vendor replied to a question I had in licensing related to building a W2G using their tool and a non-Enterprise license. The reply below answered my question clearly that even a commercial utility developed for W2G is not intended to bypass Microsoft's EULA. This is a non-issue if you have an Enterprise license.

> "Windows To Go is an enterprise feature, it is only available in Windows 8/10 Enterprise. This means that it's not completely legal when using a Non-enterprise Windows to create Windows To Go." - *a vendor of W2G building software*

Another issue with W2G to consider is the media to install W2G onto. Only Microsoft certified USB devices are recommended. Actually, by default, you will not be allowed to create a W2G on a non-certified device as seen in Figure 10.6, as you can't continue past this dialog without a certified device.

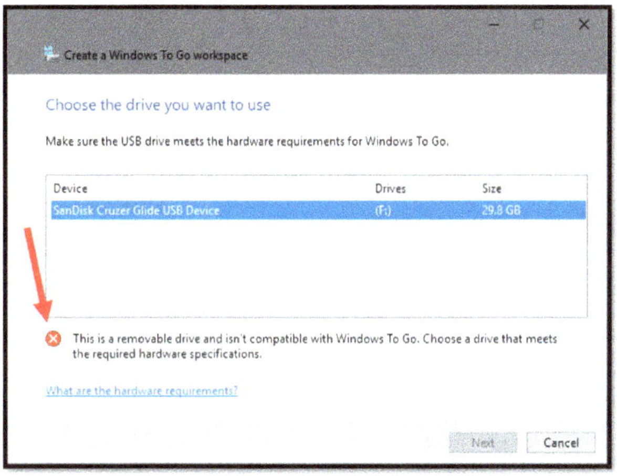

Figure 10.6 Non-certified device

Microsoft certified devices are those that are durable, built for high read/write speeds, and backed with manufacturer warranties (among a few other requirements). Unfortunately, Microsoft-certified USB devices are not inexpensive and also are not easily found in your local electronics or computer store. This means that not only do you have to have access to an Enterprise license, but also must have a certified USB device. Again, this is a non-issue since the certified USB devices are not a restricted purchase item.

Instructions to bypass both the Enterprise EULA and prepare a non-certified

USB device can be found online, but insofar as using W2G, the proper use includes having the required software license and certified device. The creation of a W2G FOS takes more time than building any version of WinFE. W2G building is not more complex to build, but practically, creating W2G is physically installing a complete Windows operating system onto an external drive. It is possible to spend hours creating one W2G, compared to a WinFE that can take less than 5 minutes.

The serious issue to be aware

Similar to WinFE, W2G boots a computer system with the internal drives OFFLINE (SAN Policy 4) as seen in Figure 10.7. And similar to WinFE, drives can be placed ONLINE/OFFLINE. The major difference is that when a drive is placed ONLINE with W2G, write protection for the drive is **OFF**.

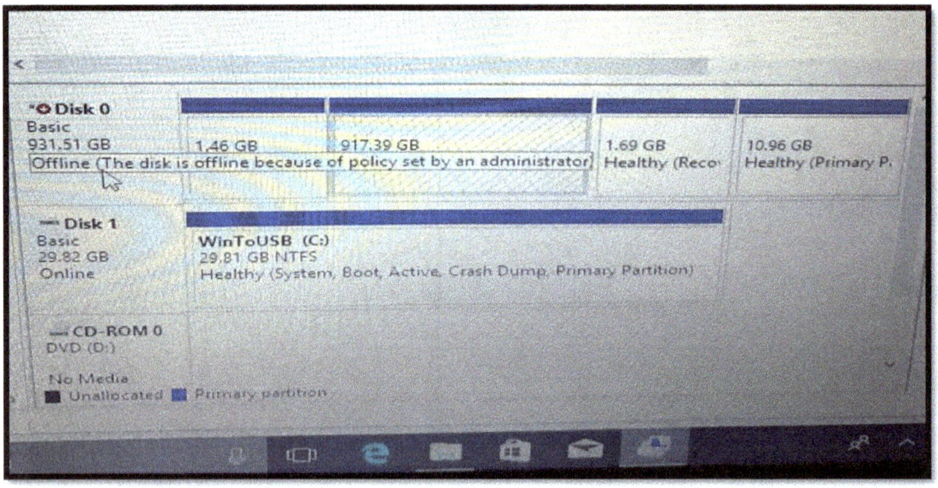

Figure 10.7 Disks are OFFLINE

CHAPTER 11: Commercial WinFE Products

There are good reasons to purchase a commercial WinFE product. Perhaps the most important reason is customer support. Secondly, you can put your trust that the WinFE was built correctly by a commercial vendor if you are unsure of being able to build your own. Both of these reasons also have counters arguments, such as you have to trust that the vendor built the WinFE correctly and that you will have customer support when you need it. Realistically, purchasing a commercial WinFE should give you reasonable assurance that the WinFE is maintained, updated, and supported.

As far as specific vendors that sell WinFE products, there are few. Some outwardly market their product as a WinFE, with slightly different terms such as "Windows Forensics Edition" or "Windows Forensic Boot Disk". Some commercial vendors do not market that their product is based on WinFE, or is actually a WinFE, but rather market their tool that runs in a forensically safe booted system. These products are typically triage or imaging tools installed on WinFE bootable USB flash drives.

In tests that I have done with some of the commercial WinFE products, I did not find anything that would give me pause that one is better than the other insofar as write protection is involved. An argument against commercial WinFE products is that I have seen one product that is no longer available, but was simply a Basic WinFE with one forensic app installed which sold for hundreds of dollars. This particular WinFE is no longer on the company's website, ending support for it. Also, some commercial WinFEs retail for hundreds of dollars may be tied with a software protection device (dongle).

Whether or not purchasing a commercial version of WinFE matters is up to the user. The write protection options may vary depending upon whether DISKPART, a proprietary application, or freely application is used in the WinFE.

CHAPTER 12: Innovative Uses of WinFE

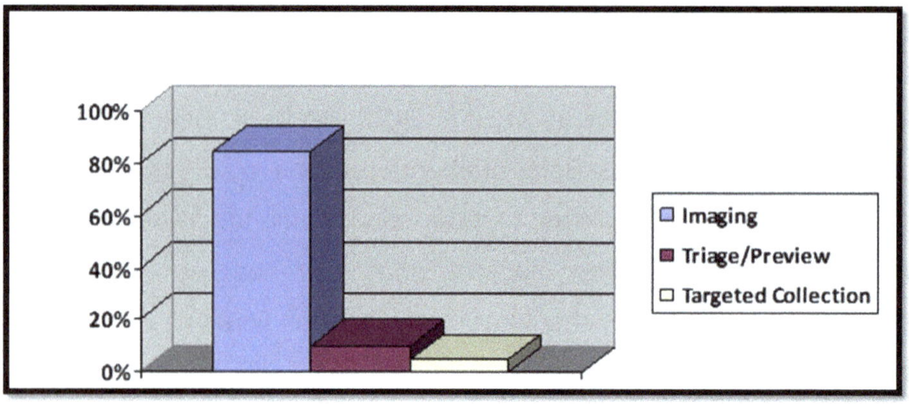

Figure 12.1 Common use of WinFE (an example of one person's needs)

What is the most likely use of WinFE for you? Once you know what you want WinFE to do, you can easily decide how to build it. In all likelihood, imaging is the primary need for a forensic operating system because that may be the only method to access the media. If that is the case, then as long as the WinFE can boot as many computers as possible, run a variety of imaging programs, then WinFE has done its job. Triage and targeted collections are two other popular features of WinFE, but again, related to accessing the media in order to either collect the data or copy/image it.

However, there are other tasks that WinFE may do that you have not thought of or considered. This chapter takes you through innovative methods of using WinFE that will increase your effectiveness as much as you can put these methods to use.

Imaging

As mentioned above and seen in Figure 12.1, a common use of WinFE, especially when there is no other way to get to the data. This is only an example of WinFE's common use, not indicative of everyone's use of WinFE.

WinFE is also a time saving with multiple machines being able to image concurrently, each with its own target drive to save the images. An example would be imaging 25 computers with WinFE, booting one-by-one, connecting a

USB in each computer, and image at the same time. This would be much faster than removing 25 hard drives and connecting to 25 write blockers to how many forensic workstations you may have.

Targeted data collection (files, folders, types of files, email, images, etc..)

Data collection, as it relates to electronic discovery, does not always imitate forensic imaging collection in criminal investigations. Typically, user-created files are simply copied from a custodian computer onto external media. These files consist of basic word processing documents, spreadsheets, email, and the like. Although forensic imaging may not be the most widely method used to collect this data, WinFE does have a place to ensure a forensic collection of specific files from media without having to image the entire media. This is not to say that file copying programs cannot copy files and maintain all metadata, but that if the most secure method of copying files is needed, WinFE can provide for it.

A custodian computer can be booted to WinFE and from the forensically sound environment, the desired user-created files that would have been simply copied while the computer was running, can now be logically imaged (with FTK Imager as an example) in the most forensically sound manner possible. Additionally, booting into the WinFE allows avoiding Administrator privilege issues typically found in corporate environments. The only additional time needed is that time it takes the computer to boot to WinFE, which is not an unreasonable amount of time for data collection.

Triage

In this section, a "triage" and "preview" are considered the same function. No matter how one may interpret different definitions of these two terms, the actual process of looking at the evidence without conducting a full analysis is very similar, if not identical, in practice, even if the goals are different.

One goal is to is to determine the media ranking in priority for analysis against other media (Figure 12.2) and another goal might be to determine whether or not evidence may exist on a media (Figure 12.3).

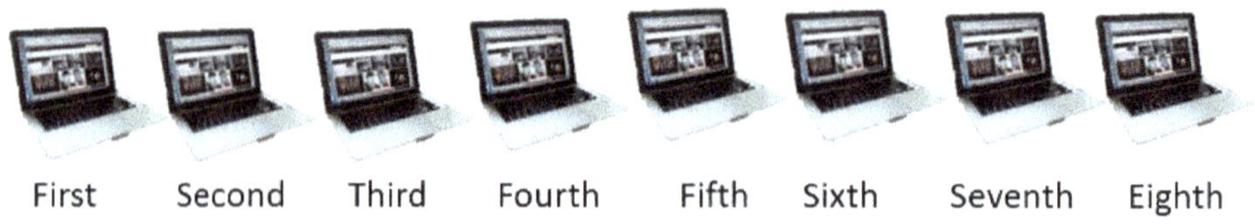

Figure 12.2 Prioritizing analysis

A triage of a computer system with WinFE covers lots of ground and situations. Law enforcement benefits with consent searches, border agencies benefit with border searches, parole officers can use in parole checks, national security response can use in different scenarios, and any place where high level information is needed for actionable intelligence.

Figure 12.3 Eliminating analysis

As with any forensically sound booted system, nearly any utility can be used to interrogate the media, which includes being to conduct keyword searches, view graphic files, or any number of limited analysis processes. The primary difference between WinFE and other types of bootable media such as Linux is that Windows-based programs can be used. As many agencies and corporations use Windows as their primary operating system, the number of persons that are able to use WinFE is certainly higher than other operating systems.

A limitation of conducting a triage/preview with WinFE is that of the tool used. **Some utilities cannot see the physical drive**, in which case, the evidence drive will need to be placed ONLINE in a READONLY mode. At that point, any software will be able to "see" the media in order to triage it. Triage/Previewing is beyond the scope of this guide and mentioned only as a topic of consideration of WinFE usage.

Limited forensic analysis

A limited forensic analysis can be considered a bit more in-depth than a triage, in that the analysis has a goal of finding evidence beyond that of what triage may find. An example would be matters where life or property are at risk and time is of the essence.

Full analysis

Using forensic applications that can run in WinFE and are capable of a full analysis, it is possible to do an entire forensic examination in WinFE on a suspect's computer system. As far as the reason to do this on the evidence machine instead of imaging the media and examining on a forensic workstation depends upon the analyst to make that decision. There are certainly some situations where this would be reasonable, and WinFE provides the ability to do it.

Data review

WinFE can be used as a platform for data review, such as reviewing a forensic image or native files. To review a forensic image, an image mounting application within WinFE can mount a forensic image to allow a reviewer to either review the image as a mounted drive or use specialized software to search the mounted image. A situation where this would be beneficial is that of reviewing forensic images or data extracted from a forensic image that contains illicit photos. When a case reviewer views illicit images on a workstation, the workstation is typically contaminated with temp and cache files, including potential malware. Reviewing under WinFE keeps the workstation untouched and safe.

A secondary method to review data with this method is to boot WinFE in a virtual machine and configure the virtual machine in a manner that the virtualized WinFE can view the evidence. With this method, the reviewer can both review in a virtual (guest) machine while at the same time, have use of their host machine.

Surreptitious acquisitions

Internal corporate investigations, national security investigations, sneak and peek warrants, battlefield intelligence, and high-tech spy-work. Each of these scenarios can be exploited with a WinFE installed on a large capacity USB flash drive. From a quick triage to full data collection, a computer can be acquired with minimal disruption to the computer's environment as disassembly is not needed, and all conducted without leaving electronic traces of the collection, as long as the computer can be booted to WinFE.

With instances of needing actionable intelligence, being able to find and collect relevant data may be impossible given large computer hard drives, or a hostile environment. Booting a machine for specific intelligence can turn a multi-terabyte data storage device into bytes of actionable intelligence, whether it be a terrorism matter or missing person case (Figure 12.4).

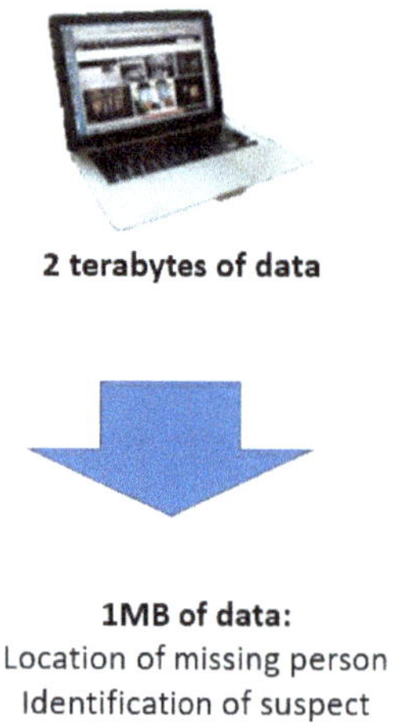

Figure 12.4 Actionable Intelligence

Educational/Training platform

Teaching digital forensics has an obstacle of students being able to do homework at home, due to varying home computer systems. Some students may have older versions of operating systems, or be using an operating system that is not being used in class. WinFE solves the majority of these issues by allowing students to use WinFE at home, using the same software and operating system that is being used in class, regardless of their home computer.

Although not every computer can be booted to WinFE, if the students at least have a system that can boot to WinFE, the class can have a common platform for coursework, homework, and practice. Just as important, since WinFE is a valid forensic tool, students can learn to build it, customize it, and use it for class and the real world.

Remote collections

WinFE provides for network connectivity through a variety of software programs (WinFE 10 is pre-installed with one application, Mini-WinFE can have network scripts added to the build). Remote collections can be made where a physical person at the evidence machine boots the evidence machine with WinFE, connects to the network/Internet, and gives control to a remote examiner. All data copied or imaged at the evidence computer's site can be shipped to the examiner for further analysis.

POW – portable forensic workstation

"POW" isn't a real acronym... but it works for this description. As a WinFE can be carried physically in your pocket, you can have a complete forensic operating system with you at all times. If a device can be booted to a WinFE, it can be triaged or analyzed. If the WinFE resides on a large enough USB, a complete image or sparsely collected data can be stored on the same USB as WinFE.

This is certainly not the best way to prepare for forensics or do forensic work, but it could be the only way in unexpected situations. In that case, it would be the best way if there was no other way to prevent losing the opportunity.

Boot Your Forensic Machine to WinFE

As WinFE is a minimalist version of your full-fledged Windows OS, it will more than likely run a bit faster than your forensic workstation. After all, there probably are a considerable number of programs and processes running each time your forensic machine is on, many of which you do not need. An option for using your imaging tools with WinFE and using your forensic machine would be to boot your forensic machine to WinFE, connect your evidence media, and image to your storage device or network. This would allow using your trusted hardware at the fastest possible use of your OS (WinFE) without the overhead of unnecessary processes running in the background.

RAIDs

WinFE is unique in imaging and/or collecting data from RAIDs. Without getting into specifics about RAIDs or the types of RAIDs, Figure 12.5 shows how WinFE can see a RAID based on whether the RAID is software or hardware based.

Briefly described, a RAID is a set of hard drives that are combined to appear as one volume. The combination is made by using software in the operating system or hardware (RAID controller) on the computer. This is a big difference, and the difference to know when using WinFE.

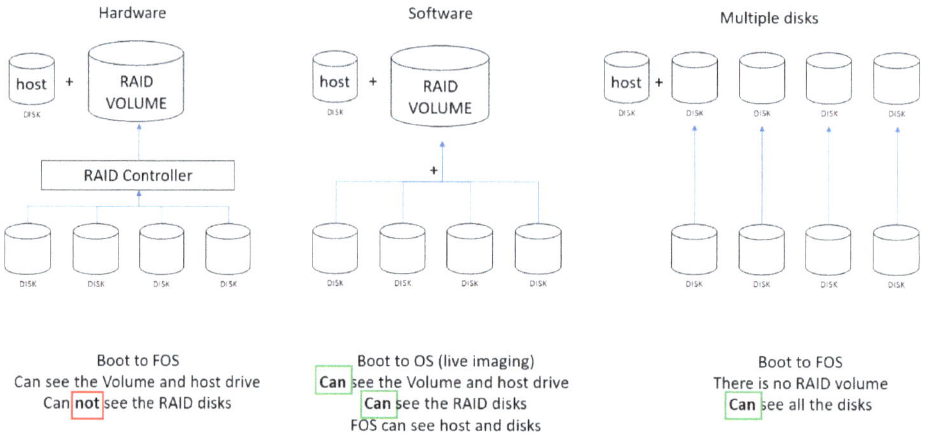

Figure 12.5 RAIDs

In the first image in Figure 12.5, if WinFE is used to boot the system, WinFE will be able to see (and image) the RAID volume, but not see the individual disks. The individual disks will need to be imaged separately outside the machine if imaging is needed.

In the second image, if WinFE is used to boot the system, WinFE will be able to see (and image) the RAID volume as well as the individual disks. This is because the operating system manages the RAID.

In the third image, if WinFE is used to boot the system, WinFE can see (and image) all the disks because they are not in a RAID. Be aware that a system can have a RAID and individual disks, so it is important to know what you are looking at. When facing multiple hard drives in a system, ask yourself questions such as, 'am I seeing a RAID volume or a single disk?'.

Something else that you come up with! Share it!

You can easily come up with something WinFE can do that has not be discussed or used by anyone else. When that happens, share the information! The more uses that WinFE is capable of doing, the more acceptance it will have in the community.

CHAPTER 13: Non-Windows Live CDs

The Live Linux Forensics CDs. CAINE, DEFT, PALADIN. Most all are fantastic tools and should be a part of your toolkit because when one doesn't work, you should have another on hand to try.

Why Linux?

Ease of setting up! Mostly, the Linux Live CDs are pre-built, turnkey, and downloadable forensic operating systems. There is nothing to set up, install, or configure as it is all done for you, including being packed with software.

Linux also works when WinFE might not. Do not get tied down to only using a Linux FOS or only using a Windows FOS. Have both and choose the best for the task at hand. More choices give you more options to handle more situations.

Linux works! Linux is a strong operating system and the write protection is solid as well. It works, so do not discount it no matter how much you may like WinFE more. No one says you can only choose one to have in your toolbox.

Why not Linux?

Not easily customizable, if at all. When you can download a large ISO file that is packed with applications, modifying the ISO and creating a new ISO is not usually going to be easy if you are not familiar with modifying or creating a Linux ISO file.

Software overload is an issue. As some Linux distributions include over a hundred software applications, it is unlikely that all users will ensure that all EULSs are in compliance for digital forensics work. Figure 13.1 shows an example of a Linux Forensic distro that clearly states that the applications may come under different licenses. Some may be shareware, demoware, freeware, home-use only, or commercial-license needed for use. If any of these applications are on your Linux Forensic CD that you are unable to properly use, then it is taking up valuable space or providing an avenue of inadvertently violating a EULA.

DEFT License

Deft is a Ubuntu customization with a collection of computer forensic programs and documents created by thousands of individuals, teams and companies. Each of these works might come under a different licence. Our Licence Policy describe the process that we follow in determining which software we will ship and by default on the deft install CD.

The Ubuntu team is committed to Free and Open Source Software. The exact details of what that means can lead people into a very long debate indeed, often ending up with both sides in violent disagreement. The short answer is that it is our absolute conviction that the world is a better (more efficient, more supportable, safer, more interesting, more compassionate, fairer… there are lots of ways to define it) place if you have the source code to all the software on your computer, and the right to USE that source code in constructive ways.

We believe that this is important even if you are not a software developer, because someone else in your family who uses your computer might find that they have that interest and talent, and because you could hire someone to exercise those rights on your behalf. We really do believe that this is the central idea that will drive innovation and development in the software industry for the next 20 years (right up until the computers take over, and who knows, maybe they will feel the same way). And we hope to be one of many teams that sticks around sustainably, making a living working in that new world. We would invite you to read more about our Free Software Philosophy and help to shape this policy further.

http://www.deftlinux.net/

Figure 13.1 EULAs in Live Linux CDs

As great of an operating system that Linux is, it is still not as familiar as Windows, particularly when so many forensic applications are Windows-based. Many Linux applications are command-line, which not only is not a strong suit of many computer users, but is easier to make an error. Figure 13.2 shows the difference between mounting a drive in Linux via command-line versus a GUI. Granted, there are GUI imaging applications in Linux, but many more command-line tools as compared to Windows.

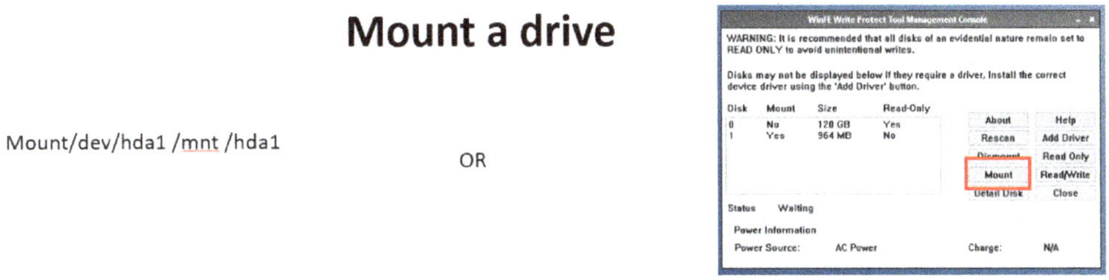

Figure 13.2 Mounting a drive comparison, Linux and Windows

Apple

Evidence machine is a Mac? Then the best choice is to use a Mac OS FOS tool. Intel based Macs can be booted to WinFE, but it is more practical in using a tool designed for Apple systems. There are some situations where your decision-making is easy as to which tool to choose, and with Apple, the decision is most always going to be to use a FOS developed specifically for a Mac.

CHAPTER 14: Bootable Media

CD, DVD, USB flash drive. USB hard drive. The one that is best depends on the computer system to acquire. The environment will dictate your choices, if you have a choice at all. When going onsite, or in the field, be prepared for anything and everything you can. That means being prepared to having to use a FOS to boot a machine for imaging when you expected that you would be able to remove the hard drive. Be prepared to acquire an Apple system when you expected to only image a Windows computer.

Preparing a selection of FOSs is not difficult. Once you build a WinFE, download a live Linux forensic OS, and have a Mac acquisition tool on hand, you can handle 99% of anything you come across. **The worst mistake is to think one of these FOSs can handle everything, or try to force one to handle something that another tool can do better.** Preferences are important, but not more important than choosing the appropriate tool.

When building a bootable media, the option to build a multi-boot FOS may sound reasonable. By multi-boot, prior to fully booting into WinFE, a boot selection menu can give you the choice of booting into a WinFE or a non-WinFE forensic operating system. This is a convenient method of having a forensic operating system, where one boot device contains multiple forensic operating systems. Personally, I prefer to have one boot device with one forensic operating system, as I typically know exactly which FOS I want the machine to boot.

Appendix I

Misty's work

Misty (http://reboot.pro/user/56459-misty/) has been instrumental in the development of the next generation of WinFE builds, most notably with Mini-WinFE. With Misty's approval, the following pages are documentation maintained by Misty at http://winfe.mistyprojects.co.uk/readme.html, re-printed here for convenience.

The text format has been slightly modified to fit this guide, with full URLs added to linked text, but the content is re-printed in full.

Introduction

This project has evolved from the Winbuilder *Mini-WinFE* project. A move has been made to the *PEBakery* build engine, with the *ChrisPE* project used as a core fileset. Use this project to create WinFE from a range of 32-bit and 64-bit Windows sources, including -

- *Windows 7*
- *Windows 7 (SP1)*
- *Windows Server 2008 R2 SP1*
- *Windows 8*
- *Windows 8.1*
- *Windows 8.1 Update*
- *Windows 10*
- *Windows 11*

Windows RTM source files are recommended. The sources in the above list have been tested, other source files may also work.

This project has been internally tested. Some of the current features include -

- No caching of Windows source files - resulting in reduced storage space requirements on the Host OS used to build the project.
- .wim support using internal *PEBakery* commands - the wimlib library is used for managing wim support. The full contents of the the Windows source and *WinPE* .wim files are not applied (extracted) to a local directory - resulting in significant time savings.
- Support for a range of shells including *bblean*, *CMD*, *LaunchBar* and *WinXShell*.
- WoW64 support.

Contents

Please note that some of the *screenshots used throughout this guide may have been taken from other projects.*

1. *Windows Forensic Environment* - About *Microsoft©* "WinFE".
2. *Windows Preinstallation Environment* - About *Microsoft©* "WinPE".
3. *Builders* - brief overview of the PEBakery build engine.
4. *Project Options* - the main settings/options.
5. *Project Scripts* - List of all scripts included with the *WinFE* download.
6. *Instructions (PEBakery)* - a detailed walkthrough for using the *WinFE* project to create *WinPE*. Also covers *PEBakery* usage.
7. *Instructions (WinBuilder)* - a detailed walkthrough for using the *WinFE* project to create *WinPE*. Also covers *WinBuilder* usage.
8. *Menu System* - an overview of the menu systems for the supported Shells. Cover creating custom sub-menus.
9. *Include Program in boot.wim*
10. *Post Configuration*
11. *Packages*
12. *Create a Bootable USB Stick* - covers using *DiskPart* (Command-line) and *Rufus* (GUI).
13. *UEFI, BIOS, GPT and MBR* - overview of *UEFI* and *BIOS*.
14. *MultiBoot WinPE*

15. *Quick Start Guide (PEBakery)* - the basic steps for using this project in the *PEBakery* build engine to create *WinPE* in just a few minutes!
16. *Quick Start Guide (WinBuilder)* - the basic steps for using this project in the *WinBuilder* build engine to create *WinPE* in just a few minutes!
17. *Quick Start - Running Mini-WinFE* - overview of using the Mini-WinFE boot disk.
18. *DiskMgr*
19. *WinFE Tests* - results from a series of tests exploring circumtances in which unplanned disk writes may occur in *WinFE*.
20. *Download/Links*
21. *Acknowledgements*

Windows Forensic Environment

The Windows Forensic Environment (a.k.a. *WinFE*) is a Windows based boot disk that can be used as a platform for digital forensic analysis. Being Windows based it enables users to run a number of Windows programs that they might already be familiar with. It is an alternative *or* addition to a number of forensically focused Linux distributions.

WinFE is a software write blocker used to prevent writes to storage devices. Usage may include gathering evidence on systems where hardware cannot be removed, triage investigations, or as an alternative to potentially expensive hardware write blockers.

Troy Larson, Senior Forensic Examiner of Microsoft©, is credited with creating the Windows Forensic Environment. *WinFE* does not appear to be available as a commercial product from Microsoft. It is however relatively easy to create *WinFE* for personal use from freely available tools. *WinFE* is in essence a Windows Preinstallation Environment (*WinPE* - see *here*) with two minor registry edits that are applied to ensure that any hard disks are not automatically mounted during the *WinPE/WinFE* boot process - minimising the risk of the contamination of data/evidence. *WinFE* is a lightweight version of Windows that can be used for many tasks - it is a complete, standalone operating system and will work independently of any other operating systems already installed.

Windows Preinstallation Environment

Windows Preinstallation Environment (*WinPE*) is a lightweight version of Windows that can be used for many tasks. It was originally designed as a 32-bit replacement for DOS - for windows deployment, backup and recovery. *WinPE* is a complete, standalone operating system and will work independently of any other operating systems already installed. See *here* for more information.

When a computer is running (booted from) a full version of Windows certain files are 'locked' - making it difficult to take a system backup or to remove a virus/malware. Consequently some tasks are best performed when the operating system is offline - this can be achieved by booting to another operating system such as *WinPE* to access the offline system.

There are two distinct methods for booting *WinPE* - RAM Boot and Flat Boot. RAM Boot is the most common method and anyone who has installed Windows Vista/7/8/8.1 will already (perhaps unknowingly) have used it. Microsoft recommend a minimum of 512 MB RAM in order to run a RAM booted version of *WinPE* - in tests it was possible to boot some versions of *WinPE* with 256 MB RAM. For more details about RAM and Flat boot *WinPE* and RAM requirements, please see here.

When *WinPE* is RAM Booted or Flat Booted from read only media it will not save any changes made to it when the system is rebooted. A benefit of this is always having a clean (virus free) *WinPE* operating system on boot.

WinPE is easy to customise. The builds prior to customisation are very limited and the UI (User Interface) is command line. It is possible to adapt these builds to use a GUI shell and other programs and utilities can be added so that various tasks can be carried out, including but not limited to -

- *Disk partitioning*
- *Deploying Windows*
- *Disk/partition imaging*
- *Data backup*
- *System/data recovery*
- *System restore*
- *Forensic analysis*
- *Password reset*
- *Offline Virus Scan*

WinPE Versions

There are a number of different versions of official Microsoft *WinPE*. The earlier versions used the same codebase as Windows XP/2003 - these are usually referred to as *WinPE* 1.*.

Earlier versions of *WinPE* (prior to the introduction of version 2.0) were aimed at enterprise customers and were not available to the general public. As of version 2.0 it was possible for non-enterprise customers to create their own *WinPE* by using the freely available Windows Automated Installation Kit (WAIK). The WAIK has now been replaced with the Windows Assessment and Deployment Kit (ADK).

Windows Operating Systems use a numbering format for identification purposes - these numbers can be used to identify the codebase from which a particular *WinPE* was created. Windows builds use the numbering format 'MajorVersion.MinorVersion.Build' - e.g. 6.1.7600. Unlike the product names associated with Windows Operating Systems (e.g. Windows 7) these numbers can refer to multiple products - version 6.1.7600 for example refers to both Windows 7 and Windows Server 2008.

WinPE versions include -

WinPE	Major.Minor.Build	Windows Operating System source
2.0	6.0.6000	Windows Vista
2.1	6.0.6001	Windows Vista (SP1) / Server 2008
3.0	6.1.7600	Windows 7 / Server 2008 R2
3.1	6.1.7601	Windows 7 (SP1) / Server 2008 R2 (SP1)
4.0	6.2.9200	Windows 8 / Server 2012

5.0	6.3.9600	Windows 8.1
5.1	6.3.9600	Windows 8.1 Update

Following the release of Windows 10, WinPE versions are identifed by MajorVersion.MinorVersion.Build numbers that generally correspond with the Windows 10 build from which they were compiled. WinPE 10.0.16299 for example corresponds with Windows 10.0.16299 (aka Version 1709 / Fall Creators Update).

There are some exceptions to this rule as the *WinPE* included in Windows 10.0.18362 (May 2019 Update (1903)) and 10.0.18363 (November 2019 Update (1909)) sources are both based on *WinPE* 10.0.18362.

Another example of the same *WinPE* version being included in multiple Windows sources is *WinPE* 10.0.19041. The following Windows 10 sources all include/use *WinPE* 10.0.19041 -

- May 2020 Update (10.0.19041 / 2004)
- October 2020 Update (10.0.19042 / 20H2)
- May 2021 Update (10.0.19043 / 21H1)
- November 2021 Update (10.0.19044 / 21H2)

WinPE 10.* versions include -

WinPE Build	WinPE Version	Windows Operating System source
10.0.10240	1507	-
10.0.10586	1511	November Update
10.0.14393	1607	Anniversary Update
10.0.15063	1703	Creators Update
10.0.16299	1709	Fall Creators Update
10.0.17134	1803	April 2018 Update
10.0.17763	1809	October 2018 Update
10.0.18362	1903	May 2019 Update (Windows 10.0.18362 / 1903) November 2019 Update (10.0.18363 / 1909)
10.0.19041	2004	May 2020 Update (10.0.19041 / 2004) October 2020 Update (10.0.19042 / 20H2) May 2021 Update (10.0.19043 / 21H1) November 2021 Update (10.0.19044 / 21H2)

There are 32 bit and 64 bit versions of all of the above *WinPE* systems. More recent versions of *WinPE* are likely to better support more recent hardware without the need for injecting drivers. *WinPE* 3.x builds are very stable and have been well tested, with a large userbase and support for a wide range of third party scripts in other projects. Unfortunately *WinPE* 3.x based builds do not offer the same level of write protection in forensic environments.

Build Engines

The *MistyPE* project is compatible with two different build engines, both of which are included in the project download -

- WinBuilder
- PEBakery

WinBuilder

Based upon information in the *WinBuilder* wiki, *WinBuilder* was developed by *Nuno Brito*, *Peter Schlang* and *Robert Kochem* between 2005 to 2011.

MistyPE has been coded to use the *WinBuilder* scripting language, a language developed specifically for the *WinBuilder* build engine. *WinBuilder.exe* version *82.0.1.0* is included in the project download and the project has been extensively tested in *WinBuilder*.

WinBuilder runs on the Windows XP and newer operating systems and does not require any additional dependencies. It has a relatively small footprint and has been around for long enough to have extensive documentation covering supported commands - see here for example.

WinBuilder version *82.0.1.0* was released around 2011. Whilst there are some bugs these are fairly well known and it's possible to work around them as a consequence. Unfortunately *WinBuilder* is no longer in development and there do not appear to be any plans to update it in the future.

Screenshot of *Mini-WinFE* running in *WinBuilder* -

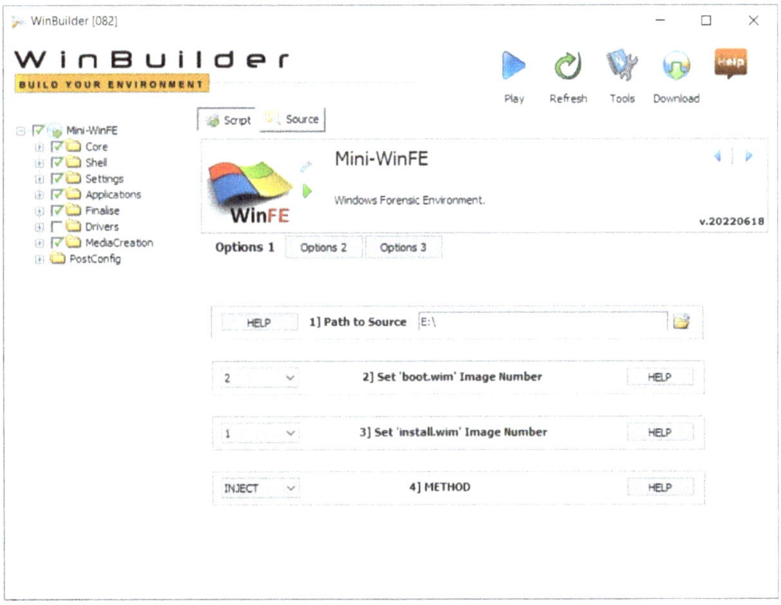

PEBakery

This *Mini-WinFE* project has been designed for use with *PEBakery* - the *PEBakery* 0.9.5.1 beta build is included in the project download. The project has been tested on more recent builds including *PEBakery* 1.0.0, however tests were limited to running on a Windows 10 host operating system. Build 1.0.0 failed to run during a brief test on Windows 8.1. **NOTE** - .Net Framework 4.7.1 and Windows 7 or newer is required to run *PEBakery* 0.9.5.1 beta.

PEBakery is in development as a *WinBuilder* replacement and can be used as an alternative to *WinBuilder* for some projects. *PEBakery* has been developed by *Hajin Jang* (aka *ied206* and *joveler*) and is in active development.

PEBakery is a very promising open source project with a similar User Interface to *WinBuilder*. In the *PEBakery* developers own words (from here) -

"...***What is PEBakery?***
PEBakery is a builder specialized in customizing Windows PE.
It is intended to be used with Win10PESE, MistyPE project.

Why PEBakery was written?
PEBakery is compatible with WinBuilder 082.
Projects like Win10PESE are dependent on WinBuilder 082, but WB082's development went discontinued.
PEBakery works as a drop-in replacement of WB082, while providing much improved envrionment..."

PEBakery is open source software, licensed under GPLv3. Please note that some elements of PEBakery are covered under different licenses - please refer to the PEBakery license file. Some links -

- MSFN topic here
- github page here

Screenshot of the *Mini-WinFE* project running in *PEBakery* -

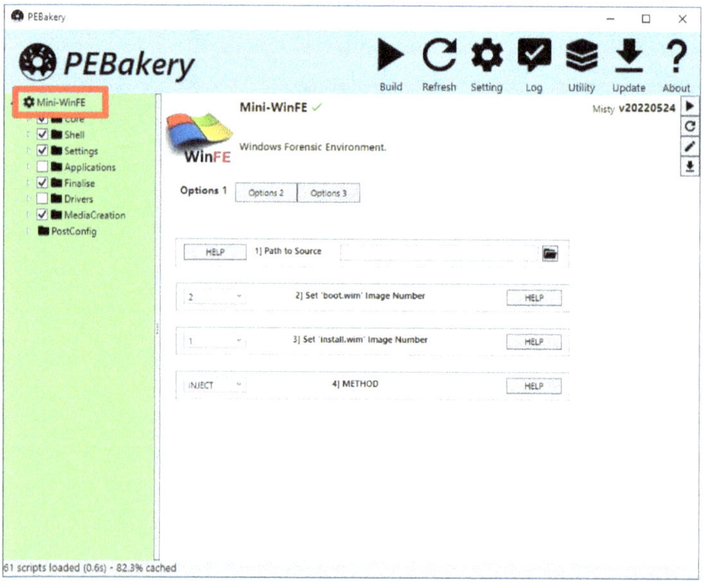

Project Options

A number of the project options are contained in the main *WinFE* project script - to display them, ensure that the script is selected by clicking on ***Mini-WinFE*** at the top of the directory tree on the left....

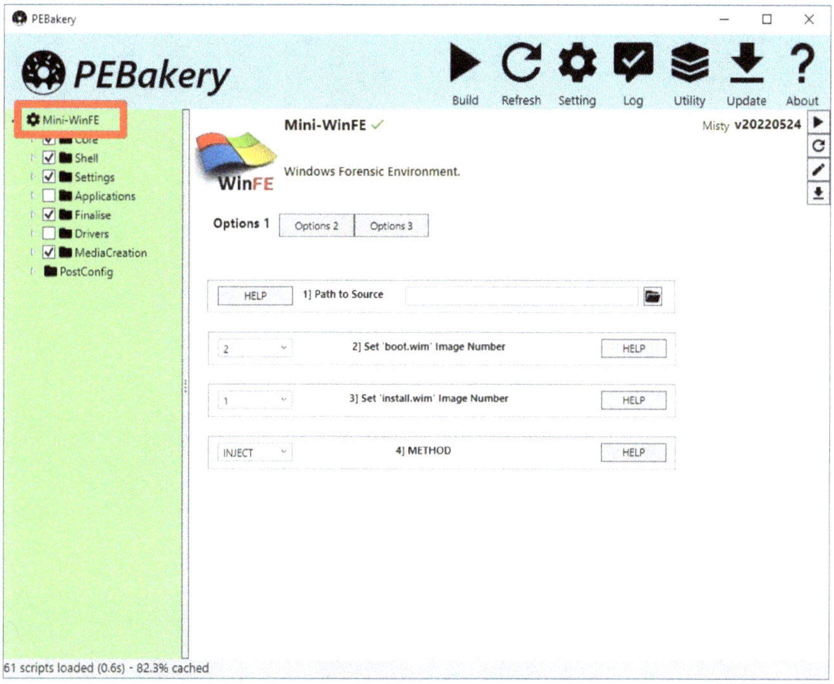

...one of the screens below will be displayed (toggle between them by clicking on the tab buttons (**Options1**, **Options2**, etc.)) -

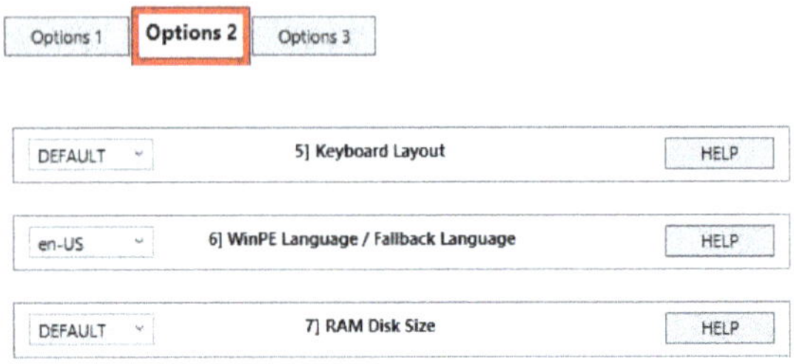

1] Path to Source

Set the path to your source files by either manually entering the path or click on the *Folder* button to set the path to your Windows Installation Media source files. Please note that if manually entering a path it must end in a backslash (\). E.g. D:\source_files\

A mounted Windows RTM .iso file is recommended. Alternatively extract the contents of a Windows .iso to a local directory. Set the path in this option to the root folder that contains the following files/directories -

- *\sources\boot.wim*
- *\sources\install.wim*
- *\bootmgr*
- *\boot*
- *\EFI*

2] Set 'boot.wim' Image number

Use image number **2** when using Windows installation media. The only time you should need to use image number **1** is when using *boot.wim* from the WAIK or *ADK* - which I consider to be more advanced usage.

If an existing cache is used, then the configuration file created when the cache was created will be read and the image number of *boot.wim* will be checked. If this is different to the image number selected in this option, then the user will be asked which image to use - either the image number from the configuration file, or the image number specified in this option.

3] Set 'install.wim' Image number

In the majority of cases, image number **1** should be selected when using Windows installation media. The only time you might need to use a different image number is when using a Windows Server source. Windows 2008 R2 (SP1) and Windows 2012 R2 releases for example contain multiple images (in *install.wim*) - image number **1** is a *Server Core Installation* and doesn't contain some of the file dependencies required in *WinFE*.

4] METHOD

Two build methods are currently supported -

- **INJECT** - a minimal fileset is extracted from *boot.wim*, reducing storage space requirements. Files extracted include registry hives, which are modified during the build process. The *INJECT* method is significantly faster than the *EXTRACT* method, however *EXTRACT* should be considered if any drivers are being integrated - please refer to the Drivers section for more information.
- **EXTRACT** - the *wimapply* command will be used to apply/extract the full contents of the selected image in *boot.wim*. This method is slower and requires more storage space, however if drivers are being integrated then this method should be considered - please refer to the Drivers section for more information.

Both of these methods involve extracting files from *boot.wim*, modifying the registry, then injecting any modified or added files back to *boot.wim*.

5] Keyboard Layout

If the **DEFAULT** setting is used, then no settings will be changed and the keyboard layout from the existing source files will be used. There are a limited range of alternative Keyboard Layout's available in this script.

6] WinPE Language / Fallback Language

This setting is only used if the source file language cannot be verified by *wimlib-imagex*.

7] RAM Disk Size

Use this option to set the size of the RAM Disk (in MB) - this is the amount of writable space on the SYSTEMDRIVE that will be available when *WinPE* is running.

This setting is ignored in WinPE 5.x if system RAM is greater than 1GB. It will only be used when RAM is less than (or equal to) 1GB.

Project Scripts

NOTE - there are currently two different *Mini-WinFE* project branches/repositories on *GitHub*. Some of the features/applications documented in this page may not be present in both branches.

- *main Branch* - forensic focus. A number of applications and settings that could potentially perform disk writes have been removed.
- *WinPE Branch* - includes more applications and options - use with caution as it is possible to use settings that will **not** write protect disks.

The *Mini-WinFE* project scripts can currently be divided into seven distinct sections -

- *Core*
- *Shell*
- *Settings*
- *Applications*
- *Finalise*
- *Drivers*
- *MediaCreation*
- *PostConfig*

A number of configurable options are contained in the main project file. The screenshots below display these options (clicking on the *HELP* button from within the project displays information about what the individual options do) -

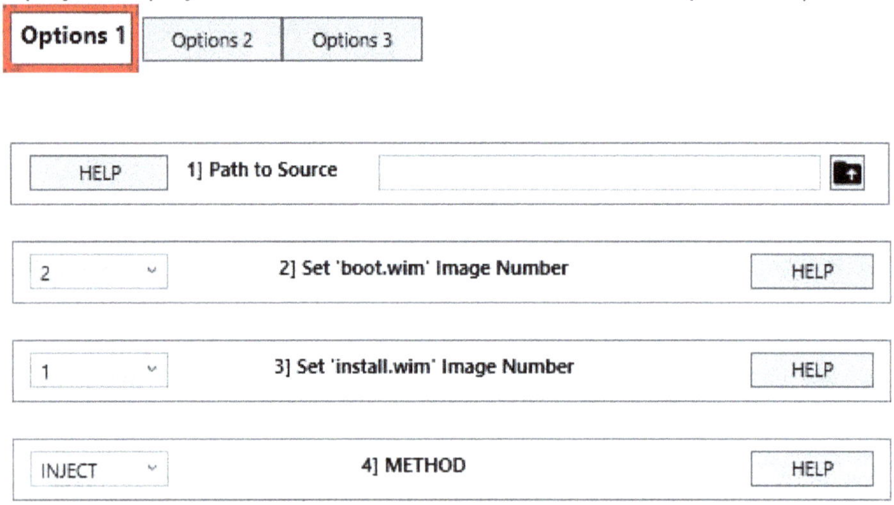

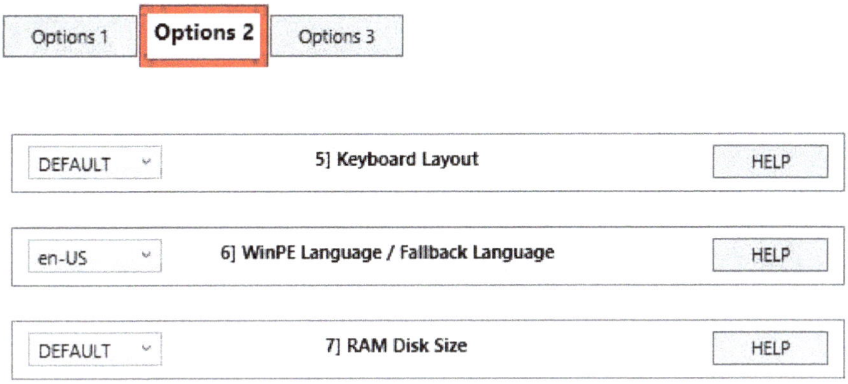

Core Scripts

Please note that only two of the scripts in this section are actually visible to the end user in the PEBakery User Interface - the remainder are hidden from view in an effort to declutter the interface.

- **Core Files** - This script cannot be disabled. Most of the work is carried out in this script, including error checks, file checks, verifying source language/build/processor architecture, and copying and extracting the required files from the selected source.
  Path - *Projects* > *WinFE* > *Core* > *A_core.script*
- **Browse for Folder** - used to add Browse for Folder dialog support. This script is hidden and is executed by other scripts to ensure that Browse for Folder support is added as required for individual applications.
  Path - *Projects* > *WinFE* > *Core* > *Browse.For.Folder.script*
- **Common Commands** - this script is hidden and is executed by other scripts as required. Supported commands include directory delete (following an error) and creating startmenu shortcuts.
  Path - *Projects* > *WinFE* > *Core* > *common.script*
- **Tweaks** - includes a range of tweaks. Click on the *?* buttons for information about the available options.
  Path - *Projects* > *WinFE* > *Core* > *D_Tweaks.script*

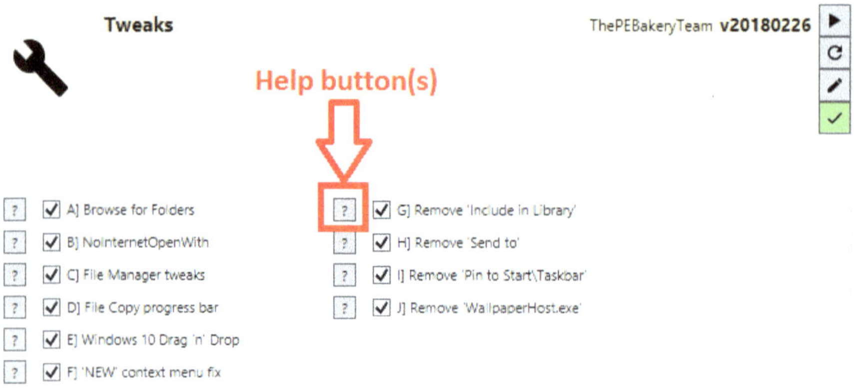

- **WoW64** - Add WoW64 support.
  Path - *Projects* > *WinFE* > *Core* > *G_WoW64.script*.
- **SysWOW64** - this script is hidden. It contains registry settings required for WoW64 support.
  Path - *Projects* > *WinFE* > *Core* > *syswow64.script*
- **Verification Checks** - this script is hidden and is executed by other program scripts for a range of checks including identification of source files.
  Path - *Projects* > *WinFE* > *Core* > *verify.script*

Shell Scripts

- **Shell** - select a shell. Current options are *WinXShell*, *bblean*, *CMD* and *LaunchBar*. The shell script is context sensitive and different options will be visible depending on the selected shell. Click on the *HELP* buttons for information about the available options. Select a shell using the available tabs. The displayed/selected shell will be used in the build.
  Path - *Projects* > *WinFE* > *Shell* > *B_shell.script*

WinXShell shell options -

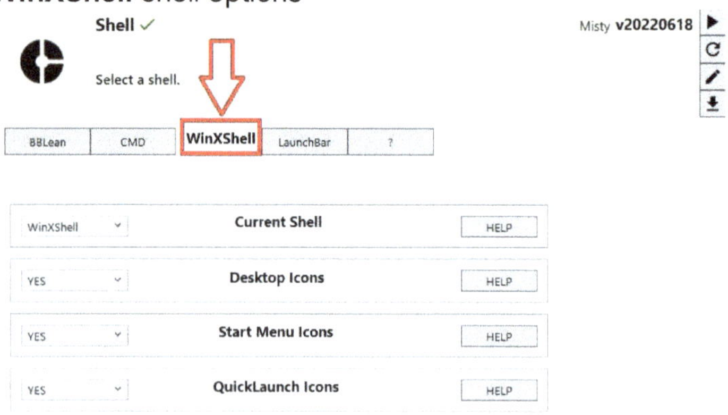

LaunchBar shell options -

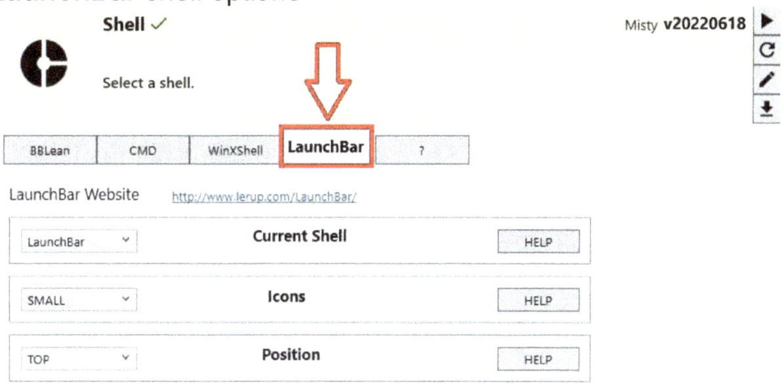

- **Default Filemanager** - set the default FileExplorer. Either *7-zip*, *Explorer++*, *Q-Dir* or *JustManager* can be selected.
  Path - *Projects* > *WinFE* > *Shell* > *D_filemanager.script*

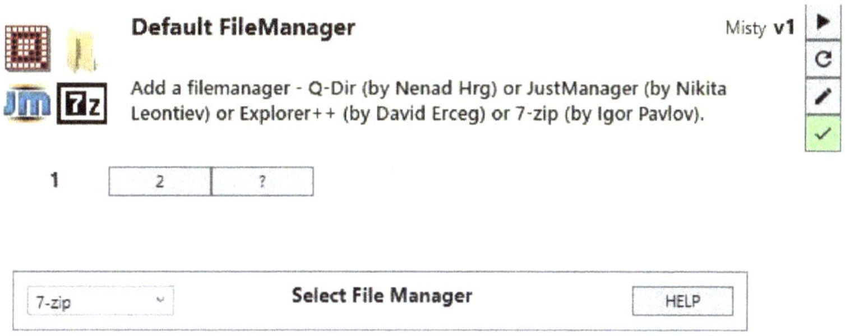

Settings Scripts

- **Network** - this script can be enabled without selecting any of the script options to give different results -
  - No options selected - will add a batch file + a menu entry to run it. The batch file runs the command *"wpeutil InitializeNetwork"* - this will Initialize network components and drivers, and set the computer name to a randomly chosen value. Running the InitializeNetwork command can cause an unnecessary delay when *WinPE* boots - adding it as a menu option ensures that the network can be started *if required*.
  - Option(s) selected - selecting any combination of script options will add *unattend.xml* to the build, with a menu entry added to *winpeshl.ini* to automatically run *wpeinit*. This will Initialize the network during the boot process. This is useful if an application requires network access - e.g. TightVNC Server.

Path - *Projects* > *WinFE* > *Settings* > *Network.script*

- **Recommended** -
  Path - *Projects* > *WinFE* > *Settings* > *Recommended.script*
  - **BootSect** - tool used to add *NTLDR* or *BOOTMGR* code to a Volume Boot Record. This script adds a batch file to the build as the required program is already included. The batch can be executed by right-clicking on a drive in Explorer.
  - **CMD Here** - Start a command prompt from the right-click context menu.
  - **Keyboard Layout** - change the keyboard layout in *WinPE* whilst it's running. Uses *wpeutil* tool that is already included in the build.
  - **ScreenRes** - This will add a menu option for changing the screen resolution. No external programs are used, however a number of xml files are added - this option simply starts a batch file that will run the *wpeinit* command to change the screen resolution to a value set in the included xml files. A number of screen resolutions are available in the batch file.
- **Wallpaper** - select a custom wallpaper. A project wallpaper can be used. Not working if *LaunchBar* or *CMD* are selected as shell.
  Path - *Projects* > *WinFE* > *Settings* > *wallpaper.script*

Applications Scripts

The following lists all of the program/application scripts that are included in the *Mini-WinFE* project download.

- **LaunchBar** - a program launcher created by *Peter Lerup*. "*...LaunchBar is a small Windows freeware program that mimics the behavior of the dockable QuickLaunch toolbar that was available in all Windows versions before Windows 7...*". Please refer to the *LaunchBar* website (see here) for more information.

  If *LaunchBar* is enabled, an option to add shortcuts to the LaunchBar menu can be selected in application scripts. Screenshot of *LaunchBar* running -

  - Included in download - YES
  - Processor Architecture - x86 and x64
- **Add Custom Batch and run at Start-up** - add a custom batch file to the build. Edit the custom batch file via a button embedded in the script.
  - Included in download - N/A
  - Processor Architecture - N/A

- **Add Custom Folders\Files** - select a directory and it's contents will be added to the build.
  - Included in download - N/A
  - Processor Architecture - N/A
- **7-Zip** (version 19.00) - File archiver. Used to extract contents from *.zip/.7z/.iso/.wim* files and numerous other file types. Can also create *.zip* and *.7z* files. Right click a file in explorer to access menu options for extracting from or creating files. *7-zip website*
  - Included in download - YES
  - Processor Architecture - x86 and x64
- **AccessGain** (version 1.1) - Used to bypass file system security checks in order to access folders protected by NTFS security permissions or by 3rd-party software. Right click on a drive in the included File Manager to access the options. This is really useful if you can't delete a file/folder due to restricted security permissions.
  - Included in download - YES
  - Processor Architecture - x86 and x64
- **BOOTICE** (version 1.3.3) - "BOOTICE is a boot-related maintenance gadget that is primarily used to install, repair, backup, and restore MBR or partition PBR of disks (images); edit Windows boot configuration files BCD; manage UEFI boot entries; and VHD/VHDX file management. In addition, there are disk sector editing, disk filling..."
  - Included in download - YES
  - Processor Architecture - x86 and x64
- **CloneDisk** (version 2.3.6) - backup/restore to/from an imagefile or clone a disk to another. Additional feature are also supported - refer to the *CloneDisk website* for more information.
  - Included in download - YES
  - Processor Architecture - x86 and x64
- **Disk Management** - Disk management console (diskmgmt.msc). Not working in *WinPE* 2.* (Vista sources). This will add an option to install diskmgmt.msc on demand. Credit to IcemanND on the msfn forum - see *here*.
  - Included in download - **N/A**
  - Processor Architecture - x86 and x64
- **DMDE** (Version 4.0.0.800) - "...is a powerful software for data searching, editing, and recovery on disks. It may recover directory structure and files in some complicated cases through the use of special algorithms when other software can't help....DMDE has a number of freeware features such as disk editor, simple partition manager (e.g. allows undelete a partition), a tool to create disk images and clones, RAID constructor, file recovery from the current panel....DMDE supports FAT12/16, FAT32, NTFS, Ext2/3/4..." The Free Edition is included in the download - please refer to the License Agreement - *here*. *DMDE website*
  - Included in download - YES
  - Processor Architecture - x86 and x64
- **Explorer++** (version 1.3.5) - file manager with multiple pane and tab support. *Explorer++ website*
  - Included in download - YES

    - Processor Architecture - x86 and x64
- **Forensic Acquisition Utilities (FAU)** - "...a collection of utilities and libraries intended for forensic or forensic-related investigative use...". Includes a dd utility for imaging systems. Combined with NetCat (also included) it can image systems over a network. FAU is the property of GMG Systems, Inc. and is being reproduced with the kind permission of the author. GMG Systems, Inc. Please refer to the FAU End User License Agreement - *here*.
    - Included in download - YES
    - Processor Architecture - x86 and x64
- **Free Shooter** (Version 2.0.7) - "...tool for taking screenshots without bloatware features, simple as life, light as air....". Capture fullscreen, active window, or a selected are of the screen. The following file types can be captured using Free Shooter - BMP, JPG, TIFF, PNG and GIF formats. Free Shooter website
    - Included in download - YES
    - Processor Architecture - x86 and x64
- **FTK Imager Lite** - Create a physical or logical image of any drive. This program can create an image using the raw, SMART or E01 formats. FTK Imager website
    - Included in download - **NO**
    - Processor Architecture - x86 and x64
- **HWiNFO** (Version 7.24.4770.0) - system diagnostic tool that can be used to check hardware. HWiNFO website
    - Included in download - YES
    - Processor Architecture - x86 and x64
- **HxD** (version 2.5.0.0) - "...HxD is a carefully designed and fast hex editor which, additionally to raw disk editing and modifying of main memory (RAM), handles files of any size....". HxD website
    - Included in download - YES
    - Processor Architecture - x86 and x64
- **ImDisk** (version 2.0.10) - ImDisk is a virtual disk driver for Windows. It can create virtual hard disk, floppy or CD/DVD drives using image files or system memory. Right click on supported image types (e.g. **.iso** files) to mount them as virtual drives. Can also be used to create disc images of real drives. ImDisk website
    - Included in download - YES
    - Processor Architecture - x86 and x64
- **IrfanView** (version 4.51.0.0) - "...IrfanView is a fast, compact and innovative FREEWARE (for non-commercial use) graphic viewer for Windows XP, Vista, 7, 8 and 10. ...". IrfanView website
    - Included in download - YES
    - Processor Architecture - x86 and x64
- **JkDefrag** (Version 3.66) - command-line disk and file defragmentation tool. A batch file with several options can be executed from the right-click context menu. JkDefrag website
    - Included in download - YES
    - Processor Architecture - x86 and x64

- **JustManager** (Version 0.1 Alpha 54) - file manager with multiple pane and tab support. JustManager website
  - Included in download - YES
  - Processor Architecture - x86 and x64
- **NT Password Editor** (version 0.7) - NT Password Editor. This program can be used to edit passwords on a Windows NT based systems (Windows 2000, XP, Vista, 7, 8). Can be used to reset forgotten passwords and allow access to locked user accounts - it can only change or remove passwords for local system accounts. This program can NOT decrypt passwords or change domain and Active Directory passwords. NT Password Edit website
  - Included in download - YES
  - Processor Architecture - x86 and x64
- **Opera** - Web Browser. Opera USB Version 12.18 is included in the download. OperaUSB website
  - Included in download - YES
  - Processor Architecture - x86 and x64
- **OSK** - On-Screen Keyboard. autoit executable based on source code by RichMinichiello available in the following forum post - https://www.autoitscript.com/forum/topic/159626-on-screen-keyboard/
  - Included in download - YES
  - Processor Architecture - x86 and x64
- **Product Key Scanner** (version 1.01) - "...Product Key Scanner is a tool that scans the Registry of Windows Operating system and finds the product keys of Windows and other Microsoft products. You can scan the Registry of your current running system, as well as you can scan the Registry from external hard drive plugged to your computer....". Product Key Scanner website
  - Included in download - YES
  - Processor Architecture - x86 and x64
- **Q-Dir** - Quad explorer file manager with multiple pane and tab support. Q-Dir website
  - Included in download - YES
  - Processor Architecture - x86 and x64
- **sDelete** - Secure delete application. "...SDelete is a command line utility that takes a number of options. In any given use, it allows you to delete one or more files and/or directories, or to cleanse the free space on a logical disk...". sDelete website
  - Included in download - **NO**
  - Processor Architecture - x86 and x64
- **Drive Snapshot** - partition backup tool. Can be used to backup and restore an operating system. This utility is not included in the download, however the script will automatically attempt to download a time limited trial version. If you have a licensed copy then copy it to the *"/Project/Cache/Programs/SnapShot"* folder. Drive Snapshot website
  - Included in download - **NO**
  - Processor Architecture - x86 and x64
- **Sumatra** (Version 3.1.2) - **.PDF** file reader. SumatraPDF website
  - Included in download - YES
  - Processor Architecture - x86 and x64

- **SwiftSearch** (version 7.5.1) - "...SwiftSearch is a lightweight program whose purpose is to help you quickly find the files you need on your Windows machine without ever requiring you to index your drives. Most search utilities that achieve similar speeds do so by indexing drives while the computer is idle, but because idleness detection is so difficult to get right, in practice they end up slowing down the whole system just to speed up search. SwiftSearch works differently: given administrator privileges, it completely bypasses the file system (only NTFS supported) and reads the file table directly every time, which speeds up search by many orders of magnitude....". SwiftSearch website
  - Included in download - YES
  - Processor Architecture - x86 and x64
- **TightVNC Server** (Version 2.8.8.0) - *VNC* server application. Boot *WinPE* and create a Remote Desktop - accessing the *WinPE* system from a *VNC* client application. Includes an option to run at boot - this is useful if booting *WinPE* on a remote/headless system. TightVNC website
  - Included in download - YES
  - Processor Architecture - x86 and x64
- **TinyHexer** (version 1.7) - Tiny hexer is a hex editor for binary files. It will also allow access and editing of disk sectors.
  - Included in download - YES
  - Processor Architecture - **x86 only**
- **wimlib** - "...wimlib is an open source, cross-platform library for creating, extracting, and modifying Windows Imaging (WIM) archives. WIM is a file archiving format, somewhat comparable to ZIP (and many other file archiving formats); but unlike ZIP, it allows storing various Windows-specific metadata, allows storing multiple "images" in a single archive, automatically deduplicates all file contents, and supports optional solid compression to get a better compression ratio. wimlib and its command-line frontend wimlib-imagex provide a free and cross-platform alternative to Microsoft's WIMGAPI, ImageX, and DISM....". wimlib website
  - Included in download - YES
  - Processor Architecture - x86 and x64
- **WinHex** - versatile Hex editor. In addition to the common hex editor functions, this software can be used for computer forensics, data recovery, system imaging and restore and disk editing. WinHex website
  - Included in download - **NO**
  - Processor Architecture - x86 and x64
- **X-Ways Forensic** - X-Ways Forensics is an advanced work environment for computer forensic examiners. X-Ways website
  - Included in download - **NO**
  - Processor Architecture - x86 and x64

Finalise

- **Subst** - add a batch file to locate the boot media (via a unique tag file created during the boot process) and use the *subst.exe* utility to assign a virtual drive letter. This is useful if using custom scripts/utilities/shortcuts

with a hardcoded path.
Path - *Projects* > *WinFE* > *Finalise* > *Subst.script*

- **WinFE** - Add the registry settings required to create a Windows Forensic Environment. *Erwan Labalec*'s *DiskMgr* or *Colin Ramsden's*'s *Protect.exe* (Write Protect Tool) will be added to the build - this provides a User Interface for toggling disk attributes.
  Path - *Projects* > *WinFE* > *Finalise* > *winfe.script*
- **Shell - Finalise** - This script cannot be disabled. Menu entries are configured via this script , *winpeshl.ini* is created, and files are injected to *boot.wim*.
  Path - *Projects* > *WinFE* > *Finalise* > *xxxShell.script*

Drivers

Only one script is included in this section -

- **Drivers** - Use this script to integrate drivers to the build. *Get WAIK Tools* is used to download *DISM*. ~~There are two options in the script~~ -
  - **EXTRACT** - the contents of the image selected in *boot.wim* will be fully extracted and *DISM* will be used to inject the drivers to the offline image. If this method is selected then setting option 4 in the main project script (**METHOD**) as *EXTRACT* is recommended - this will fully extract *boot.wim* early in the build process.
  - ~~**MOUNT** - *DISM* will be used to mount the image selected in *boot.wim* > inject drivers to the mounted image > unmount the image.~~ (**NOTE** - the MOUNT option has been temporarily removed)

  Path - *Projects* > *WinFE* > *Drivers* > *drivers.script*

MediaCreation

The script in this section can either be selected during the build process, or can be executed independently afterwards - as long as the build completed successfully. Files in the %BaseDir%\WinFE.Files\ISO.ROOT\ directory (where *%BaseDir%* refers to the directory from which *PEBakeryLauncher.exe* is running) are added to the .iso file.

- **Create ISO** - this script includes a number of options, the default settings will create a RAM bootable ISO file using MKISOFS - for use on BIOS and UEFI based systems. It's also possible to create a Flat Boot *WinPE* (*WinPE* 2.x/3.x only) or even a multiboot ISO file with options for RAM Boot and Flat Boot - bootable on UEFI and BIOS based systems.

To execute the Create ISO script following a build, simply select the script in the directory tree and click on the *Run Script* button

PEBakery screenshot (the *Run Script* button is located to the right of the title bar) -

WinBuilder screenshot (the *Run Script* button is located to the right of the script icon bar) –

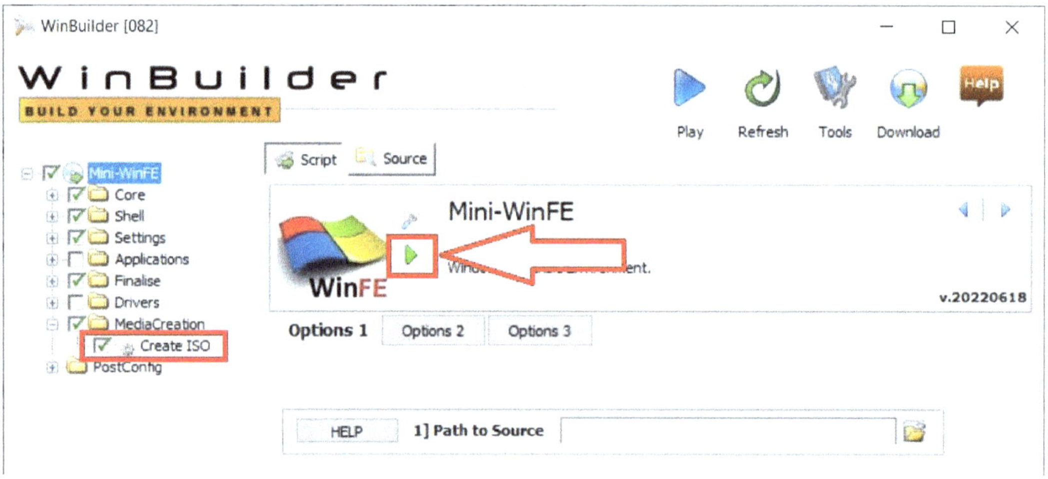

PostConfig

The scripts in this section cannot be executed during the build process and is designed for post processing.

- **Advanced Options** - Can be used to mount/unmount the registry hives created when the *WinFE* project has finished the build process. This script can also be used to inject (add) additional files to *boot.wim* and carry out some additional tasks.
- **Add Package** - Use this script to add a *Mini-WinFE* compatible *Package* to the project (refer to the *Packages* section for more information) -

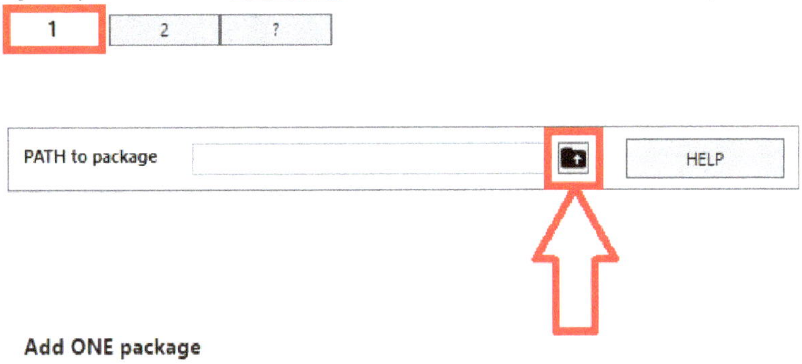

Applications not included in the project download

The majority of applications currently supported in *Mini-WinFE* are included in the project download. The exceptions are -

- *FTK Imager*
- *sDelete*
- *Drive Snapshot*
- *WinHex*
- *X-Ways Forensic*

sDelete - EULA prevents redistribution with the project. This application will be downloaded automatically if selected during the build process and added to a local file cache.

Drive SnapShot - evaluation versions can be downloaded to a local file cache prior to building Mini-WinFE by running "Download automatically (RECOMMENDED)". Alternatively, the application can be added by browsing to the file using the folder button in the "PATH to 32-bit" and "PATH to 64-bit" section and then selecting *ADD TO CACHE*. Adding the application using *ADD TO CACHE* option is covered in more detail in the *FTK Imager* section below.

FTK Imager - The FTK Imager licence prevents redistribution. FTK Imager files will need to be copied from a local source/installation. The application can be added by browsing to the executable file using the folder button in the "PATH to 32-bit" and

"PATH to 64-bit" section and browsing/selecting *FTK Imager.exe*. Do not try to add the installer, the target is *FTK Imager.exe* extracted from the installer.

Click on the folder icon -

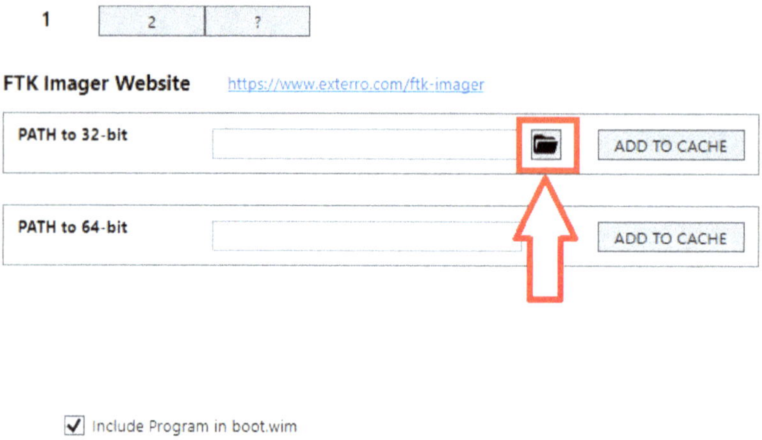

Browse to the executable -

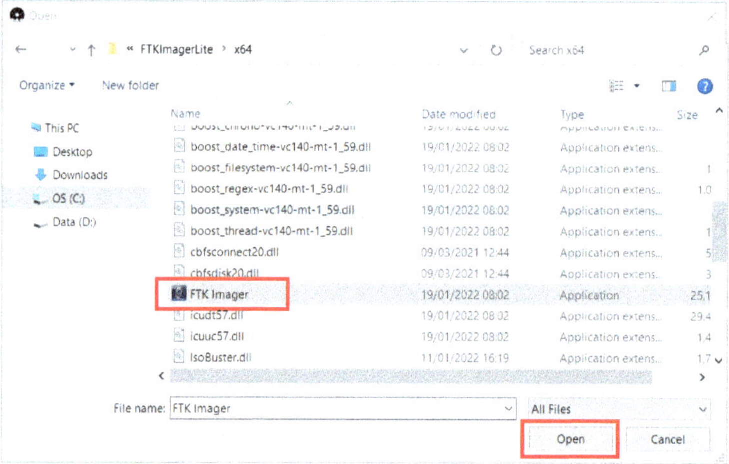

Click on the *ADD TO CACHE* button -

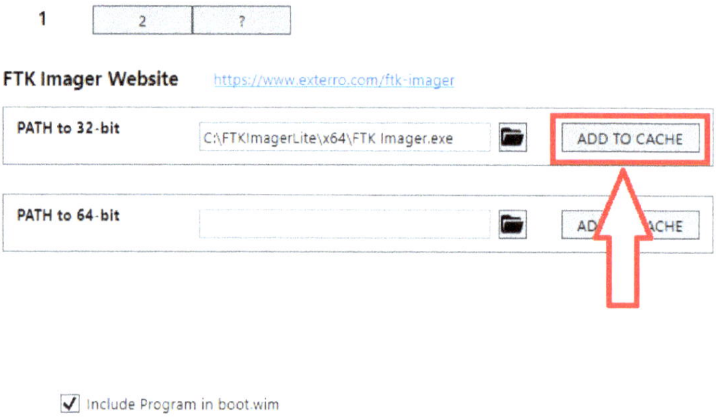

WinHex - The licence prevents redistribution. An evaluation version can be downloaded by clicking on the *Download Evaluation version automatically > ADD TO CACHE* button. Alternatively, the application can be added by browsing to the executable file(s) using the folder button in the "PATH to 32-bit" and "PATH to 64-bit" section(s) and browsing/selecting the relevant file (*WinHex.exe*/*WinHex64.exe*). Adding the application using the *ADD TO CACHE* option is covered in more detail in the *FTK Imager* section above.

X-Ways Forensic - The licence prevents redistribution. The application can be added by browsing to the executable file(s) using the folder button in the "PATH to 32-bit" and "PATH to 64-bit" section(s) and browsing/selecting the relevant file (*xwforensics.exe*/*xwforensics64.exe*). Adding the application using the *ADD TO CACHE* option is covered in more detail in the *FTK Imager* section above.

Instructions (PEBakery)

Please note that any screenshots in this documentation may differ from the current release.

You will require the following in order to build *WinFE* -

- **Administrator privileges** - registry hives will need to be mounted and edited during the build process, and other processes also require administrator privileges.
- .Net Framework 4.7.2 and Windows 7 or newer (required to run PEBakery).
- Free disk space - 1GB should be more than adequate as Windows source files are not cached during the build process.
- Windows Installation Media - either a CD/DVD, a mounted disk image or the files copied to an accessible folder.

WinFE uses the *WinBuilder* scripting language to automate a number of tasks to create a working *WinPE*. New commands have been implemented in *PEBakery* and this project is ***NOT*** compatible with *WinBuilder*.

Before running *PEBakery* please be aware that, *in the WinFE project*, the following project directory (and sub directories) will, if they exist, be deleted during the start of the build process (**Note** - *%BaseDir%* is a *PEBakery* variable for the folder from which the *PEBakery* executable *PEBakeryLauncher.exe* is running).

- %BaseDir%\WinFE.Files\
- %BaseDir%\ProjectTemp\

Sections in this page -

- *Updating PEBakery*
- *PEBakery Basics*
- *Project Options*

Updating PEBakery

Pre-compiled *PEBakery* testbuild downloads are available here.

PEBakery version *0.9.5.1 beta5* is included in the project download. *PEBakery* is in active development and you may want to update to new versions as they are released. I recommend deleting all traces of the previous version before extracting a new test build to the directory containing the *WinFE* project files. Assuming *WinFE* is in the C:\WinFE\ path, delete the following files/folders -

- C:\WinFE\PEBakeryLauncher.exe (file)
- C:\WinFE\Binary (folder)
- C:\WinFE\Database (folder)

Now extract the files from the updated *PEBakery* build/release to the *WinFE* root folder (the folder containing the *Projects* directory). Using the path from the example above, the project should now contain the following (the C:\WinFE\Database folder will be created when PEBakery is first started) -

- C:\WinFE\PEBakeryLauncher.exe (file)
- C:\WinFE\Binary (folder)

PEBakery Basics

The *PEBakery* Interface is divided into several sections -

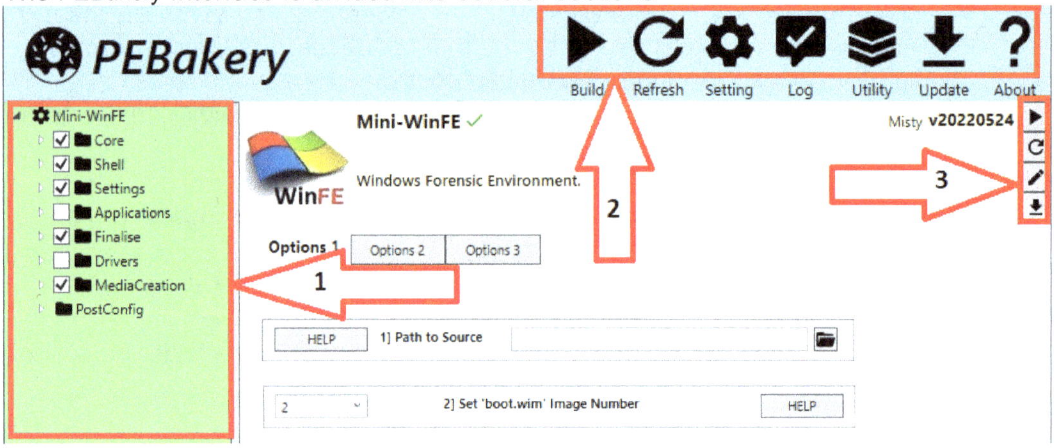

1. Expandable folder tree with a list of project scripts in the left panel. Tick the box in the folder tree next to the script that you want to include in the build. Untick any boxes next to scripts to be excluded from the build process.
2. *PEBakery* settings/options buttons in the top panel. Buttons from left to right -
    - *Build* - run the project.
    - *Refresh* - Refresh all scripts in the *PEBakery* cache. Any edits to scripts made since *PEBakery* was started, or scripts added to the project, will take effect. If a script is added to the project directory for example, it will not be displayed in the folder tree until the *Refresh* button is pressed.
    - *Setting* - *PEBakery* build engine settings with numerous options.
    - *Log* - display log files.

- *Utility* - can be used to check/generate code for writing scripts.
- *Update* - not yet implemented.
- *About* - contains information about the build version and software licence(s).

3. Script settings/options buttons to the right of the script titlebar. From top to bottom -
    - *Run Script* - run the selected plugin without running the full project. Useful for pre/post processing scripts.
    - *Refresh Script* - refresh the selected scripts in the *PEBakery* cache. E.g. if the script file has been edited since *PEBakery* was started.
    - *Edit Script* - open the selected script in a text editor (or other default program associated with .script files).
    - *Syntax Check* - useful for developers to check the code for syntax errors. If default *PEBakery* settings are used then this button will be displayed in green if there are no errors in the script, or orange if there are any syntax errors.

When *PEBakeryLauncher.exe* is first run, you should see a screen similar to the following (the folder tree on the left can be expanded so that individual script options can be selected or disabled as required) -

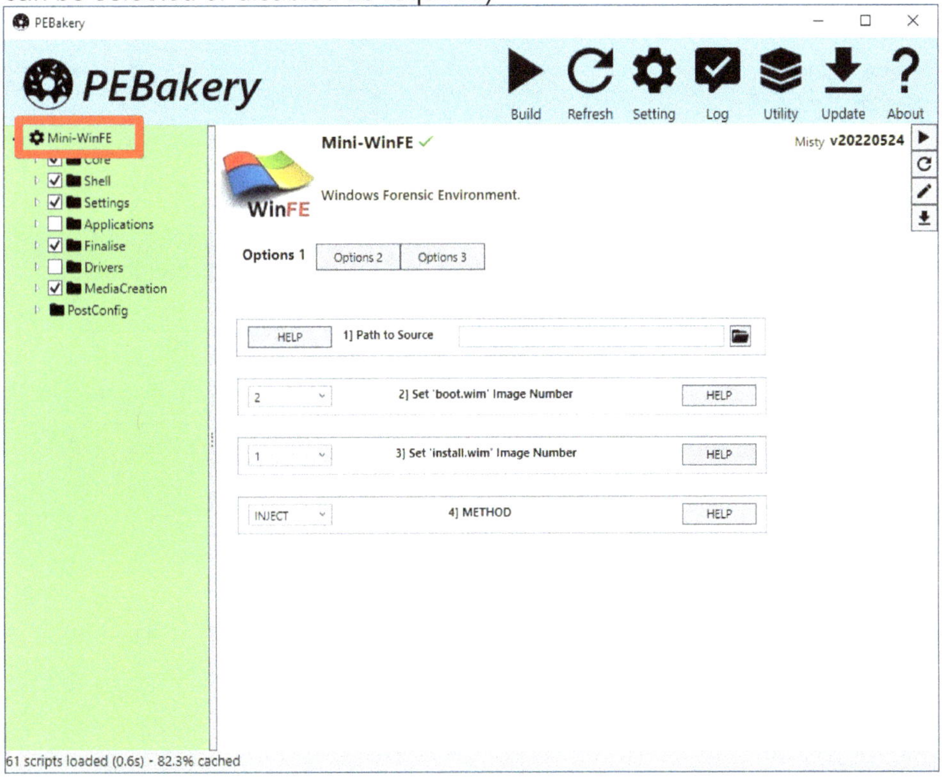

Set the path to your source files by either manually entering the path (1) or click on the *Folder* button (2) to set the path to your Windows Installation Media source files. Please note that if manually entering a path it must end in a backslash (\). E.g.

D:\source_files\

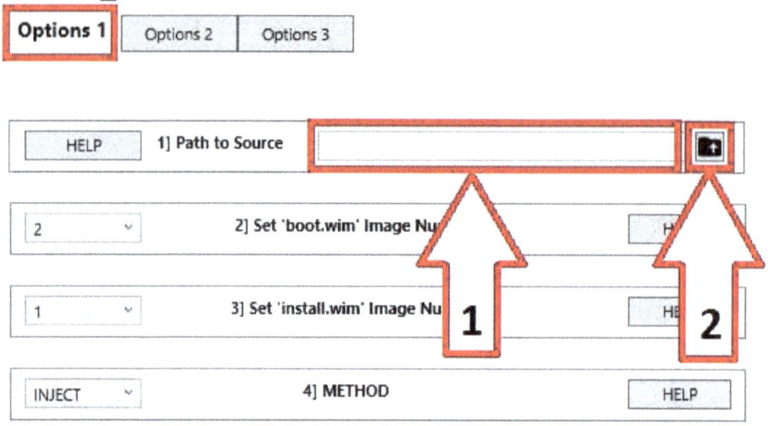

A mounted Windows RTM .iso file is recommended as source. Alternatively extract the contents of a Windows .iso to a local directory. Set the path in this option to the root folder that contains the following files/directories -

- *\sources\boot.wim*
- *\sources\install.wim*
- *\bootmgr*
- *\boot*
- *\EFI*

Expand the folder tree on the left and view and select individual project script options as required (refer to the Project Scripts section for details about all included project scripts) -

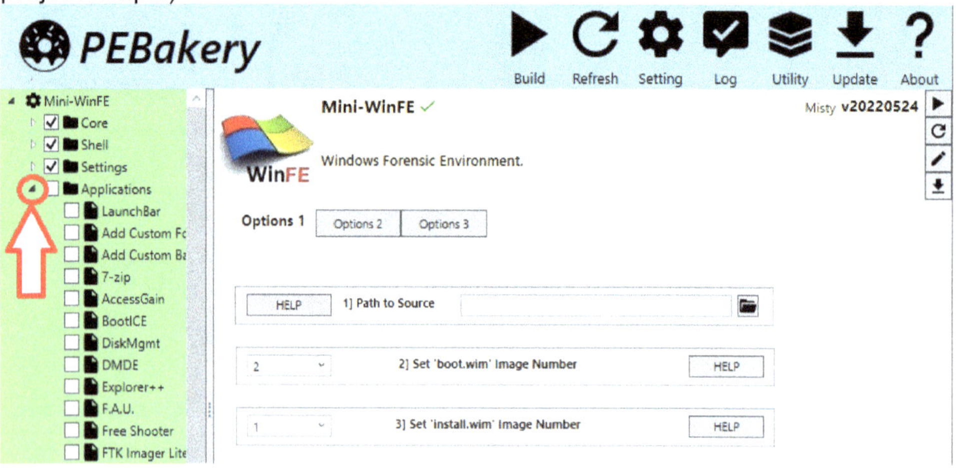

To start the build process, click on the *Build* button in the top row of buttons -

A progress bar will be displayed for individual project scripts as they are processed -

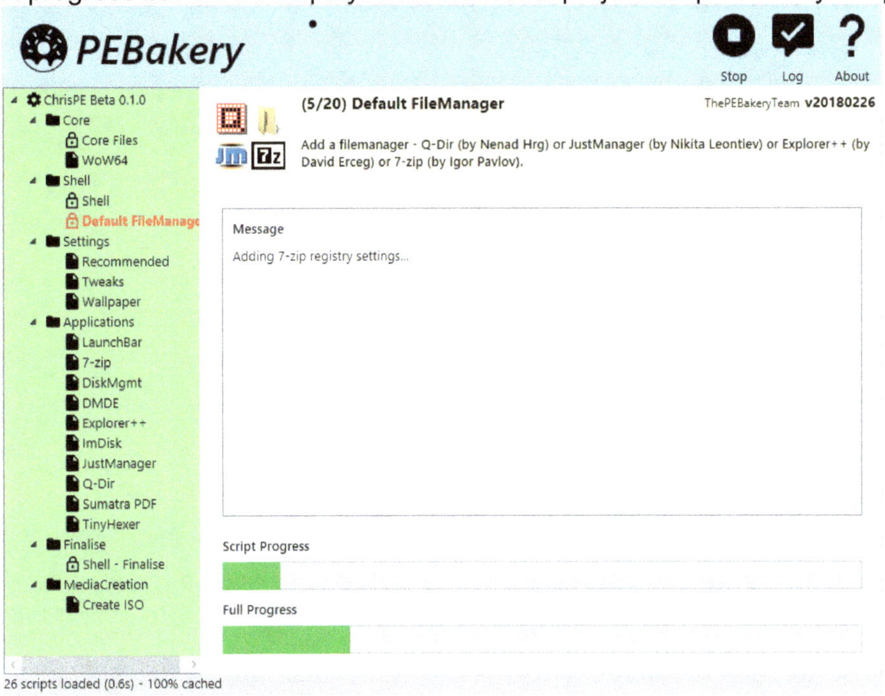

The source for project scripts can be viewed by clicking on the *Edit Script* button to the right of the script title bar (note - you may need to associate a default program to open *.script* files) –

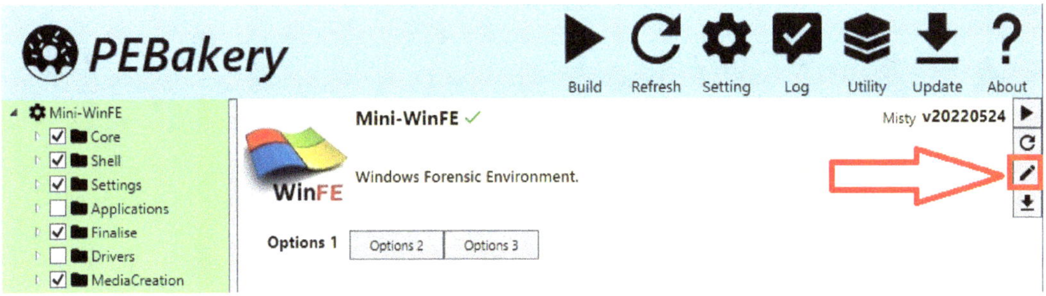

PEBakery has built in logging support with a database store containing logs for previous builds. These logs are very useful for troubleshooting problems with both the project and *PEBakery*. Logs can be accessed via the *Log* button in the top row of buttons -

Use the tabs to toggle between *System Log* and *Build Log* pages - -

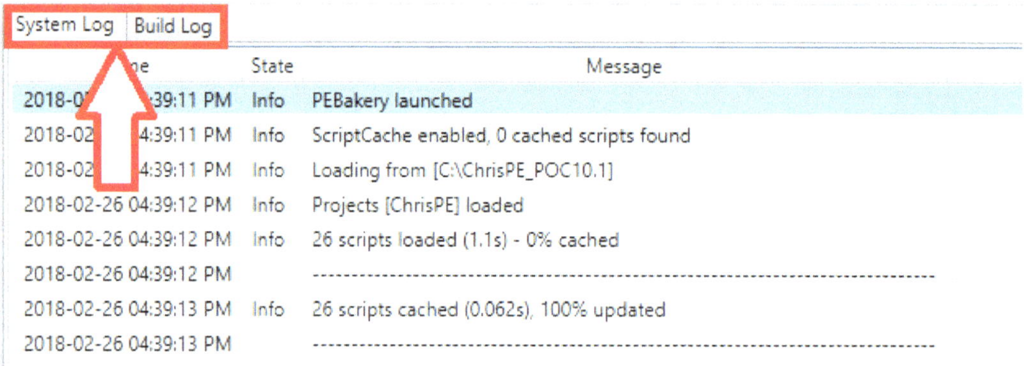

In the *Build Log* tab, use the pick list in the *Select Build* field to select the required build log and then click on the *Export* button to save the log file (*.html* and plain *.txt* files are supported) -

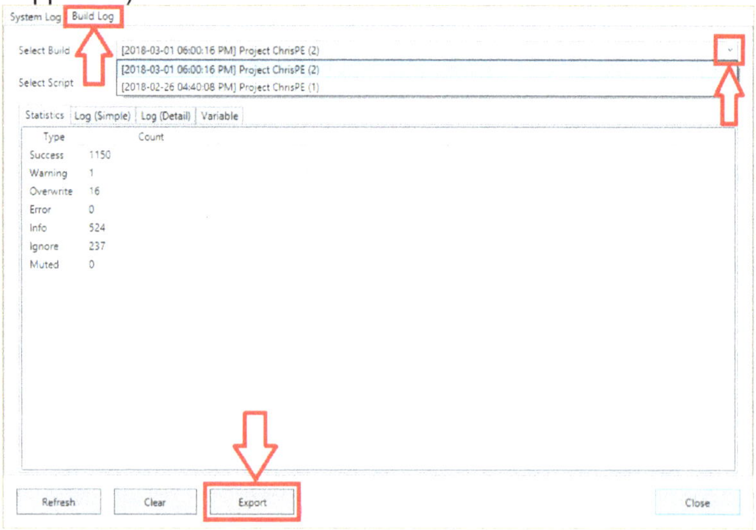

Project Options

Individual project scripts can contain a range of options. In *Mini-WinFE* the interface has been kept as simple as possible with options reduced to a minimum. A number of options are set in the main project script and can be viewed by selecting *Mini-WinFE* at the top of the folder tree in the left panel -

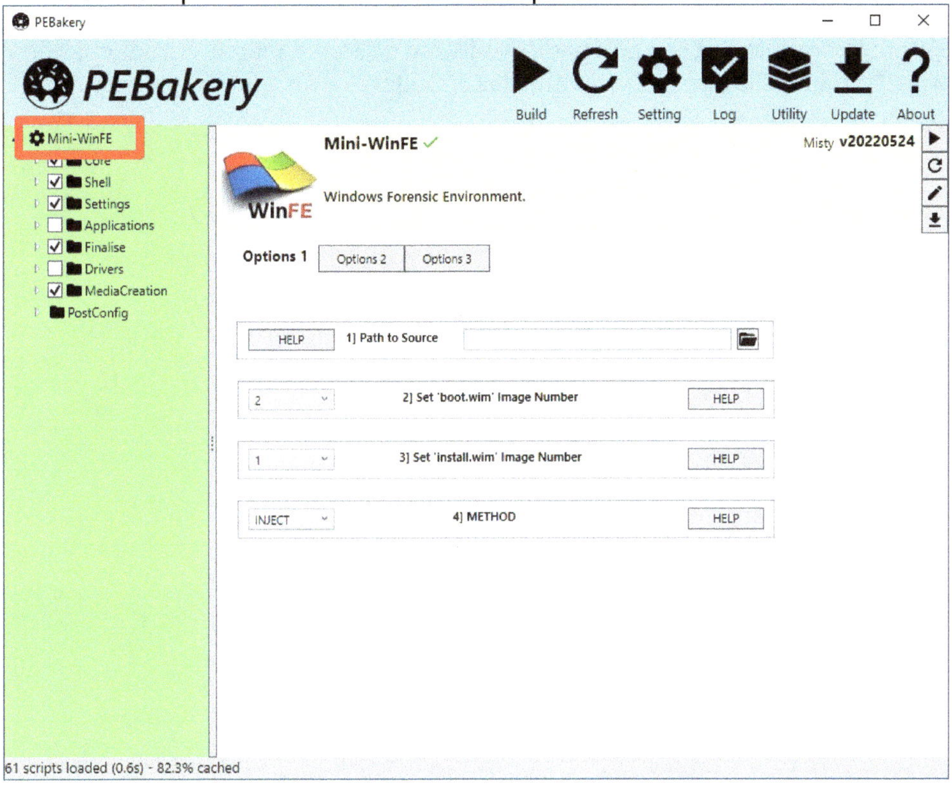

Multiple scripts, including the main project script, use pick lists with a range of pre-defined options -

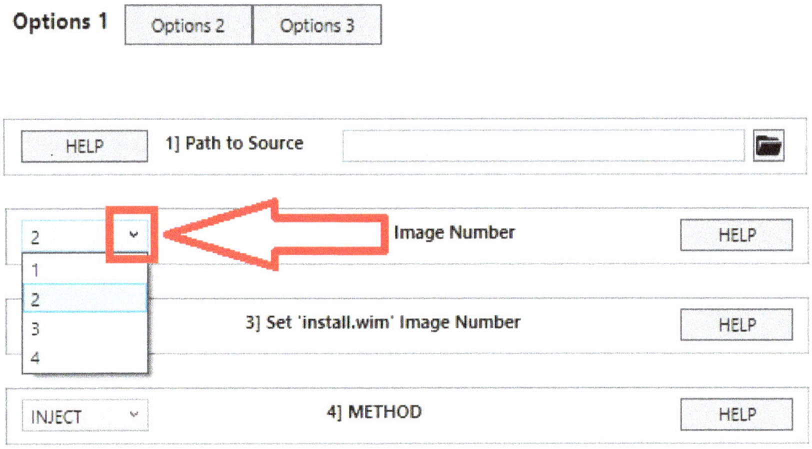

A number of scripts in the *WinFE* project have a tab style interface with additional options -

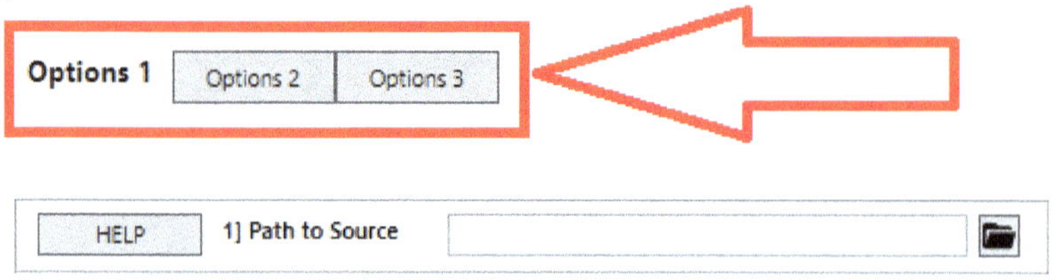

To see more information about any of the available options that can be set/changed in the *WinFE* project, click on the relevant **HELP** button -

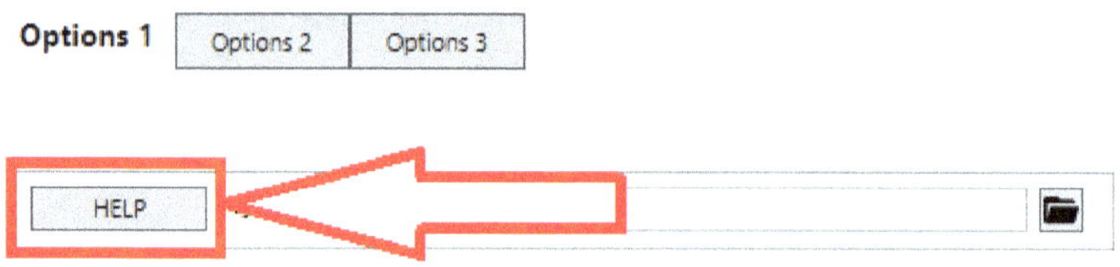

Selecting **HELP** for this option will display the following information -

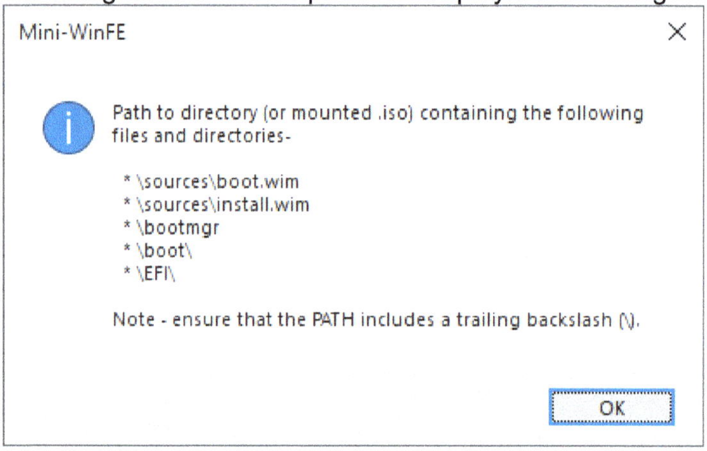

Some scripts use a **?** help button -

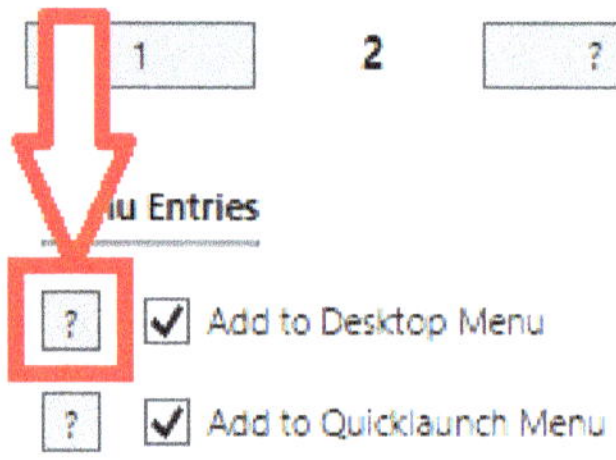

A number of *Applications* .scripts have an option to *Include Program in boot.wim*. For more information about this option see *here*.

***Mini-WinFE* supports custom menus. For more information about this option see *here*.**

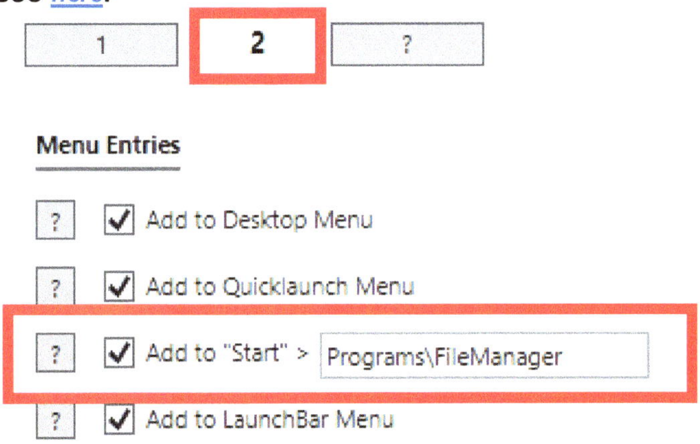

Instructions (WinBuilder)

Please note that any screenshots in this documentation may differ from the current release.

You will require the following in order to build *WinFE* -

- **Administrator privileges** - registry hives will need to be mounted and edited during the build process, and other processes also require administrator privileges.
- Free disk space - 1GB should be more than adequate as Windows source files are not cached during the build process.
- Windows Installation Media - either a CD/DVD, a mounted disk image or the files copied to an accessible folder.

Mini-WinFE uses the *WinBuilder* scripting language to automate a number of tasks to create a working *WinPE*.

Before running *WinBuilder* please be aware that, *in the Mini-WinFE project*, the following project directory (and sub directories) will, if they exist, be deleted during the start of the build process (**Note** - *%BaseDir%* is a *WinBuilder* variable for the folder from which the *WinBuilder* executable *WinBuilder.exe* is running).

- %BaseDir%\WinFE.Files\
- %BaseDir%\ProjectTemp\

Sections in this page -

- *WinBuilder Basics*
- *Project Options*

WinBuilder Basics

When *WinBuilder.exe* is first run, you should see a screen similar to the following (the folder tree on the left can be expanded so that individual script options can be selected or disabled as required) -

The **Source** button to used in other projects to set the path to your Windows Installation Media source files (this option is not used in *Mini-WinFE*) -

Use the **Script** button to return to the main interface -

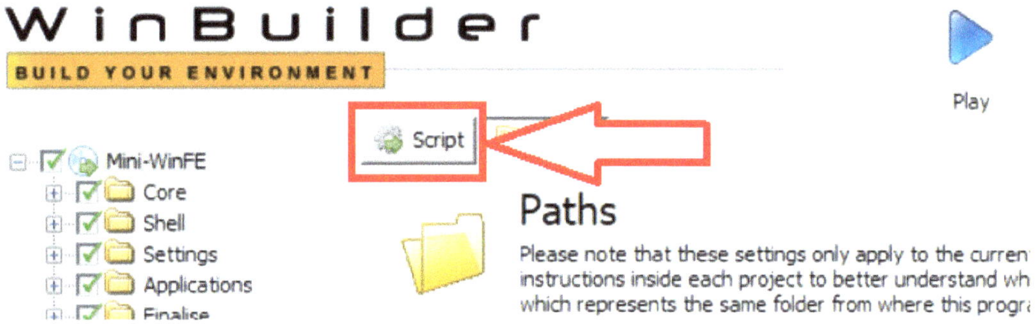

When *WinBuilder.exe* is first run, you should see a screen similar to the following (the folder tree on the left can be expanded so that individual script options can be selected or disabled as required) -

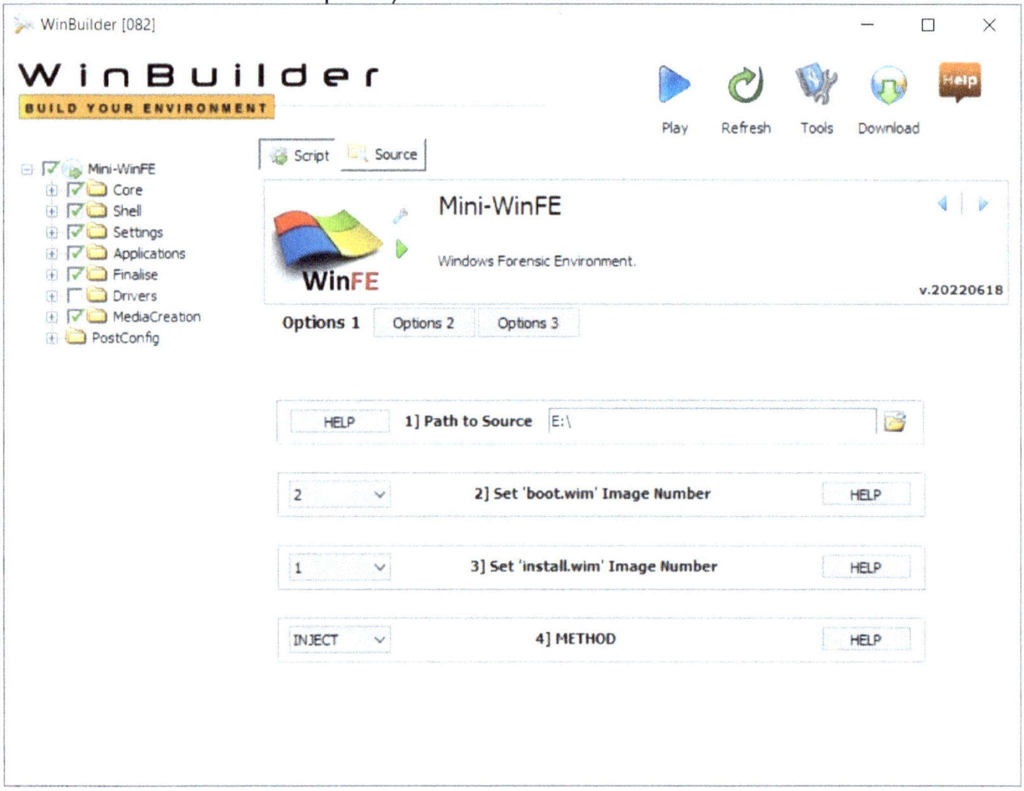

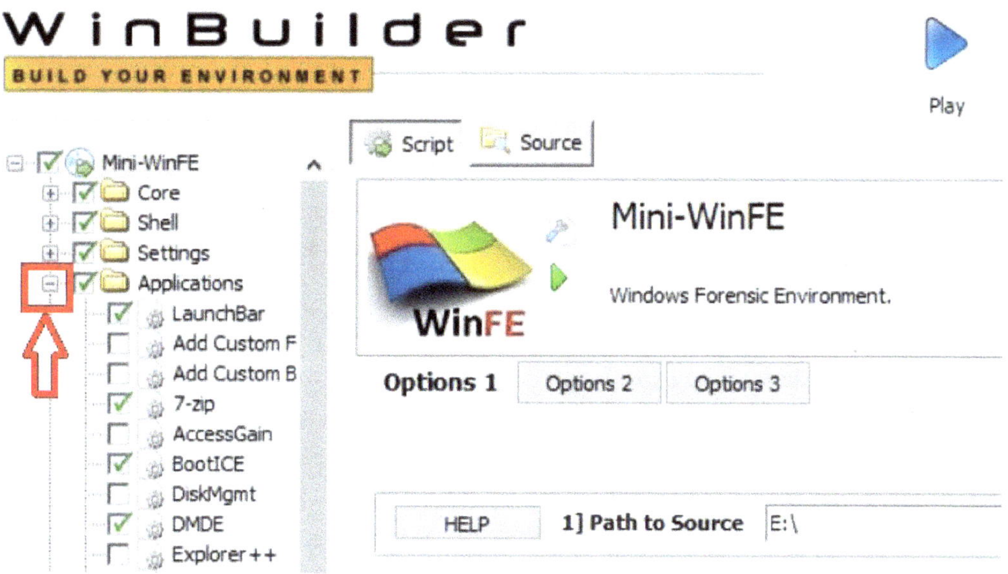

Select the main project script in the folder tree and set the path to your source files by either manually entering the path (1) or click on the *Folder* button (2) to set the path to your Windows Installation Media source files. Please note that if manually entering a path it must end in a backslash (\). E.g. D:\source_files\

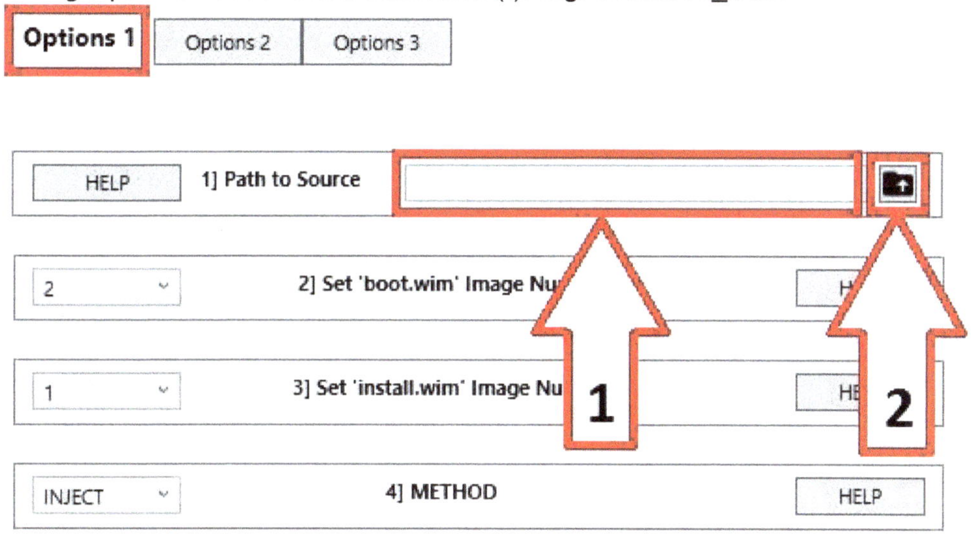

A mounted Windows RTM .iso file is recommended as source. Alternatively extract the contents of a Windows .iso to a local directory. Set the path in this option to the root folder that contains the following files/directories -

- *\sources\boot.wim*

- *\sources\install.wim*
- *\bootmgr*
- *\boot*
- *\EFI*

To start the build process, click on the big blue *Play* button in the top right of the screen -

A progress bar will be displayed for individual project scripts as they are processed.

If there are any errors during the build process then view the log file for further information by clicking on the **Log** button (see below). You can close the log by clicking back on the **Script** button (to the left of the **Log** button) -

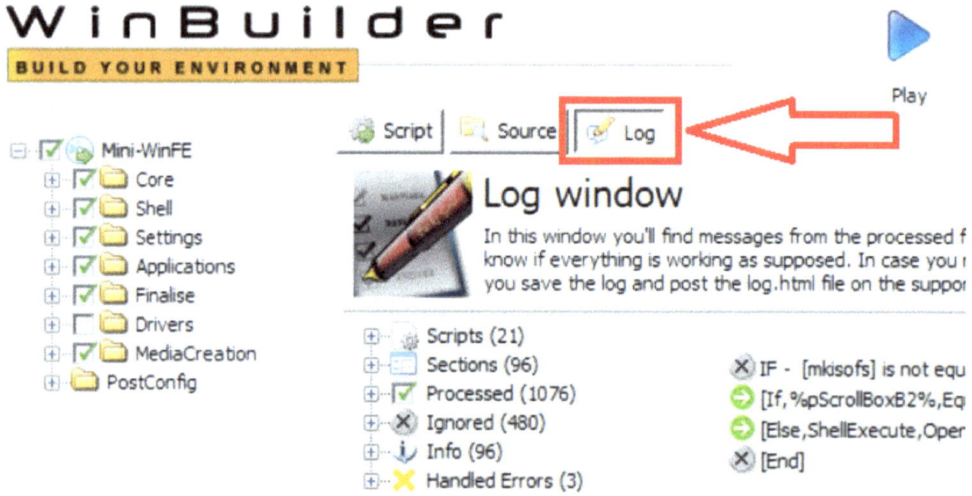

The source for project scripts can be viewed by clicking on the scripts icon –

This will open a range of options including the built in text editor which is displayed by clicking on the **Source** button –

Return to the project by clicking on the ✕ button in the top right of the screen.

Project Options

Individual project scripts can contain a range of options. In *Mini-WinFE* the interface has been kept as simple as possible with options reduced to a minimum. A number of options are set in the main project script and can be viewed by selecting *Mini-WinFE* at the top of the folder tree in the left panel -

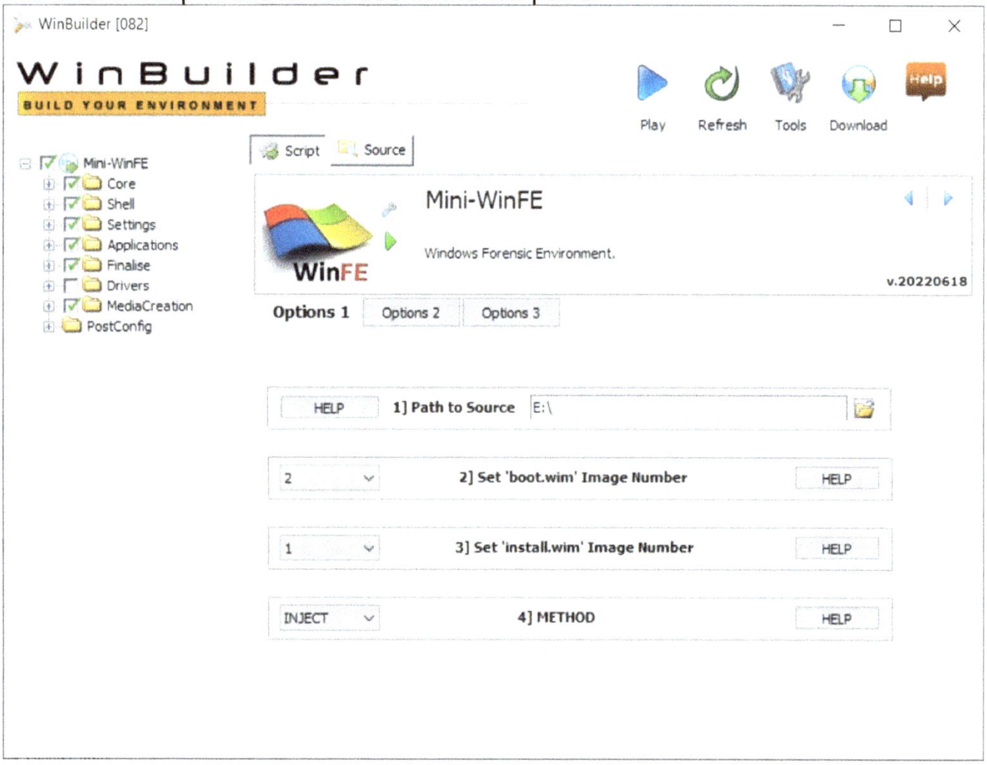

Multiple scripts, including the main project script, use pick lists with a range of pre-defined options -

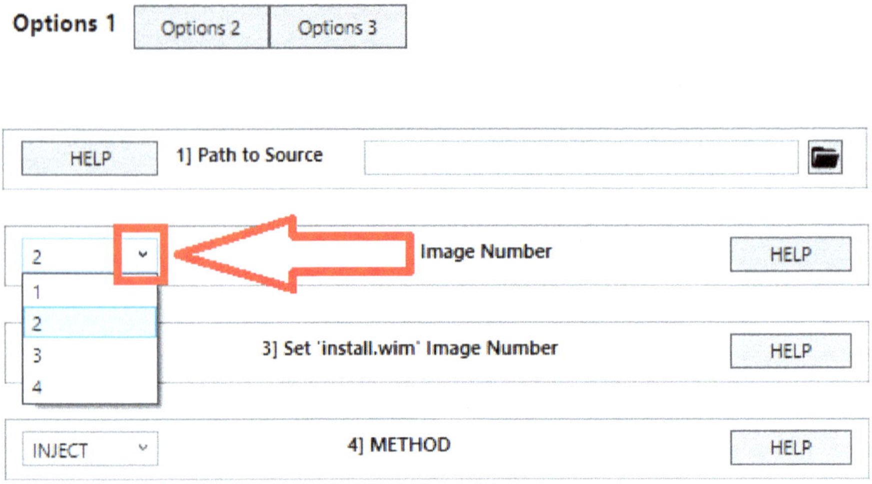

A number of scripts in the *WinFE* project have a tab style interface with additional options -

To see more information about any of the available options that can be set/changed in the *WinFE* project, click on the relevant **HELP** button -

Selecting **HELP** for this option will display the following information -

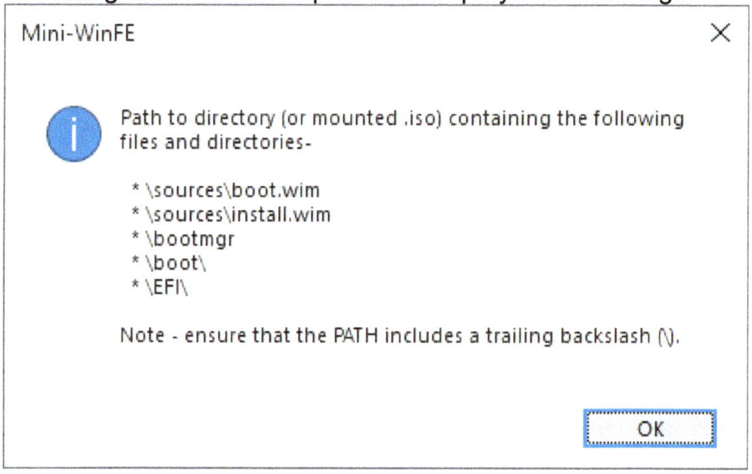

Some scripts use a **?** help button -

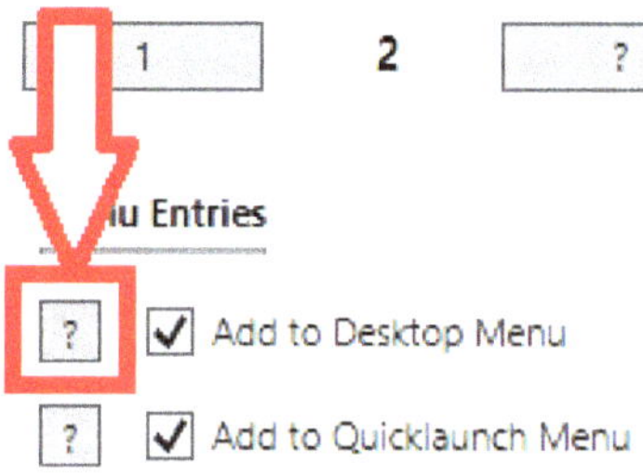

A number of *Applications* .scripts have an option to *Include Program in boot.wim*. For more information about this option see *here*.

Mini-WinFE **supports custom menus. For more information about this option see here.**

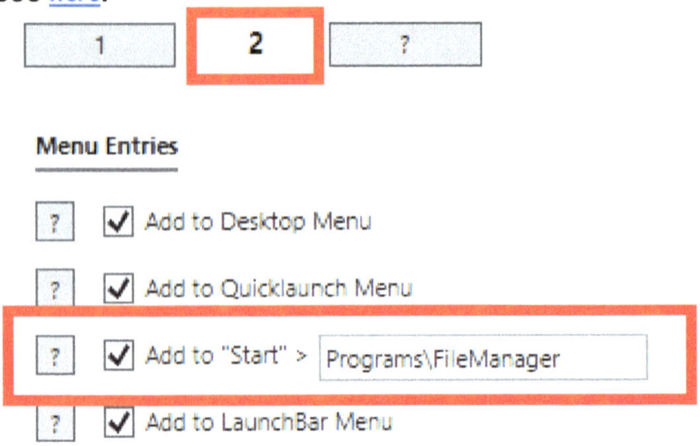

WinFE Menu System

WinFE currently has support for the following four shells -

- *bblean*
- *CMD*
- *LaunchBar*
- *WinXShell*

Each shell has a different menu system - except the *CMD* shell, which does not have any menu support. *WinXShell* for example supports Desktop shortcuts, QuickLaunch shortcuts and a Start menu. The *bblean* menu is accessible via the Windows button or by right-click on the desktop. *LaunchBar* uses a Quick Launch style menu bar not dissimilar to the Mac OSX Dock.

The menu can be customised to create sub-menus. Select an application script in the directory tree to the left of the *PEBakery* interface and select tab 2 (if present) to access the menu options -

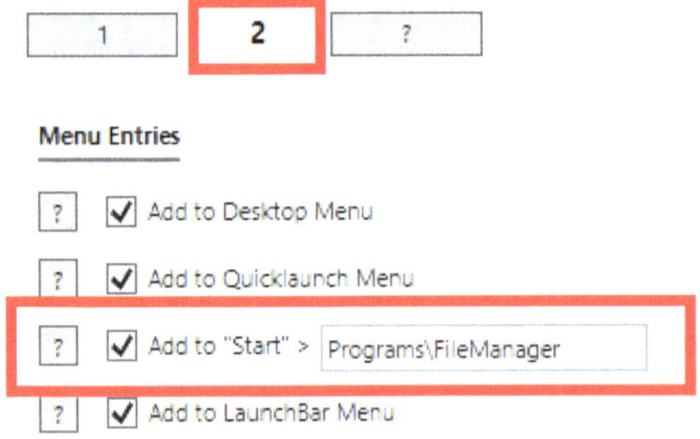

Current options -

- *Add to Desktop Menu* - select to add a Desktop shortcut for the application (*WinXShell* only).
- *Add to Quicklaunch Menu* - select to add a Quicklaunch shortcut for the application (*WinXShell* only).
- *Add to "Start" >* - use the textbox in this option to create custom menu entries (sub-menus) for the *bblean*, *LaunchBar* and *WinXShell* shells.
- *Add to LaunchBar Menu* - applies only to a second instance of *LaunchBar* (e.g. when the *Applications* > *LaunchBar* script is selected in the build).

Screenshot of a *WinXShell* start menu –

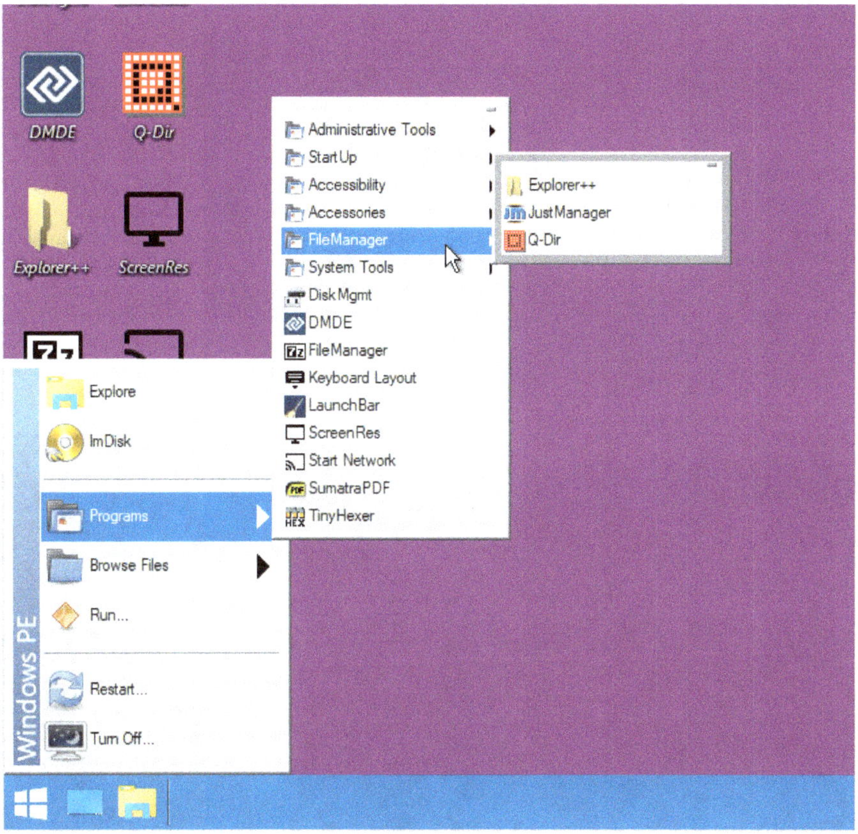

In the screenshots below, the *Add to "Start" >* option has been set with the following values in the textbox (**bold** text entries below) -

- *Shell > Default Filemanager* - **Programs**
- *Settings > Network* - **Programs**
- *Settings > Recommended* - **Programs**
- *Applications > LaunchBar* - **Programs**
- *Applications > 7-zip* - **Programs**
- *Applications > DiskMgmt* - **Programs**
- *Applications > DMDE* - **Programs**
- *Applications > Explorer++* - **Programs\FileManager**
- *Applications > ImDisk* - N/A (left empty)

- *Applications* > *JustManager* - **Programs\FileManager**
- *Applications* > *Q-Dir* - **Programs\FileManager**
- *Applications* > *Sumatra PDF* - **Programs**
- *Applications* > *TightVNC Server* - **Programs**
- *Applications* > *TinyHexer* - **Programs**
- *Finalise* > *WinFE* - N/A (left empty)

Screenshot of *bblean* menu. Note that *ImDisk* is displayed at the root of the Start menu as the entry in the *Add to "Start"* > field was left blank. Also note the Programs\FileManager sub-menu created by the entries in the *Add to "Start"* > field in the *Explorer++*, *JustManager* and *Q-Dir* scripts - -

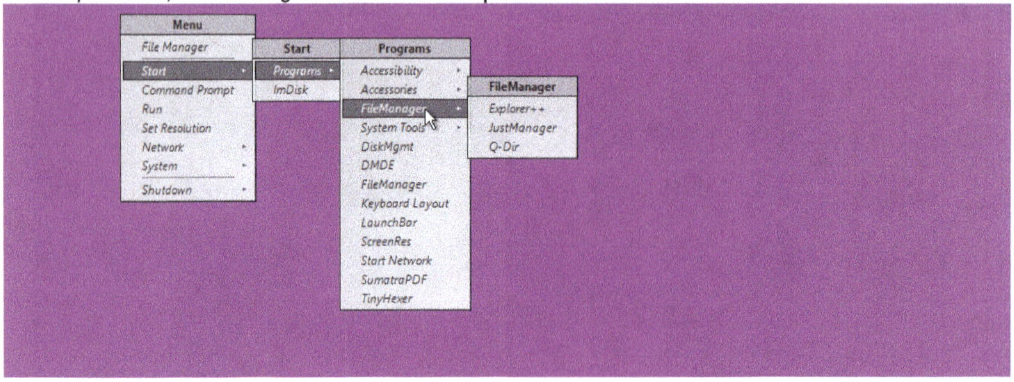

Screenshot of *LaunchBar* menu. Note that *ImDisk* is displayed at the root of the LaunchBar as the entry in the *Add to "Start"* > field was left blank –

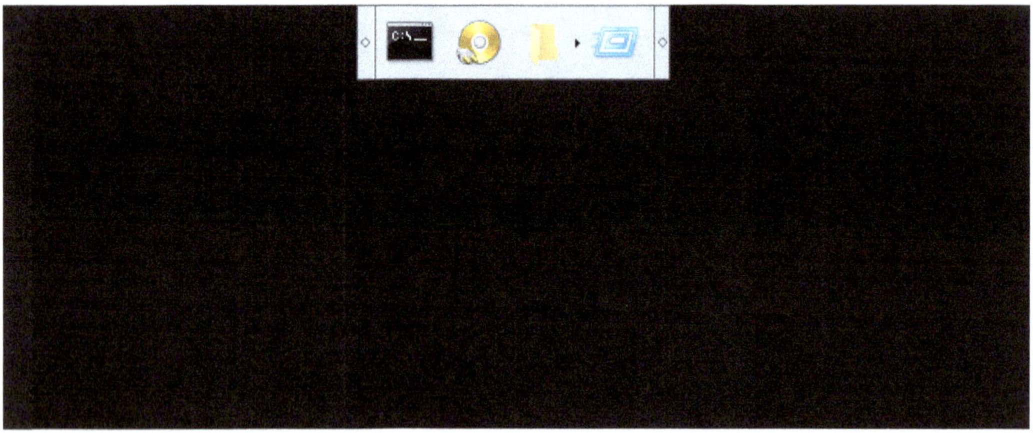

Screenshot of *LaunchBar* menu displaying sub-menus. Note the Programs\FileManager sub-menu created by the entries in the *Add to "Start"* > field in the *Explorer++*, *JustManager* and *Q-Dir* scripts -

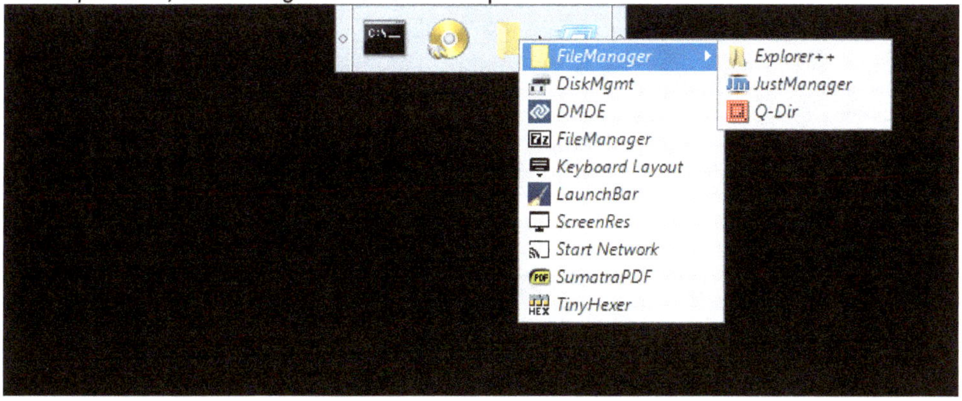

Screenshot of *WinXShell* Start Menu. Note that *ImDisk* is displayed at the root of the Start menu as the entry in the *Add to "Start"* > field was left blank. Also note the Programs\FileManager sub-menu created by the entries in the *Add to "Start"* > field in the *Explorer++*, *JustManager* and *Q-Dir* scripts –

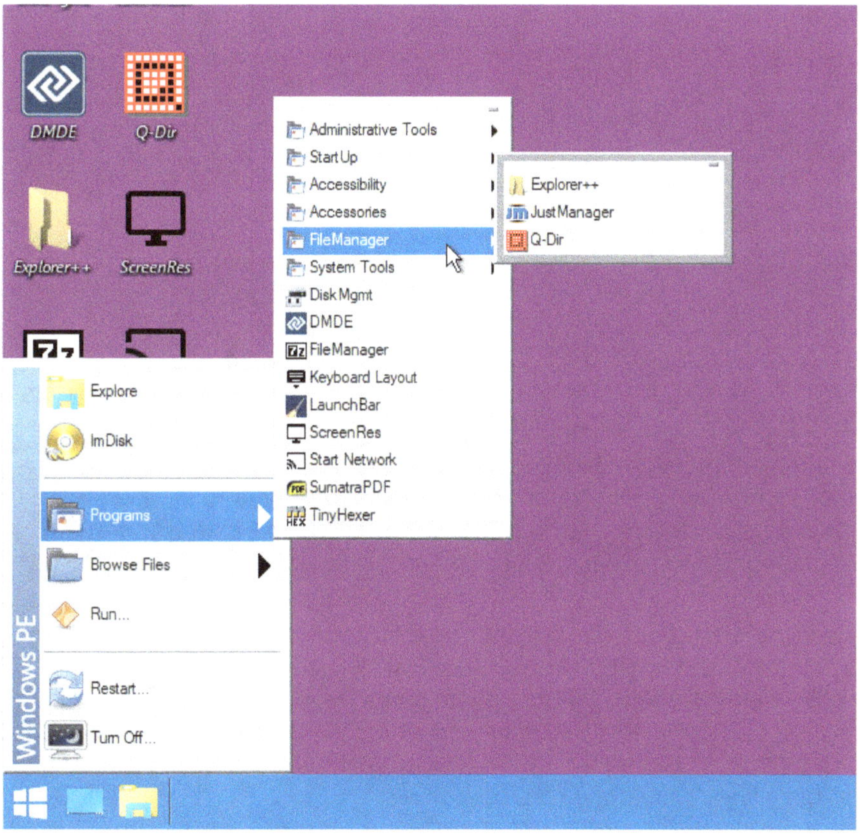

Screenshot of *LaunchBar* running in *WinXShell* -

Include Program in boot.wim

A number of *Applications* .scripts have an option to *Include Program in boot.wim*. E.g. -

If the *Include Program in boot.wim* option is enabled then the selected application will be added to *boot.wim* - increasing the size of *WinPE* and the system RAM requirements.

If a light build of *WinPE* is required, then consider disabling this option at the individual application script level - allowing control over which applications are included or excluded from *boot.wim*. None of the applications included in the initial *WinFE* release are particularly large and this is unlikely to be an issue at the time of writing, however as the project develops larger applications are likely to be added.

Any applications included in boot.wim will increase RAM usage due to the file size increase in *boot.wim* when adding additional files. FTK Imager version 3.1.1.8 for example is 74 MB when unpacked. Although not currently included/supported in the project, this program can run in a *WinPE* environment. Disabling the *Include Program in boot.wim* option has other advantages - the main one being the ability to update individual programs without having to rebuild *boot.wim*.

If the *Include Program in boot.wim* option is disabled, the application will be added to one of the following directories (depending on the *WinPE* Processor Architecture) -

- \WinFE.Files\ISO.ROOT\Programs.x86\ (32-bit *WinPE* builds)
- \WinFE.Files\ISO.ROOT\Programs.x64\ (64-bit *WinPE* builds)

Paths are relative to *PEBakeryLauncher.exe*. The contents of \WinFE.Files\ISO.ROOT\ will be added to the root of the CD\DVD image if the Create ISO script is enabled. Alternatively, manually copy the \WinFE.Files\ISO.ROOT\Programs.x**\ directory to the root of a USB drive.

If any of the *Applications* scripts have the *Include Program in boot.wim* option disabled, then a menu shortcut will be added to the build that will launch a batch file to search for a unique file created during the build process. The unique file uses a name based on the build date and time. *Find Programs* shortcut icon -

Batch file launched when the *Find Programs* menu option is selected, running in *WinPE* (note the name of the tag file in this build - 2018-13-19-15.56.tag) -

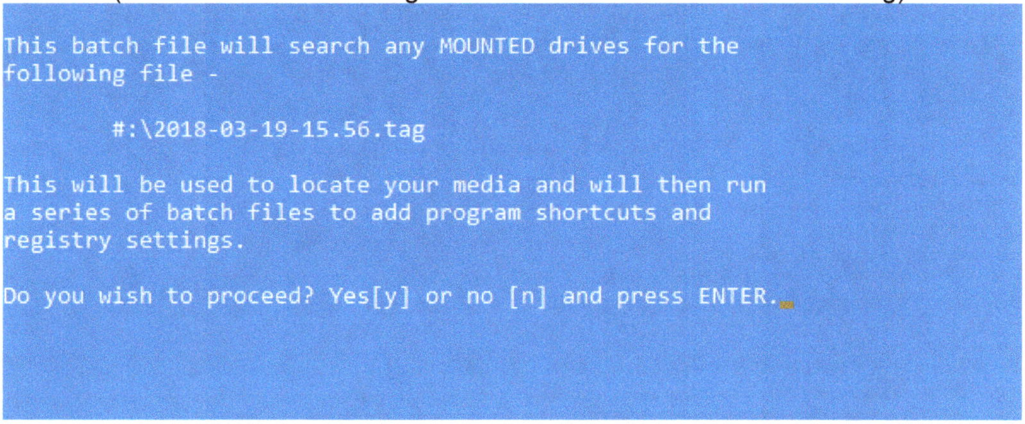

This batch file will search any MOUNTED drives for the
following file -
#:\2018-03-19-15.56.tag
This will be used to locate your media and will then run
a series of batch files to add program shortcuts and
registry settings.
Do you wish to proceed? Yes[y] or no [n] and press ENTER.

NOTE - if you plan to PXE boot your *WinFE* build then there are significant advantages in enabling the *Include Program in boot.wim* option as it may not be possible to access other media from this environment.

Running the *Find Programs* menu option will run a batch file which will search for a unique file. If this unique file is located in the root of a mounted drive then a series of other batch files will be executed. These will create menu entries in the selected shell's start menu (and may also add registry entries and start *LaunchBar*). Menu entries will be added to the *Start* > *ExternalMedia* submenu.

WinXShell prior to running the *Find Programs* menu option (*ExternalMedia* submenu is empty) -

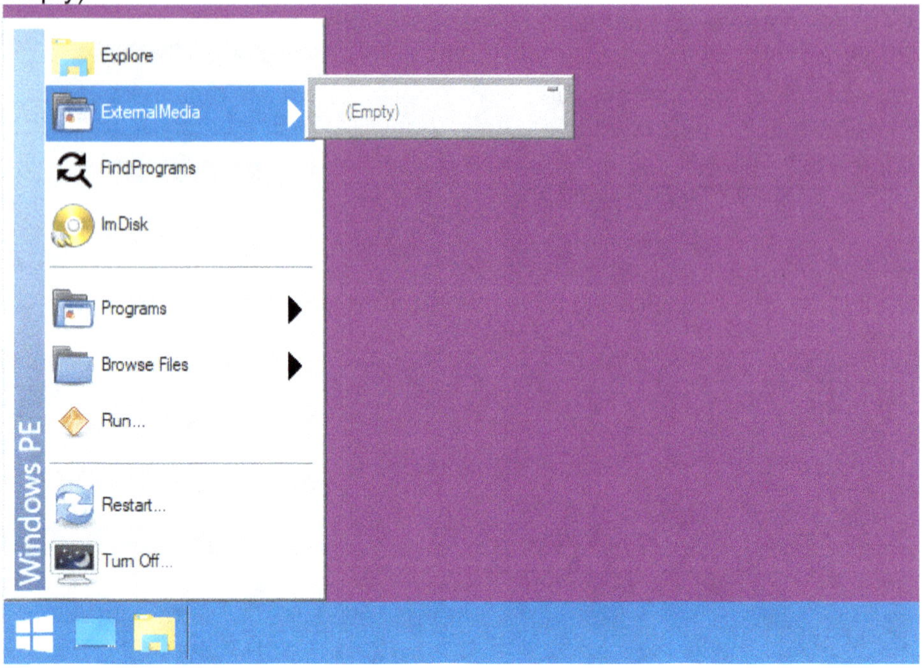

WinXShell after running the *Find Programs* menu option –

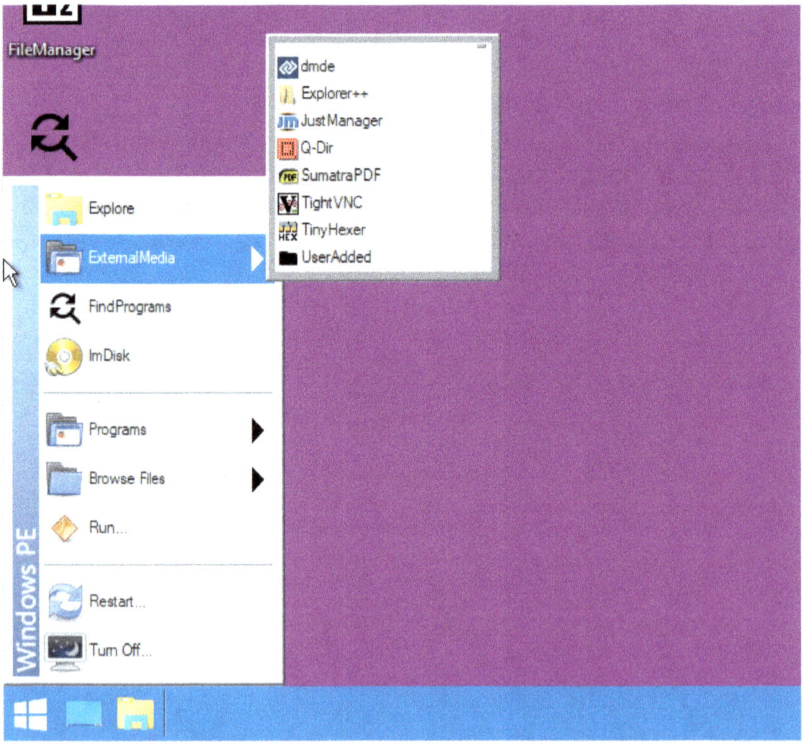

LaunchBar prior to running the *Find Programs* menu option (*ExternalMedia* submenu is empty) –

LaunchBar after running the *Find Programs* menu option –

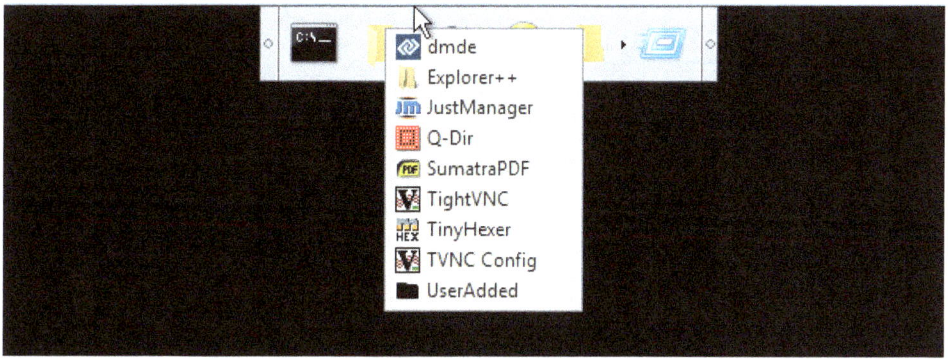

BBLean prior to running the *Find Programs* menu option (*ExternalMedia* submenu is empty) –

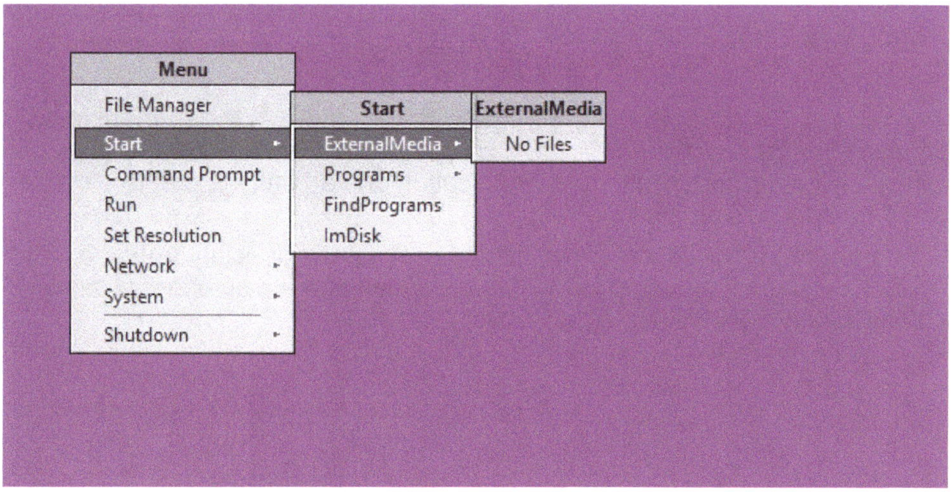

BBLean after running the *Find Programs* menu option -

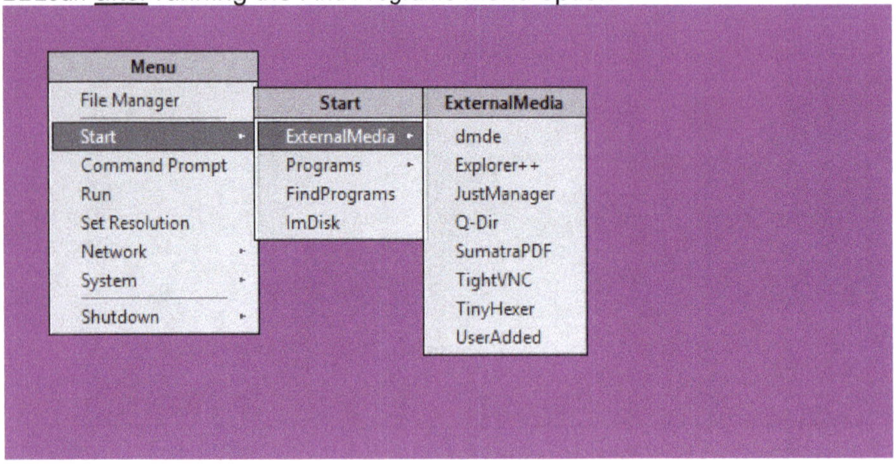

Post Configuration

A number of project scripts can be executed post build - this currently includes all *Applications* scripts distributed with the project. In addition to the *Applications* scripts, the following can also be executed post build -

- *Drivers > Drivers*
- *MediaCreation > Create ISO*
- *PostConfig > Advanced Options*

The ability to add applications and features following a project build without rebuilding the entire project may save time and may also be of use to developers for testing puposes. To take advantage of this feature a project run must already have been completed. In it's current implementation, running a script post build will check for the presence of the following file -

- \WinFE.Files\project.settings.ini

This file will then be parsed to check for a number of varibles required in the build process.

Running *Applications* scripts post build will create menu entries in the shell selected in the previous project run. If an *Applications* script has the *Include in boot.wim* option disbled then it will be copied to the relevant location and an entry to create a menu shortcut will be added to a batch file.

To execute a script post build, simply select the script in the directory tree and click on the *Run Script* button to the right of the title bar. The following screenshot shows the *Run Script* button in the *MediaCreation > Create ISO* script -

The *PostConfig* > *Advanced Options* script also contains a range of post build options -

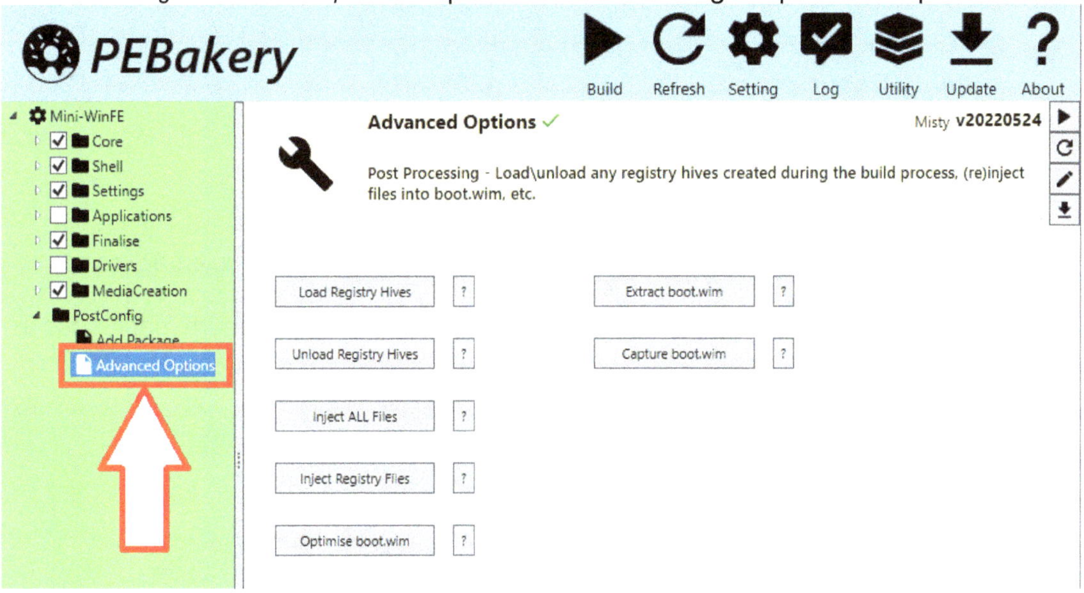

Packages

NOTE - Packages are currently limited - more will be added over time. At the time of writing a limited set of compatible packages is available here

A basic package system has been introduced in *WinFE* to make it easier to add third party scripts to the project. Packages can be added via the *PostConfig* > *Add Package* script. There are two options at the time of writing -

- *Tab 1* - add a single package.
- *Tab 2* - add multiple packages.

Both options use the command-line *7z.exe* executable (included in the project download) to extract the selected file(s) to the *WinFE* root directory. The option to select a single package will check for a marker file to ensure that the file/package is compatible with *Mini-WinFE*. The option to add multiple packages will NOT check the selected package(s) for project compatibility so please ensure that any target is a compatible *Mini-WinFE* package.

Packages are compressed using *7-zip* LZMA compression - the *PostConfig > Add Package* script will only work with files with a *.7z* extension.

The following screenshot shows *Tab 1* settings - used to add a single package. Manually enter a path to a package or use the file browser button -

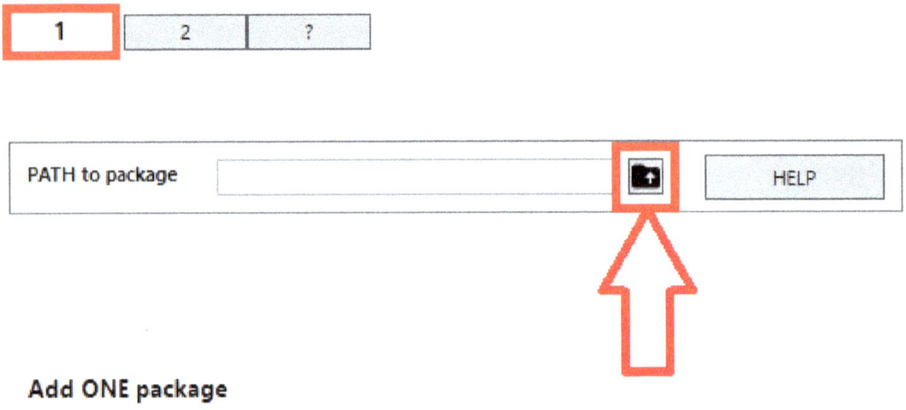

The following screenshot shows *Tab 2* settings - used to add multiple packages. Manually enter a path to the directory containing your package(s) or use the directory browser button. If manually entereing a path, please ensure that it ends in a backslash ("\") -

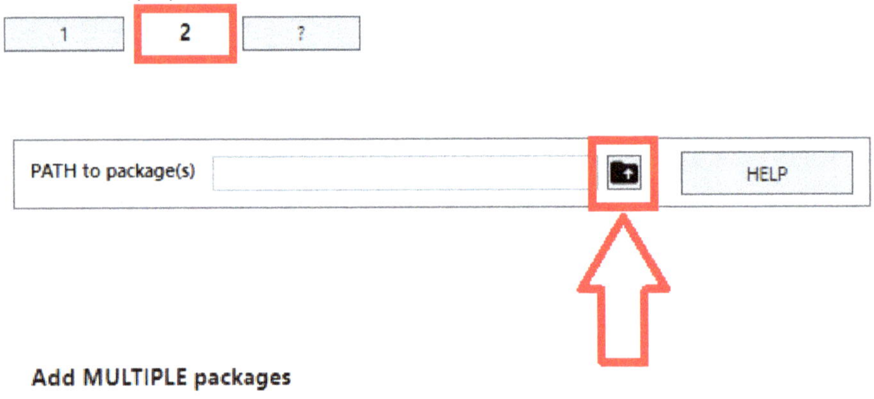

After entering/selecting a valid PATH, click on the *Run Script* button to add the package(s) to the project -

Create a Bootable USB Stick

There are a number of different methods for creating a bootable USB stick, including -

- Diskpart
- Rufus
- Other Tools/Methods

Diskpart

The following is a walkthrough of the steps required for creating a bootable USB stick using the command-line *DiskPart* tool. The actions include wiping the disk before creating and formatting a new partition and making the partition active - as this could potentially result in data loss make sure that the correct disk is selected. *DiskPart* works by targeting an object (either a disk, volume or partition) - making it have *"focus"* (see here).

The drive will need to be manually selected. Use the command **List disk** to show all available disks -

```
DISKPART> list disk

  Disk ###  Status         Size     Free     Dyn  Gpt
  --------  -------------  -------  -------  ---  ---
  Disk 0    Online          149 GB    31 KB
  Disk 1    Online         7681 MB      0 B
  Disk 2    Online          698 GB    31 KB
```

It should be possible to identify your USB stick based on it's size or other attributes. In this walkthrough the *"target"* was identified as disk 1. Select disk 1 by entering the command **sel disk 1** -

```
DISKPART> sel disk 1

Disk 1 is now the selected disk.
```

To double check the correct disk has been selected, use the command **detail disk** to display more detailed attributes -

```
DISKPART> detail disk

Disk ID: 00000000
Type   : USB
Status : Online
Path   : 0
Target : 0
LUN ID : 0
Location Path : UNAVAILABLE
Current Read-only State : No
Read-only  : No
Boot Disk  : No
Pagefile Disk  : No
Hibernation File Disk  : No
Crashdump Disk  : No
Clustered Disk  : No

  Volume ###  Ltr  Label        Fs     Type        Size     Status
  ----------  ---  -----------  -----  ----------  -------  ---------
  Volume 4     G   SANDISK_USB  FAT32  Removable   7671 MB  Healthy
```

Use the **clean** command to wipe the disk (a limited number of sectors will be erased - removing all partition information and effectively wiping the whole disk). Alternatively the command **clean all** could be used to zero the whole of the disk. As either of these commands will for all intents and purposes delete everything on the selected drive, make sure this is your USB stick and not your hard drive before proceeding! -

```
DISKPART> clean

DiskPart succeeded in cleaning the disk.
```

To create a primary partition using all available disk space, use the command **create partition primary**

```
DISKPART> create partition primary

DiskPart succeeded in creating the specified partition.
```

The remaining tasks need to be carried out on the newly created partition. Use the command **select part 1** to select the new partition -

```
DISKPART> select part 1

Partition 1 is now the selected partition.
```

Use the **active** command to make the partition bootable -

```
DISKPART> active

DiskPart marked the current partition as active.
```

To (quick) format the selected partition with a FAT32 file system, with a volume label WinPE_USB, use command **format fs=fat32 label=WinPE_USB quick**. Where **fs=** selects the file system to be used (options are **fat32**, **ntfs**), **label=** is the volume label to assign to the drive, and **quick** completes a fast format -

```
DISKPART> format fs=fat32 label=WinPE_USB quick

  100 percent completed

DiskPart successfully formatted the volume.
```

To mount the new partition (to assign a drive letter) use the command **assign** -

```
DISKPART> assign

DiskPart successfully assigned the drive letter or mount point.
```

Now copy the files and folder from %BaseDir%\WinFE.Files\ISO.ROOT\ to the USB stick.
The following files/folders should be present on the USB stick -

- \bootmgr
- \boot
- \boot\BCD
- \boot\boot.sdi
- \sources\boot.wim

That's it.

Rufus

Rufus (see *here*) is a relatively simple tool that can be used to create a bootable USB drive from an ISO file.

Start *Rufus* > select the target device, use the default settings > make sure that *"Create a bootable disk using:"* is selected > click on the disc icon next to *"ISO Image"* > browse to your WinPE.iso file > then click on start -

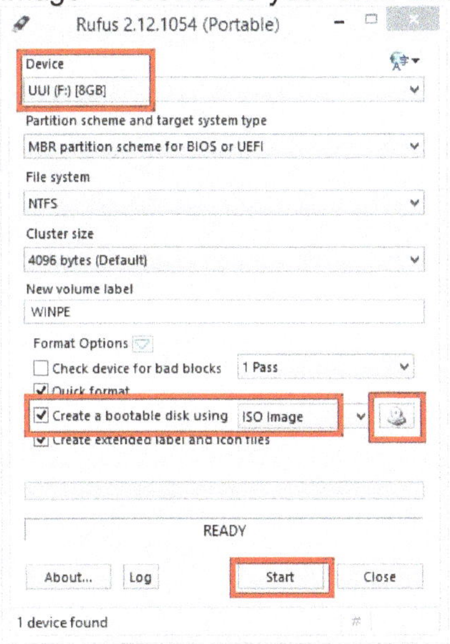

You will see a warning -

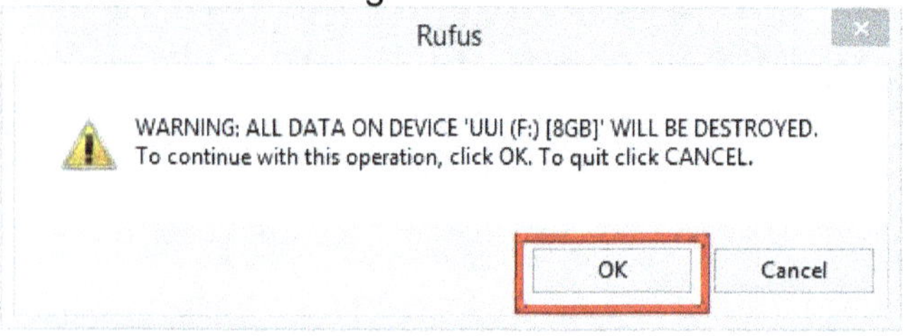

That's pretty much it - *Rufus* will make the USB stick bootable and will unpack the contents of the ISO files selected earlier.

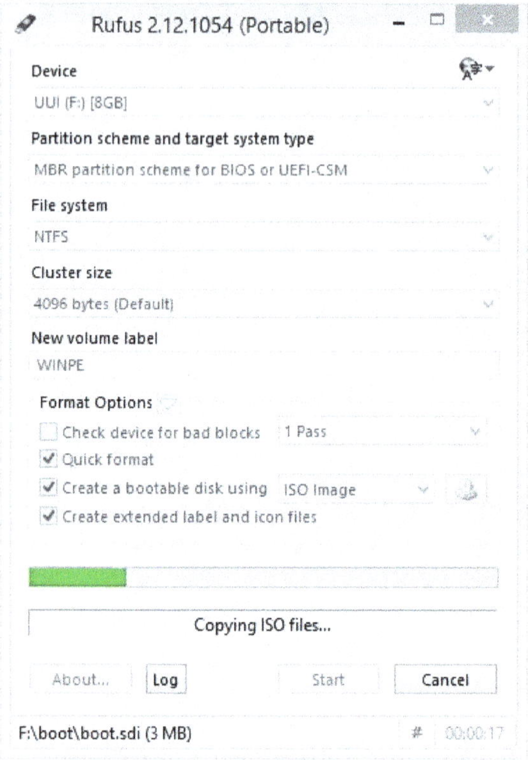

Other Tools/Methods

As an alternative to using *DiskPart* or *Rufus*, try one of the following -

- RMPrepUSB (see here)
- WiNToBootic (see here)

UEFI, BIOS, GPT and MBR

This page contains the following sections -

UEFI and BIOS

BIOS and *UEFI* are different firmware interfaces used to initialise computer hardware - running before the operating system itself is loaded/booted.

The Basic Input/Output System (*BIOS*) has been the standard firmware used in IBM Compatible PC's since the release of the first IBM PC in the 1980's. Whilst it has evolved over the years it has some limitations imposed by its original design - this appears to be leading to it being gradually replaced with *UEFI*.

An AT-compatible *BIOS* runs in 16-bit processor mode with only 1 MB of addressable RAM. The *BIOS* runs in real mode and passes control to the operating system. Windows and most other modern Operating Systems run in protected mode - allowing them to access more than 1 MB RAM. Modern Operating Systems therefore do not use *BIOS* services after the OS has loaded and it is only used in the early stages to initialise hardware, identify the boot device and load the Operating System.

There are a number of articles stating that *BIOS* systems cannot use/access more than 2 TiB of hard disk storage space - this is misleading and is not necessarily true. The hard disk partition table stores partition offset and size in sectors using Logical Block Addressing. The size and offset is limited to a 4 byte hexadecimal value - this means that the maximum number of sectors accessible on a *MBR* type hard disk is 0xFFFFFFFF (hexadecimal) or 4,294,967,296 (decimal). Assuming a sector size of 512 bytes this equals a maximum accessible size of 2 Tebibytes.

Hard disks are now available with a 4 KiB (4096 byte) sector size - 4,294,967,296 (maximum number of sectors) x 4096 bytes (sector size) = 17,592,186,044,416 bytes, or 16 Tebibytes. *MBR* disks can therefore theoretically be as large as 16 TiB. Unfortunately Windows operating systems cannot boot from a native 4 KiB sectored device - hence the misconception of the 2 TiB limit.

Some of the misconceptions about *BIOS* and *UEFI* limitations that are in actual fact Operating System or disk partition scheme limitations. Whilst Windows might limit the boot device to a maximum size of 2 TiB on *MBR* type disks, far larger secondary disks are supported for storage purposes.
The Unified Extensible Firmware Interface (*UEFI*) is a development of Intel's EFI specification. The *GPT* partitioning scheme is part of the (U)EFI specification and is supported in all *UEFI* based systems. Booting from *MBR* partitioned disks is not necessarily supported on *UEFI* systems, however some vendors have implemented legacy support for *MBR* disks.

UEFI is free from some of the AT-compatible *BIOS* limitations mentioned earlier. It can for example address far more than 1MB of RAM and runs in the full 32-bit or 64-bit processor mode (depending on Processor support). In theory a 64-bit *UEFI* system should be able to address 2^64 bytes of RAM (16 exabytes, or 16.8 million terabytes) - due to processor limitations this would not currently be possible even if the physical size of RAM did not make it completely impractical. In conjunction with *GPT* partitioned disks it can also boot operating systems from partitions larger than 2 TB.

The *UEFI* wiki (see here) currently lists the following advantages over a traditional *BIOS* system -

- Ability to boot from large disks (over 2 TB) with a GUID Partition Table, *GPT*.

- CPU-independent architecture
- CPU-independent drivers
- Flexible pre-OS environment, including network capability
- Modular design

UEFI systems can understand file systems - FAT32 is supported (the specification also requires support for FAT12/16 on removable media). Vendors can include support for other file systems.

Whilst the available Windows documentation appears to be steering towards the use of *GPT* partitioned disks on *UEFI* systems, it is also possible to boot Windows from a *MBR* partitioned disk. It is however worth mentioning that it is may not be possible to install Windows to a *MBR* partitioned disk on a *UEFI* system - unless it has a *BIOS* mode available and running (see here).

GPT and MBR

Hard disks generally use one of two partitioning schemes, these being Master Boot Record (*MBR*) and GUID Partition Table (*GPT*). *MBR* partitioned disks were introduced in the 1980's and are supported on all *BIOS* based systems. *BIOS* based systems generally do not support booting from *GPT* partitioned disks, however due to the *GPT* specification requiring a protective *MBR* it is possible to install some third party boot loaders to the first sector of a *GPT* disk.

The Master Boot Record is always located in the very first sector of a hard disk - sector 0. This 512 byte sector contains executable code used to load operating systems, in addition to the partition table which contains all partition information (size, starting sector, filesystem ID, etc.). The partition table can only contain a maximum of four partition entries. It's possible to create up to four primary partitions or one extended partition with up to three primary partitions. The Extended Partition can be subdivided into logical volumes, however the partition information for these logical volumes is not actually contained in the *MBR*. Only one primary partition entry can be marked with a boot flag.

The size of individual partition entries in the partition table is limited to 16-bytes with 32-bit values describing the partition offset and size. This in turn limits the maximum usable storage space to 2 TiB on disks with a 512 byte sector size. Due to Windows code not being able to boot from sectors larger than 512 bytes, the boot device is also limited to 2 TiB. Whilst this may once have appeared to be more than adequate, modern technology has evolved to the point where disks with larger sector sizes and capacities above 2 TiB are available and affordable.

GPT partitioned disks are free from this limitation. In fact, according to the *UEFI* forum, a *GPT* disk uses 64-bit values to store partition information and can support partitions up to 9.4 zettabytes in size. Additionally *GPT* disks can also support far more partitions than *MBR* disks - in theory there is no limit on the number of partitions, however a number of Operating Systems including Windows limit the maximum number of partitions to 128.

The *GPT* specification requires the first sector of the disk (sector 0) to contain a protective Master Boot Record. On *UEFI* systems this is not actually used - it appears to have been implemented for legacy support and to prevent *MBR* based utilities from overwriting *GPT* disks - without the protective *MBR* the disk may appear not to be initialised, or not to be partitioned.

Because of the use of a protective *MBR* on *GPT* disks, it's possible to boot some operating systems from a *GPT* disk on a *BIOS* system. In order to do so the Protective *MBR* must be edited or a third party boot loader can be installed to it. If a third party boot loader is used then it must be *GPT* aware - e.g. Grub 2.

Windows Limitations

Windows limits the maximum number of partition entries on *GPT* partitioned disks to 128.

Due to current file system limitations the maximum partition size is limited to 256 TB.

32-bit Windows Vista and Windows 7 are not *UEFI* aware and cannot be booted on *UEFI* systems (in *UEFI* Mode).

32-bit versions of Windows 8/8.1 support *UEFI*, however they cannot be booted on a 64-bit system in *UEFI* mode as the Windows version must match the processor architecture. A 32-bit Windows operating system can only be booted on a system with a 32-bit processor when in *UEFI* mode and a 64-bit Windows operating system can only be booted on a system with a 64-bit processor. Note that 32-bit *UEFI* systems are something of a rarity.

Further Reading

- *Windows and GPT FAQ*
- *GUID Partition Table* - *GPT* wiki page
- *Unified Extensible Firmware Interface* - *UEFI* wiki page
- *Booting from GPT* - looks interesting and lists some hacks for booting Windows from a *GPT* disk on a *BIOS* based system
- *Master Boot Record* - *MBR* wiki
- *An Examination of The Microsoft® Windows™ 7 and 8 GPT 'Protective' MBR and EFI Partitions*
- *Questions about USB Booting on UEFI systems* - reboot.pro forum thread
- *Questions about USB Booting on UEFI systems* - post containing a number of useful links

MultiBoot WinPE

It's possible to create a boot menu to enable more than one version of *WinPE* to be booted from the same device by using the command-line bcdedit tool - which is available in all version of Windows since the release of Windows Vista. *BCDEdit* usage is covered *here* for those interested.

WinPE 2.x/3.x/4.0/5.x/10.x all use the Boot Configuration Database (*BCD*) for boot data - this replaced the *boot.ini* file used in previous Windows NT versions (including Windows 2000/XP/2003). Unlike *boot.ini*, which used plain text entries, the *BCD* store is a registry hive - when opened with a text editor the contents are unreadable. Whilst there are some third party GUI tools capable of editing *BCD* stores, bcdedit.exe is easy to script - the batch file examples included in this section should make the process easier.

It's possible to create a *WinPE* multiboot USB thumbdrive or CD/DVD using an existing *WinFE* build. The following example setups will hopefully give you some idea of the flexibility of this approach -

- A RAM Boot *WinPE* 3.1 + a Flat Boot *WinPE* 3.1 for use on low RAM systems.
- A RAM Boot *WinPE* 3.1 + a RAM Boot *WinFE* 4.0 for Forensic Acquisitions.
- *WinPE* 2.1/3.0/3.1/4.0/5.0/5.1 - all RAM Boot + *WinPE* 5.1 Flat Boot.

Note - it's not possible to multiboot more than one flat boot *WinPE* unless installing each version to a separate partition.

The following series of batch scripts can be used to create a store and add individual boot entries.

BIOS Entries

In the examples below we will create a boot menu for *x86.wim* (RAM boot), *x64.wim* (RAM boot) and a Flat Boot *WinPE* for use on *BIOS* firmware (note the paths to *winload.exe*. This will hopefully give you an idea of the steps involved so that you can adapt them for your own setup (changing the filenames as appropriate).

After creating the *BIOS BCD* store it should be copied to the \boot folder.

The first step is to create a new *BCD* store –

```
@echo off
setlocal
:: Do not use spaces in paths and do
:: NOT wrap in quotes

set BCDEDIT=%SYSTEMROOT%\system32\bcdedit.exe
set BCDSTORE="%~dp0BCD"
::____________________________________
%BCDEDIT% /createstore %BCDSTORE%
echo.
endlocal
pause
```

Now add an entry for bootmgr –

```
@echo off
setlocal
:: Do not use spaces in paths and do
:: NOT wrap in quotes

set BCDEDIT=%SYSTEMROOT%\system32\bcdedit.exe
set BCDSTORE="%~dp0BCD"
::____________________________________
%BCDEDIT% /store %BCDSTORE% /create {bootmgr}
```

```
%BCDEDIT% /store %BCDSTORE% /set {bootmgr} description "Boot
Manager"
%BCDEDIT% /store %BCDSTORE% /set {bootmgr} device boot
%BCDEDIT% /store %BCDSTORE% /set {bootmgr} timeout 20
echo.
endlocal
pause
```

Add an entry for x86.wim –

```
@echo off
setlocal
:: Do not use spaces in paths and do
:: NOT wrap in quotes

set BCDEDIT=%SYSTEMROOT%\system32\bcdedit.exe
set BCDSTORE="%~dp0BCD"
::___________________________________
ECHO Creating ramdisksdidevice entry...
for /f "tokens=2 delims={}" %%g in ('%BCDEDIT% /store
%BCDSTORE% /create /device') do set ramdisk={%%g}
%BCDEDIT% /store %BCDSTORE% /set %ramdisk% ramdisksdidevice
boot
%BCDEDIT% /store %BCDSTORE% /set %ramdisk% ramdisksdipath
\boot\boot.sdi

Echo Adding RAM Boot WinPE entry...
```

Add an entry for x64.wim –

```
@echo off
setlocal
:: Do not use spaces in paths and do
:: NOT wrap in quotes

set BCDEDIT=%SYSTEMROOT%\system32\bcdedit.exe
set BCDSTORE="%~dp0BCD"
::___________________________________
ECHO Creating ramdisksdidevice entry...
for /f "tokens=2 delims={}" %%g in ('%BCDEDIT% /store
%BCDSTORE% /create /device') do set ramdisk={%%g}
%BCDEDIT% /store %BCDSTORE% /set %ramdisk% ramdisksdidevice
boot
%BCDEDIT% /store %BCDSTORE% /set %ramdisk% ramdisksdipath
\boot\boot.sdi

Echo Adding RAM Boot WinPE entry...
```

```
for /f "tokens=2 delims={}" %%g in ('%BCDEDIT% /store
%BCDSTORE% /create /application osloader') do set GUID={%%g}
%BCDEDIT% /store %BCDSTORE% /set %GUID% systemroot \Windows
%BCDEDIT% /store %BCDSTORE% /set %GUID% detecthal Yes
%BCDEDIT% /store %BCDSTORE% /set %GUID% winpe Yes
%BCDEDIT% /store %BCDSTORE% /set %GUID% osdevice
ramdisk=[boot]\sources\x64.wim,%ramdisk%
%BCDEDIT% /store %BCDSTORE% /set %GUID% device
ramdisk=[boot]\sources\x64.wim,%ramdisk%
%BCDEDIT% /store %BCDSTORE% /set %GUID% path
\windows\system32\winload.exe
%BCDEDIT% /store %BCDSTORE% /set %GUID% description "64-bit
Windows PE RAMBoot (BIOS)"
%BCDEDIT% /store %BCDSTORE% /displayorder %guid% /addlast
echo.
endlocal
pause
```

Add an entry for a Flat Boot WinPE –

```
@echo off
setlocal
:: Do not use spaces in paths and do
:: NOT wrap in quotes

set BCDEDIT=%SYSTEMROOT%\system32\bcdedit.exe
set BCDSTORE="%~dp0BCD"
::___________________________________
Echo Adding FlatBoot WinPE entry...
for /f "tokens=2 delims={}" %%g in ('%BCDEDIT% /store
%BCDSTORE% /create /application osloader') do set guid={%%g}
%BCDEDIT% /store %BCDSTORE% /set %guid% path
\Windows\system32\winload.exe
%BCDEDIT% /store %BCDSTORE% /set %guid% device boot
%BCDEDIT% /store %BCDSTORE% /set %guid% osdevice boot
%BCDEDIT% /store %BCDSTORE% /set %guid% systemroot \Windows
%BCDEDIT% /store %BCDSTORE% /set %guid% description "Windows
PE FLATBoot (BIOS)"
%BCDEDIT% /store %BCDSTORE% /set %guid% winpe yes
%BCDEDIT% /store %BCDSTORE% /set %guid% detecthal yes
%BCDEDIT% /store %BCDSTORE% /displayorder %guid% /addlast
echo.
endlocal
pause
```

Now putting this all together in one script (the text below has become wrapped - see here for an easier to read version) –

```
@echo off
setlocal
:: Do not use spaces in paths and do
:: NOT wrap in quotes

set BCDEDIT=%SYSTEMROOT%\system32\bcdedit.exe
set BCDSTORE="%~dp0BCD"
::____________________________________
Echo Creating BCD Store...
%BCDEDIT% /createstore %BCDSTORE%
Echo Adding {bootmgr} entry...
%BCDEDIT% /store %BCDSTORE% /create {bootmgr}
%BCDEDIT% /store %BCDSTORE% /set {bootmgr} description "Boot
Manager"
%BCDEDIT% /store %BCDSTORE% /set {bootmgr} device boot
%BCDEDIT% /store %BCDSTORE% /set {bootmgr} timeout 20
Echo Creating ramdisksdidevice entry...
for /f "tokens=2 delims={}" %%g in ('%BCDEDIT% /store
%BCDSTORE% /create /device') do set ramdisk={%%g}
%BCDEDIT% /store %BCDSTORE% /set %ramdisk% ramdisksdidevice
boot
%BCDEDIT% /store %BCDSTORE% /set %ramdisk% ramdisksdipath
\boot\boot.sdi
Echo Adding RAM Boot WinPE entry...
for /f "tokens=2 delims={}" %%g in ('%BCDEDIT% /store
%BCDSTORE% /create /application osloader') do set GUID={%%g}
%BCDEDIT% /store %BCDSTORE% /set %GUID% systemroot \Windows
%BCDEDIT% /store %BCDSTORE% /set %GUID% detecthal Yes
%BCDEDIT% /store %BCDSTORE% /set %GUID% winpe Yes
%BCDEDIT% /store %BCDSTORE% /set %GUID% osdevice
ramdisk=[boot]\sources\x86.wim,%ramdisk%
%BCDEDIT% /store %BCDSTORE% /set %GUID% device
ramdisk=[boot]\sources\x86.wim,%ramdisk%
%BCDEDIT% /store %BCDSTORE% /set %GUID% path
\windows\system32\winload.exe
%BCDEDIT% /store %BCDSTORE% /set %GUID% description "32-bit
Windows PE RAMBoot (BIOS)"
%BCDEDIT% /store %BCDSTORE% /displayorder %guid% /addlast
Echo Creating ramdisksdidevice entry...
for /f "tokens=2 delims={}" %%g in ('%BCDEDIT% /store
%BCDSTORE% /create /device') do set ramdisk={%%g}
%BCDEDIT% /store %BCDSTORE% /set %ramdisk% ramdisksdidevice
boot
%BCDEDIT% /store %BCDSTORE% /set %ramdisk% ramdisksdipath
\boot\boot.sdi
Echo Adding RAM Boot WinPE entry...
```

```
for /f "tokens=2 delims={}" %%g in ('%BCDEDIT% /store
%BCDSTORE% /create /application osloader') do set GUID={%%g}
%BCDEDIT% /store %BCDSTORE% /set %GUID% systemroot \Windows
%BCDEDIT% /store %BCDSTORE% /set %GUID% detecthal Yes
%BCDEDIT% /store %BCDSTORE% /set %GUID% winpe Yes
%BCDEDIT% /store %BCDSTORE% /set %GUID% osdevice
ramdisk=[boot]\sources\x64.wim,%ramdisk%
%BCDEDIT% /store %BCDSTORE% /set %GUID% device
ramdisk=[boot]\sources\x64.wim,%ramdisk%
%BCDEDIT% /store %BCDSTORE% /set %GUID% path
\windows\system32\winload.exe
%BCDEDIT% /store %BCDSTORE% /set %GUID% description "64-bit
Windows PE RAMBoot (BIOS)"
%BCDEDIT% /store %BCDSTORE% /displayorder %guid% /addlast
Echo Adding FlatBoot WinPE entry...
for /f "tokens=2 delims={}" %%g in ('%BCDEDIT% /store
%BCDSTORE% /create /application osloader') do set guid={%%g}
%BCDEDIT% /store %BCDSTORE% /set %guid% path
\Windows\system32\winload.exe
%BCDEDIT% /store %BCDSTORE% /set %guid% device boot
%BCDEDIT% /store %BCDSTORE% /set %guid% osdevice boot
%BCDEDIT% /store %BCDSTORE% /set %guid% systemroot \Windows
%BCDEDIT% /store %BCDSTORE% /set %guid% description "Windows
PE FLATBoot (BIOS)"
%BCDEDIT% /store %BCDSTORE% /set %guid% winpe yes
%BCDEDIT% /store %BCDSTORE% /set %guid% detecthal yes
%BCDEDIT% /store %BCDSTORE% /displayorder %guid% /addlast
echo.
endlocal
pause
```

UEFI Entries

In the examples below we will create a boot menu for *x86.wim* (RAM boot), *x64.wim* (RAM boot) and a Flat Boot *WinPE* for use on *UEFI* firmware - the entries are almost identical to those used on *BIOS* firmware with the only difference being the path to *winload.exe* being changed to *winload.efi*.

After creating the *UEFI BCD* store it should be copied to the \EFI\Microsoft\boot directory.

The first step is to create a new BCD store –

```
@echo off
setlocal
:: Do not use spaces in paths and do
:: NOT wrap in quotes

set BCDEDIT=%SYSTEMROOT%\system32\bcdedit.exe
set BCDSTORE="%~dp0BCD"
::_____________________________________________________
```

```
%BCDEDIT% /createstore %BCDSTORE%
echo.
endlocal
pause
```

Now add an entry for bootmgr –

```
@echo off
setlocal
:: Do not use spaces in paths and do
:: NOT wrap in quotes

set BCDEDIT=%SYSTEMROOT%\system32\bcdedit.exe
set BCDSTORE="%~dp0BCD"
::____________________________________
%BCDEDIT% /store %BCDSTORE% /create {bootmgr}
%BCDEDIT% /store %BCDSTORE% /set {bootmgr} description "Boot
Manager"
%BCDEDIT% /store %BCDSTORE% /set {bootmgr} device boot
%BCDEDIT% /store %BCDSTORE% /set {bootmgr} timeout 20
echo.
endlocal
pause
```

Add an entry for *x86.wim* –

```
@echo off
setlocal
:: Do not use spaces in paths and do
:: NOT wrap in quotes

set BCDEDIT=%SYSTEMROOT%\system32\bcdedit.exe
set BCDSTORE="%~dp0BCD"
::____________________________________
ECHO Creating ramdisksdidevice entry...
for /f "tokens=2 delims={}" %%g in ('%BCDEDIT% /store
%BCDSTORE% /create /device') do set ramdisk={%%g}
%BCDEDIT% /store %BCDSTORE% /set %ramdisk% ramdisksdidevice
boot
%BCDEDIT% /store %BCDSTORE% /set %ramdisk% ramdisksdipath
\boot\boot.sdi

Echo Adding RAM Boot WinPE entry...
for /f "tokens=2 delims={}" %%g in ('%BCDEDIT% /store
%BCDSTORE% /create /application osloader') do set GUID={%%g}
%BCDEDIT% /store %BCDSTORE% /set %GUID% systemroot \Windows
```

```
%BCDEDIT% /store %BCDSTORE% /set %GUID% detecthal Yes
%BCDEDIT% /store %BCDSTORE% /set %GUID% winpe Yes
%BCDEDIT% /store %BCDSTORE% /set %GUID% osdevice
ramdisk=[boot]\sources\x86.wim,%ramdisk%
%BCDEDIT% /store %BCDSTORE% /set %GUID% device
ramdisk=[boot]\sources\x86.wim,%ramdisk%
%BCDEDIT% /store %BCDSTORE% /set %GUID% path
\windows\system32\winload.efi
%BCDEDIT% /store %BCDSTORE% /set %GUID% description "32-bit
Windows PE RAMBoot (UEFI)"
%BCDEDIT% /store %BCDSTORE% /displayorder %guid% /addlast
echo.
endlocal
pause
```

Add an entry for x64.wim –

```
@echo off
setlocal
:: Do not use spaces in paths and do
:: NOT wrap in quotes

set BCDEDIT=%SYSTEMROOT%\system32\bcdedit.exe
set BCDSTORE="%~dp0BCD"
::____________________________________
ECHO Creating ramdisksdidevice entry...
for /f "tokens=2 delims={}" %%g in ('%BCDEDIT% /store
%BCDSTORE% /create /device') do set ramdisk={%%g}
%BCDEDIT% /store %BCDSTORE% /set %ramdisk% ramdisksdidevice
boot
%BCDEDIT% /store %BCDSTORE% /set %ramdisk% ramdisksdipath
\boot\boot.sdi

Echo Adding RAM Boot WinPE entry...
for /f "tokens=2 delims={}" %%g in ('%BCDEDIT% /store
%BCDSTORE% /create /application osloader') do set GUID={%%g}
%BCDEDIT% /store %BCDSTORE% /set %GUID% systemroot \Windows
%BCDEDIT% /store %BCDSTORE% /set %GUID% detecthal Yes
%BCDEDIT% /store %BCDSTORE% /set %GUID% winpe Yes
%BCDEDIT% /store %BCDSTORE% /set %GUID% osdevice
ramdisk=[boot]\sources\x64.wim,%ramdisk%
%BCDEDIT% /store %BCDSTORE% /set %GUID% device
ramdisk=[boot]\sources\x64.wim,%ramdisk%
%BCDEDIT% /store %BCDSTORE% /set %GUID% path
\windows\system32\winload.efi
%BCDEDIT% /store %BCDSTORE% /set %GUID% description "64-bit
Windows PE RAMBoot (UEFI)"
%BCDEDIT% /store %BCDSTORE% /displayorder %guid% /addlast
echo.
endlocal
```

```
pause
```

Add an entry for a Flat Boot WinPE –

```
@echo off
setlocal
:: Do not use spaces in paths and do
:: NOT wrap in quotes

set BCDEDIT=%SYSTEMROOT%\system32\bcdedit.exe
set BCDSTORE="%~dp0BCD"
::___________________________________
Echo Adding FlatBoot WinPE entry...
for /f "tokens=2 delims={}" %%g in ('%BCDEDIT% /store
%BCDSTORE% /create /application osloader') do set guid={%%g}
%BCDEDIT% /store %BCDSTORE% /set %guid% path
\Windows\system32\winload.efi
%BCDEDIT% /store %BCDSTORE% /set %guid% device boot
%BCDEDIT% /store %BCDSTORE% /set %guid% osdevice boot
%BCDEDIT% /store %BCDSTORE% /set %guid% systemroot \Windows
%BCDEDIT% /store %BCDSTORE% /set %guid% description "Windows
PE FLATBoot (UEFI)"
%BCDEDIT% /store %BCDSTORE% /set %guid% winpe yes
%BCDEDIT% /store %BCDSTORE% /set %guid% detecthal yes
%BCDEDIT% /store %BCDSTORE% /displayorder %guid% /addlast
echo.
endlocal
pause
```

Now putting this all together in one script (the text below has become wrapped - see here for an easier to read version) –

```
@echo off
setlocal
:: Do not use spaces in paths and do
:: NOT wrap in quotes

set BCDEDIT=%SYSTEMROOT%\system32\bcdedit.exe
set BCDSTORE="%~dp0BCD"
::___________________________________
Echo Creating BCD Store...
%BCDEDIT% /createstore %BCDSTORE%
Echo Adding {bootmgr} entry...
%BCDEDIT% /store %BCDSTORE% /create {bootmgr}
%BCDEDIT% /store %BCDSTORE% /set {bootmgr} description "Boot
Manager"
%BCDEDIT% /store %BCDSTORE% /set {bootmgr} device boot
%BCDEDIT% /store %BCDSTORE% /set {bootmgr} timeout 20
```

```
Echo Creating ramdisksdidevice entry...
for /f "tokens=2 delims={}" %%g in ('%BCDEDIT% /store
%BCDSTORE% /create /device') do set ramdisk={%%g}
%BCDEDIT% /store %BCDSTORE% /set %ramdisk% ramdisksdidevice
boot
%BCDEDIT% /store %BCDSTORE% /set %ramdisk% ramdisksdipath
\boot\boot.sdi
Echo Adding RAM Boot WinPE entry...
for /f "tokens=2 delims={}" %%g in ('%BCDEDIT% /store
%BCDSTORE% /create /application osloader') do set GUID={%%g}
%BCDEDIT% /store %BCDSTORE% /set %GUID% systemroot \Windows
%BCDEDIT% /store %BCDSTORE% /set %GUID% detecthal Yes
%BCDEDIT% /store %BCDSTORE% /set %GUID% winpe Yes
%BCDEDIT% /store %BCDSTORE% /set %GUID% osdevice
ramdisk=[boot]\sources\x86.wim,%ramdisk%
%BCDEDIT% /store %BCDSTORE% /set %GUID% device
ramdisk=[boot]\sources\x86.wim,%ramdisk%
%BCDEDIT% /store %BCDSTORE% /set %GUID% path
\windows\system32\winload.efi
%BCDEDIT% /store %BCDSTORE% /set %GUID% description "32-bit
Windows PE RAMBoot (UEFI)"
%BCDEDIT% /store %BCDSTORE% /displayorder %guid% /addlast
Echo Creating ramdisksdidevice entry...
for /f "tokens=2 delims={}" %%g in ('%BCDEDIT% /store
%BCDSTORE% /create /device') do set ramdisk={%%g}
%BCDEDIT% /store %BCDSTORE% /set %ramdisk% ramdisksdidevice
boot
%BCDEDIT% /store %BCDSTORE% /set %ramdisk% ramdisksdipath
\boot\boot.sdi
Echo Adding RAM Boot WinPE entry...
for /f "tokens=2 delims={}" %%g in ('%BCDEDIT% /store
%BCDSTORE% /create /application osloader') do set GUID={%%g}
%BCDEDIT% /store %BCDSTORE% /set %GUID% systemroot \Windows
%BCDEDIT% /store %BCDSTORE% /set %GUID% detecthal Yes
%BCDEDIT% /store %BCDSTORE% /set %GUID% winpe Yes
%BCDEDIT% /store %BCDSTORE% /set %GUID% osdevice
ramdisk=[boot]\sources\x64.wim,%ramdisk%
%BCDEDIT% /store %BCDSTORE% /set %GUID% device
ramdisk=[boot]\sources\x64.wim,%ramdisk%
%BCDEDIT% /store %BCDSTORE% /set %GUID% path
\windows\system32\winload.efi
%BCDEDIT% /store %BCDSTORE% /set %GUID% description "64-bit
Windows PE RAMBoot (UEFI)"
%BCDEDIT% /store %BCDSTORE% /displayorder %guid% /addlast
Echo Adding FlatBoot WinPE entry...
for /f "tokens=2 delims={}" %%g in ('%BCDEDIT% /store
%BCDSTORE% /create /application osloader') do set guid={%%g}
%BCDEDIT% /store %BCDSTORE% /set %guid% path
\Windows\system32\winload.efi
%BCDEDIT% /store %BCDSTORE% /set %guid% device boot
```

```
%BCDEDIT% /store %BCDSTORE% /set %guid% osdevice boot
%BCDEDIT% /store %BCDSTORE% /set %guid% systemroot \Windows
%BCDEDIT% /store %BCDSTORE% /set %guid% description "Windows
PE FLATBoot (UEFI)"
%BCDEDIT% /store %BCDSTORE% /set %guid% winpe yes
%BCDEDIT% /store %BCDSTORE% /set %guid% detecthal yes
%BCDEDIT% /store %BCDSTORE% /displayorder %guid% /addlast
echo.
endlocal
pause
```

Quick Start Guide

Please note that the screenshots below may differ from the current *WinFE* release.

Whilst *Mini-WinFE* has been designed to be as simply as possible, it has not been possible to create a "one-button push" method. It should however be very simple to create a *WinPE* in a matter of minutes. To do so you will need -

- **Administrator privileges** - registry hives will need to be mounted and edited during the build process, and other processes also require administrator privileges.
- .Net Framework 4.7.2 and Windows 7 or newer (required to run PEBakery).
- Free disk space - 1GB should be more than adequate as Windows source files are not cached during the build process.
- Windows Installation Media - either a CD/DVD, a mounted disk image or the files copied to an accessible folder.

Instructions -

1. Download the *WinFE* .zip package and extract the contents to a local folder - preferably a folder without spaces in the path. In the examples below the project files have been extracted to C:\WinFE\ with the Projects directory in the C:\WinFE\Projects path.
2. Run *PEBakeryLauncher.exe* (C:\WinFE\PEBakeryLauncher.exe) to start *PEBakery*.
3. Set the path to your source files by either manually entering the path (1) or click on the *Folder* button (2) to set the path to your Windows Installation Media source files. Please note that if manually entering a path it must end in a backslash (\). E.g. D:\source_files\

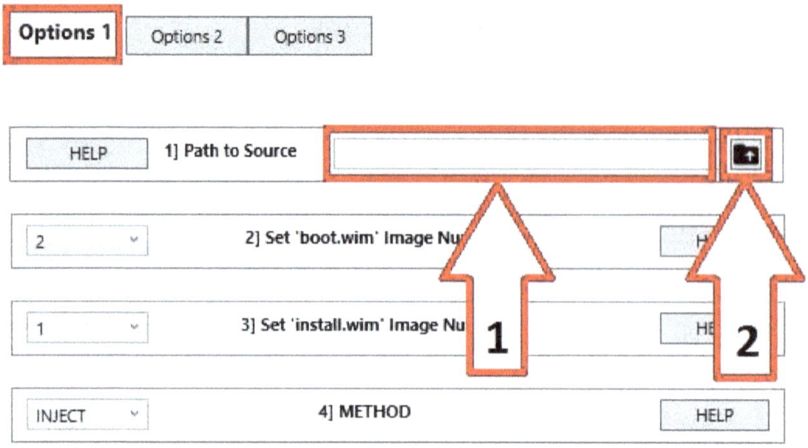

A mounted Windows RTM .iso file is recommended as source. Alternatively extract the contents of a Windows .iso to a local directory. Set the path in this option to the root folder that contains the following files/directories -

- *\sources\boot.wim*
- *\sources\install.wim*
- *\bootmgr*
- *\boot*
- *\EFI*

4. Now expand the folder tree on the left and view and select individual project script options as required (refer to the *Project Scripts* section for details about all included project scripts).
5. I recommend selecting the MediaCreation\Create ISO project script - this can then be used to create a bootable CD/DVD or USB.
6. To start the build process, click on the *Build* button in the top row of buttons -

7. A progress bar will be displayed for individual project scripts as they are processed -

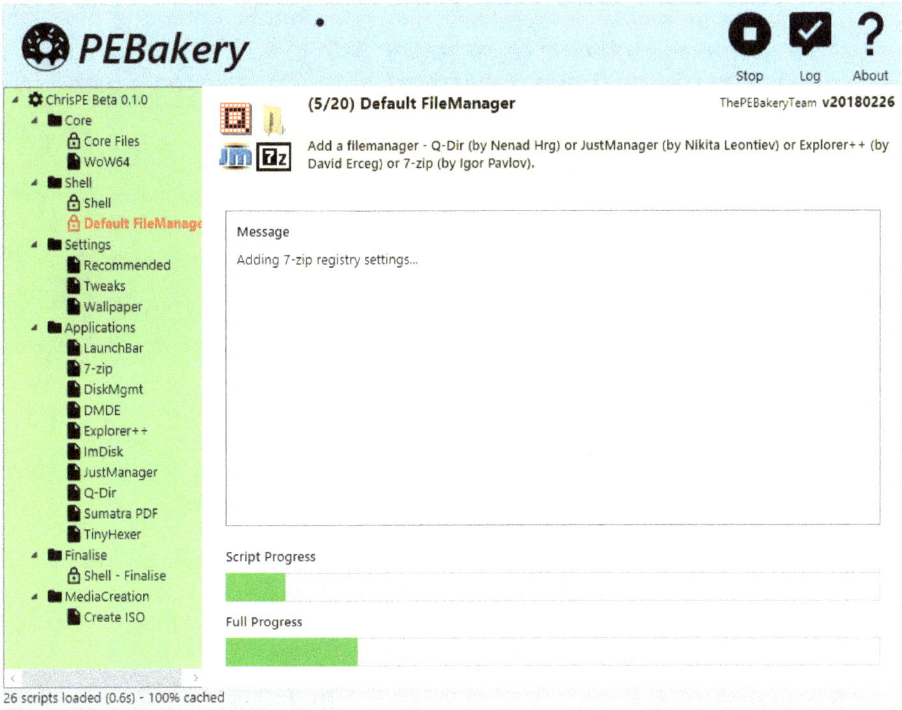

That's it. Provided the MediaCreation\Create ISO script was selected you should now have a bootable ISO image file (*\WinFE.Files\WinPE.iso* - the path is relative to *PEBakeryLauncher.exe*) that can be burnt to CD/DVD. Alternatively see *here* for an easy method to create a bootable USB device.

Quick Start Guide

Please note that the screenshots below may differ from the current *WinFE* release.

Whilst *Mini-WinFE* has been designed to be as simply as possible, it has not been possible to create a "one-button push" method. It should however be very simple to create a *WinPE* in a matter of minutes. To do so you will need -

- **Administrator privileges** - registry hives will need to be mounted and edited during the build process, and other processes also require administrator privileges.
- Free disk space - 1GB should be more than adequate as Windows source files are not cached during the build process.
- Windows Installation Media - either a CD/DVD, a mounted disk image or the files copied to an accessible folder.

Instructions -

1. Download the *WinFE* .zip package and extract the contents to a local folder - preferably a folder without spaces in the path. In the examples below the project files have been extracted to C:\WinFE\ with the Projects directory in the C:\WinFE\Projects path.
2. Run *WinBuilder.exe* (C:\WinFE\WinBuilder.exe) to start *WinBuilder*.

3. Set the path to your source files by either manually entering the path (1) or click on the *Folder* button (2) to set the path to your Windows Installation Media source files. Please note that if manually entering a path it must end in a backslash (\). E.g. D:\source_files\

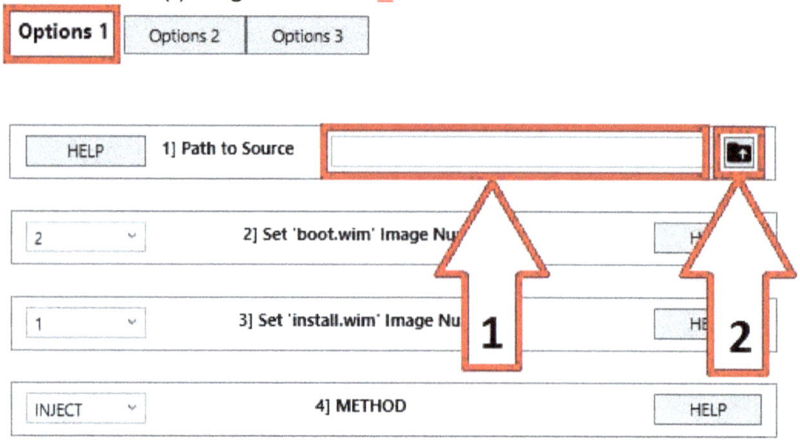

A mounted Windows RTM .iso file is recommended as source. Alternatively extract the contents of a Windows .iso to a local directory. Set the path in this option to the root folder that contains the following files/directories -

- *\sources\boot.wim*
- *\sources\install.wim*
- *\bootmgr*
- *\boot*
- *\EFI*

4. Now expand the folder tree on the left and view and select individual project script options as required (refer to the *Project Scripts* section for details about all included project scripts).
5. I recommend selecting the MediaCreation\Create ISO project script - this can then be used to create a bootable CD/DVD or USB.
6. To start the build process, click on the *Play* button in the top row of buttons -

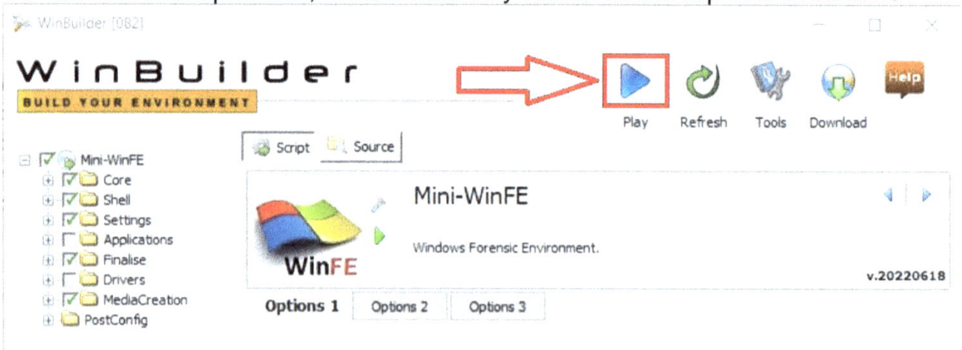

7. A progress bar will be displayed for individual project scripts as they are processed -

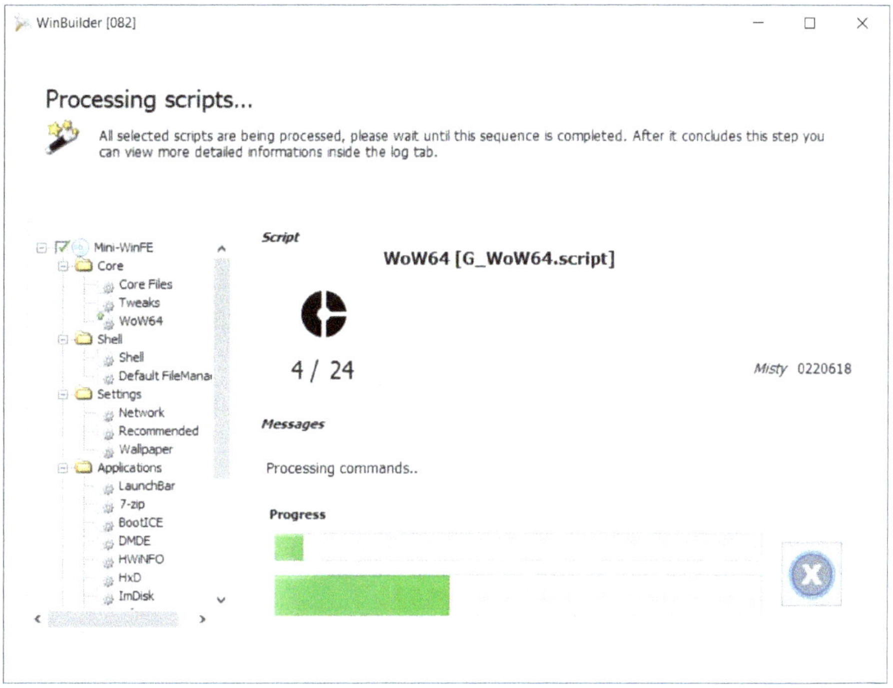

That's it. Provided the MediaCreation\Create ISO script was selected you should now have a bootable ISO image file (*\WinFE.Files\WinPE.iso* - the path is relative to *WinBuilder.exe*) that can be burnt to CD/DVD. Alternatively see *here* for an easy method to create a bootable USB device.

Quick Start - Running Mini-WinFE

This page contains the following sections -

- *DiskMgr/protect Overview*
- *Menu System - BlackBox Lean*
- *Menu System - LaunchBar*
- *Menu System - WinXShell*
- *SAN Policy Overview*
- *Pre build 6.2.9200 (Windows Vista/2008/7)*
- *Post build 6.2.9200 (Windows 8/2012/8.1/10)*
- *WARNING*

DiskMgr/protect Overview

The project can be configured to ensure that when *Mini-WinFE* is booted, either *DiskMgr.exe* or *protect.exe* will be automatically launched before any other programs. Either of these tools can be used to check the current status of any disks attached to the system, and can also be used to change disk attributes in order to ensure that any evidence disks are set as *Read Only* and *Offline* - reducing the risk of evidence contamination.

Screenshot of *DiskMgr.exe* running in *WinFE* 10.0.22000 (the program was launched automatically via *winpeshl.ini* during the boot process) -

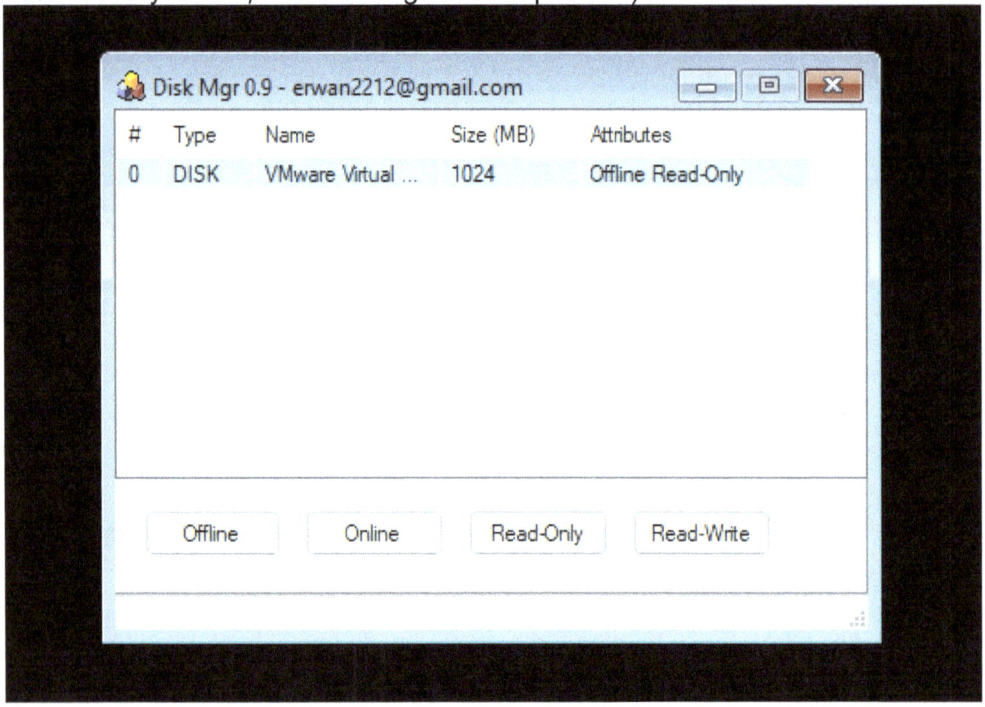

Screenshots of *protect.exe* running in *WinFE* 10.0.22000 (the program was launched automatically via *winpeshl.ini* during the boot process). Press the *OK* button to select the language -

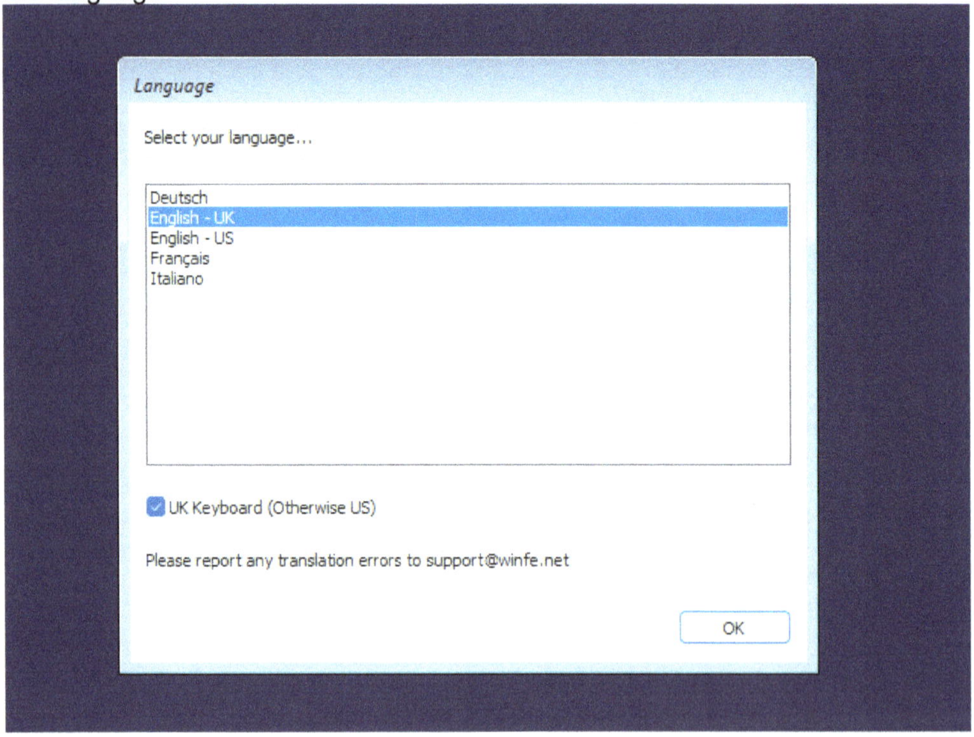

Press the *OK* button on the warning screen to run the program -

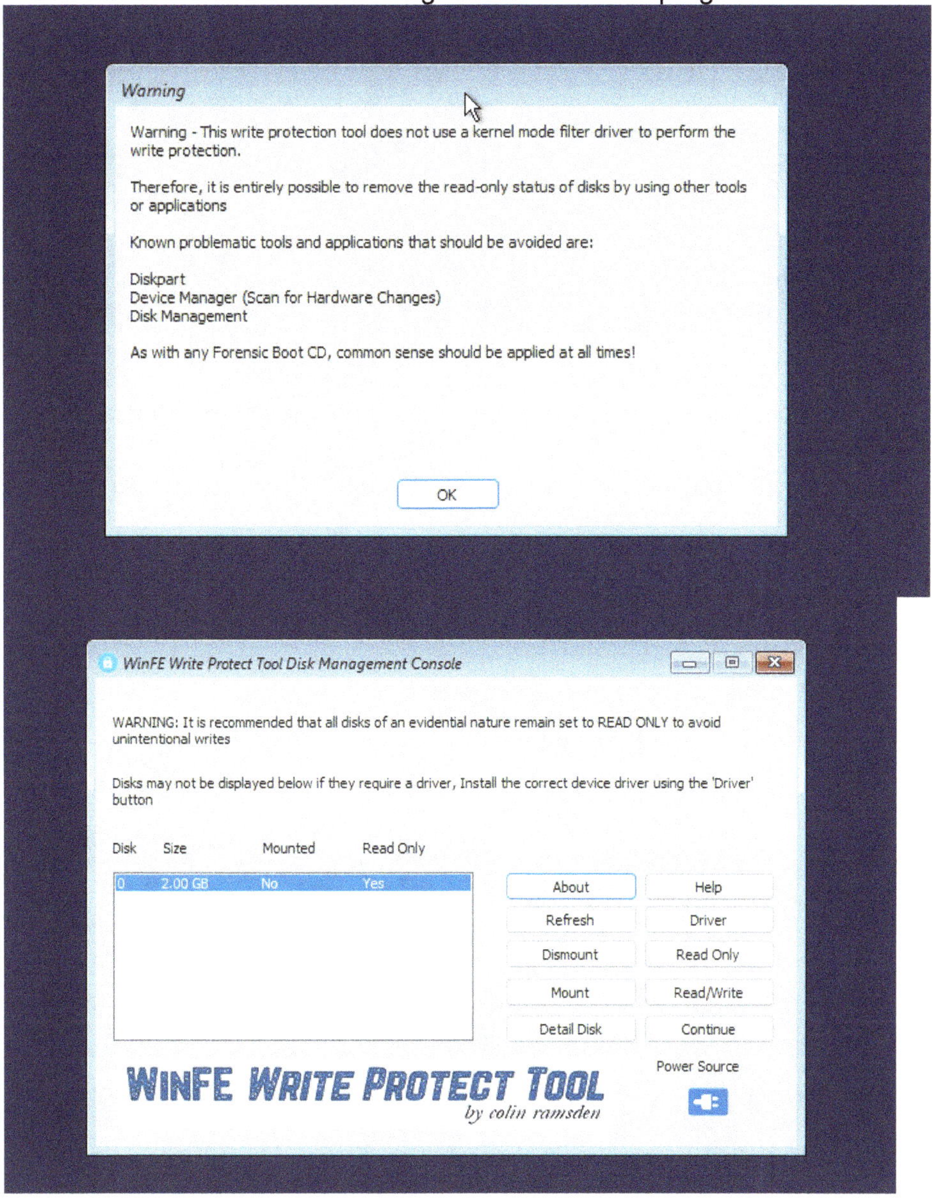

After ensuring that disk attributes are set as required, close down *DiskMgr.exe* / *protect.exe* to use *Mini-WinFE*

More detailed information about *protect.exe* usage and features is available on Colin's WinFE site - https://www.winfe.net/

Menu System - BlackBox Lean

To select a menu option, right-click anywhere on the desktop or alternatively press the *Windows* key. This will display a menu similar to the following -

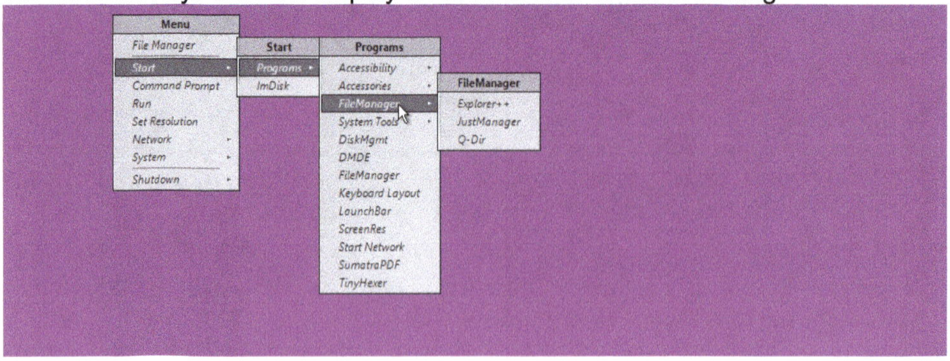

The majority of the programs and utilities supported in *Mini-WinFE* are accessible via the *Start* > *Programs* menu

The *BlackBox Lean* shell also supports keyboard shortcuts. *Mini-WinFE* supports the following shortcuts at the time of writing -

- [*Windows*] + [*E*] - launch file manager
- [*Windows*] + [*R*] - Run dialog

Menu System - LaunchBar

Screenshot of *LaunchBar* running in *Mini-WinFE* -

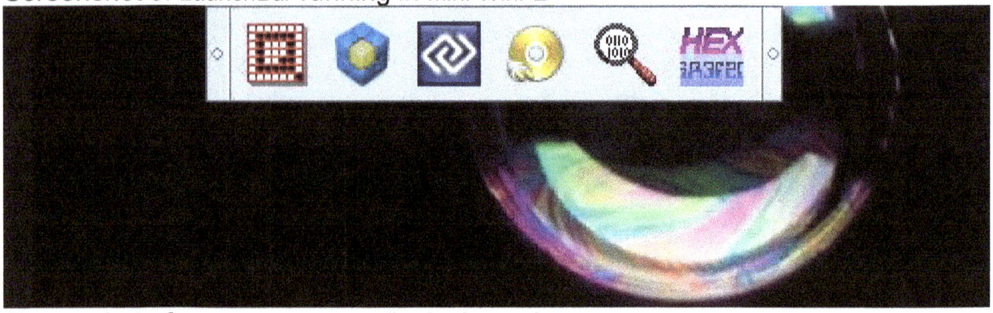

Screenshot of *LaunchBar* menu displaying sub-menus -

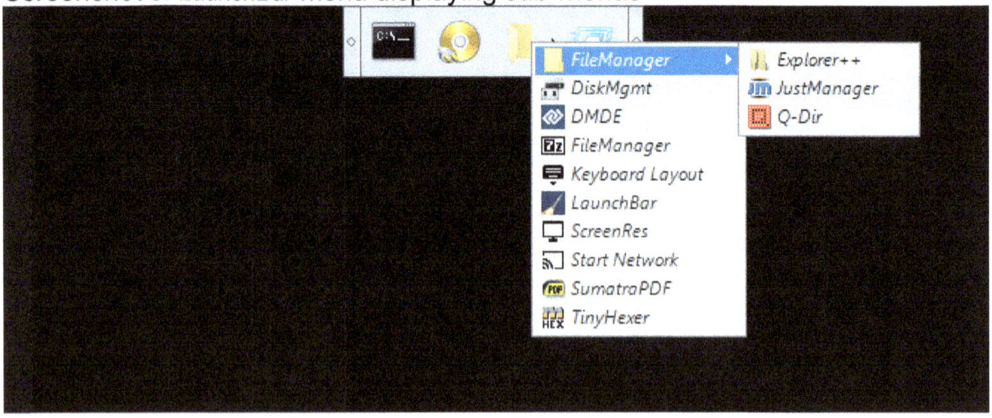

Menu System - WinXShell

Screenshot of *WinXShell* Start Menu -

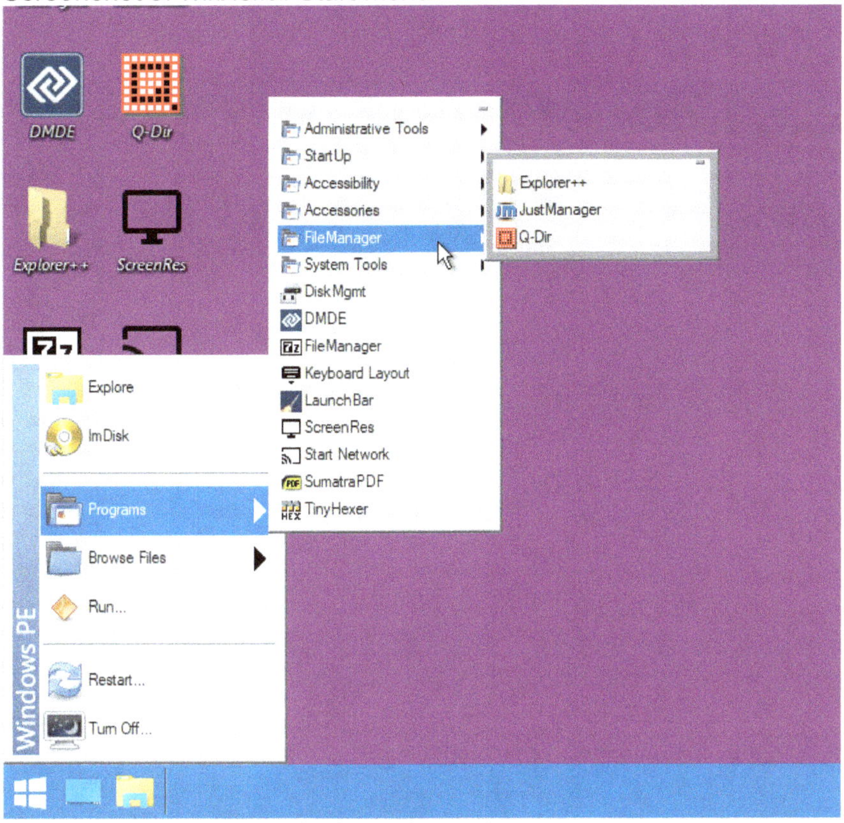

WinXShell also supports desktop shortcuts.

SAN Policy Overview

WinFE registry settings are automatically applied in *Mini-WinFE* - the project does allow the *SAN Policy* settings to be set to either 3 or 4. *SAN Policy* 4 settings were introduced with the release of Windows 8 (*WinFE* 4.0).

- *SAN Policy* **3** - Doesn't mount storage devices.
- *SAN Policy* **4** - Makes internal disks offline. Note. All external disks and the boot disk are online.

Please be aware that there are some reports of internal disks not being write protected if *SAN Policy* 4 settings are used. If using *Mini-WinFE* there is no reason to set the *SAN Policy* as 4 as either the *DiskMgr.exe* or *protect.exe* tools can be used to manually change disk attributes as required - for example setting USB attached storage as *Read-Write* and *Online* so that evidence can be captured/saved.

Pre build 6.2.9200 (Windows Vista/2008/7)

WinFE based on earlier (than build 6.2.9200) versions of Windows do not apply the same level of write protection as more recent versions of Windows. The following screenshot shows *DiskMgr.exe* running in *WinFE* 3.1 (build 6.1.7601 (Windows 7 SP1 source)). The program was launched automatically via *winpeshl.ini* during the boot process -

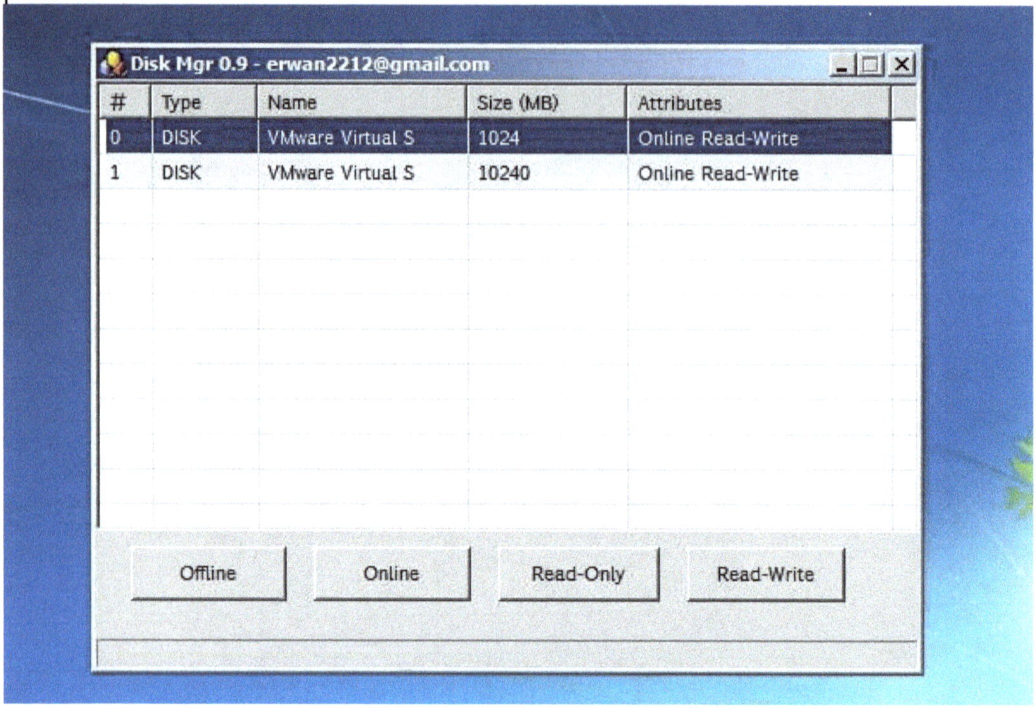

As displayed in the screenshot above, the disk attributes are set as *Online* and *Read-Write*. Whilst it is possible to use *DiskMgr* (or *protect.exe*) to change the attributes of any evidence disks to *Offline* and *Read-Only* at this stage, the write protection will obviously not have been applied earlier in the boot process. In tests this resulted in a disk signature being written at offset 0x1B8 on any disks not already containing a disk signature. In the unlikely event of two disks on the same system containing the same disk signature, one would presumably automatically be changed to avoid a collision.

All Windows NT Operating Systems will automatically write a unique disk signature at offset 0x1B8 - this is a well-documented feature of these Operating Systems. If an evidence disk has at some point been attached to a running Windows NT system then it is likely to already contain a disk signature at offset 0x1B8 - the only exception being if the disk signature has since been overwritten. Provided that an evidence disk is set as *Offline* and *Read-Only* using either *DiskMgr* or *wprotect.exe* before any other actions are performed, write protection will be applied and the only exception *might* be the writing of a disk signature earlier in the boot process.

In summary, the *WinFE* registry settings set volume attributes as *Offline* in builds pre-dating 6.2.9200 and have no effect on disk attributes. Whilst it is possible to manually set disk attributes as *Offline* and *Read-Only* using either *DiskMgr* or *protect.exe*, the registry settings do not apply these settings.

Post build 6.2.9200 (Windows 8/2012/8.1/10)

As displayed in the screenshots in the DiskMgr/protect Overview section of this page, *WinFE* 10.0.22000 applies write protection early in the boot process - before any programs are launched via *winpeshl.ini*. In the tests carried out by the author, all Windows versions since build 6.2.9200 (Windows 8) appear to provide robust write protection. This write protection is applied early enough in the boot process that a disk signature is not written to any disks that do not already have a signature at offset 0x1B8.

WARNING

Significant effort has been taken to ensure that *Mini-WinFE* can be safely used as a software write blocker. Please be aware that it may be possible to bypass write protection with some tools - care should therefore be taken.

Please ensure that you validate your *Mini-WinFE* build and tools.

DiskMgr

DiskMgr has been developed primarily for use in a Windows Forensic Environment (*WinFE*) to provide a user friendly method of changing the following *DISK* attributes -

- *Offline*
- *Online*
- *Read-Only*
- *Read-Write*

DiskMgr is similar in use to *Colin Ramsden's* "*Write Protect*" application (see here). *DiskMgr* is available in native Windows 32-bit and 64-bit versions.

The Microsoft *DiskPart* application has historically been used in *WinPE* to manipulate *DISK* attributes. Unfortunately, if *WinFE* registry settings have been applied, then *DiskPart* may fail to change certain *DISK* attributes, as displayed in the textbox below (output is from *DiskPart* version 6.1.7601) –

```
DISKPART> attribute disk
Current Read-only State : No
Read-only  : No
Boot Disk  : No
Pagefile Disk  : No
Hibernation File Disk  : No
Crashdump Disk  : No
Clustered Disk  : No

DISKPART> attribute disk set readonly

DiskPart failed to set disk attributes.
```

DiskMgr utilises the Microsoft API to set/change *DISK* attributes. The program has a very simple User Interface with an information panel displaying a list of *DISKS* and some basic information (including attributes) -

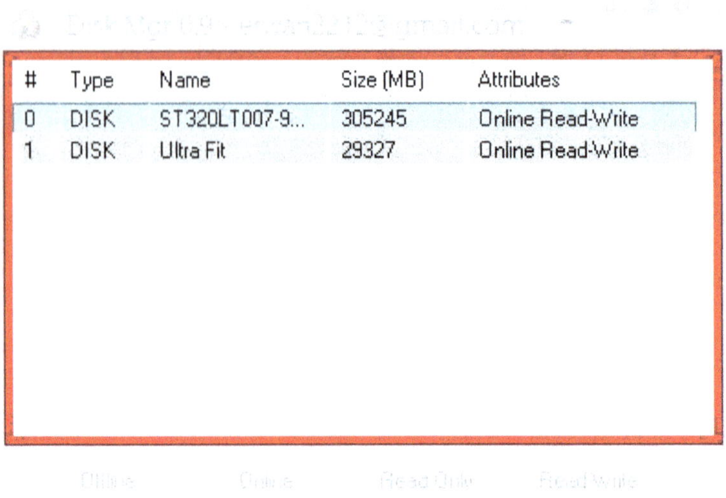

Right-clicking in the information window will display context sensitive options, including *Show Disk/Part Informations* -

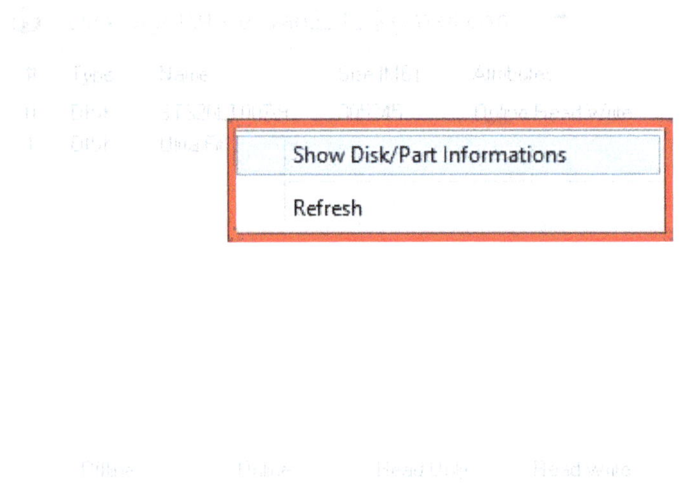

Sample output from the *Show Disk/Part Informations* option -

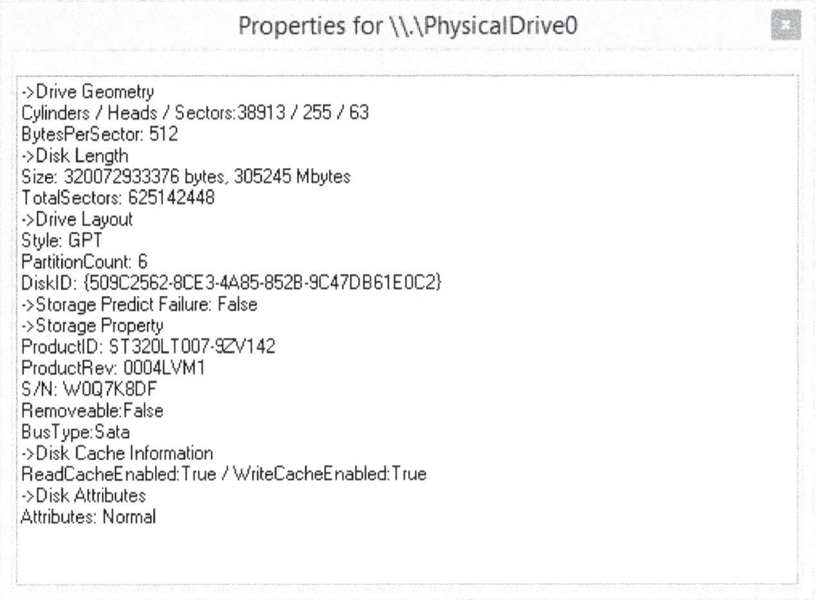

Underneath the information panel is a row of buttons for changing attributes -

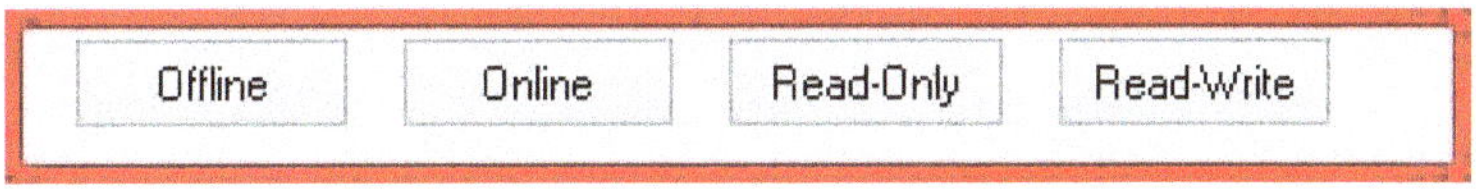

And below is a brief summary of these options -

- *Offline* - change the target *DISK* attribute to *Offline*. This option will dismount any volumes on the target *DISK*.
- *Online* - change the target *DISK* attribute to *Online*. This option will automatically mount any volumes on the target *DISK* - even if the *NoAutoMount* registry setting has been applied.
- *Read-Only* - set the target *DISK* attribute to *Read-Only*, write protecting the disk and any volumes on it. If the disk is *Online* when this setting is applied, then *DiskMgr* will temporarily *Offline* the disk before applying the changes.

- *Read-Write* - set the target *DISK* attribute to *Read-Write*, removing any write protection from the disk and any volumes on it. If the disk is *Online* when this setting is applied, then *DiskMgr* will temporarily *Offline* the disk before applying the changes.

Pressing any of the buttons will display a prompt before committing any changes. Below is a sample output from selecting the *Read-Write* option -

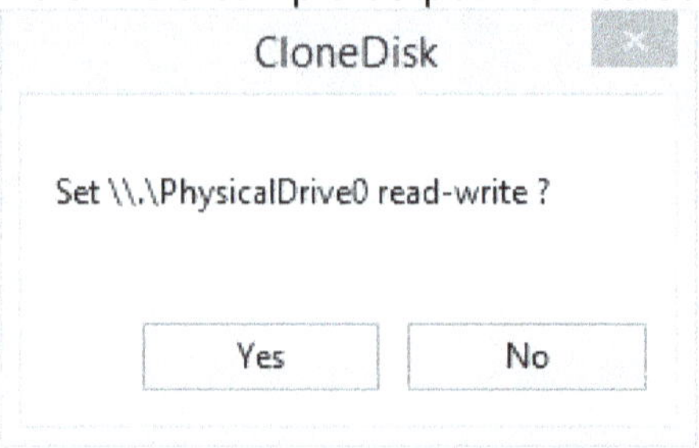

And below is the prompt displayed when selecting the *Online* option -

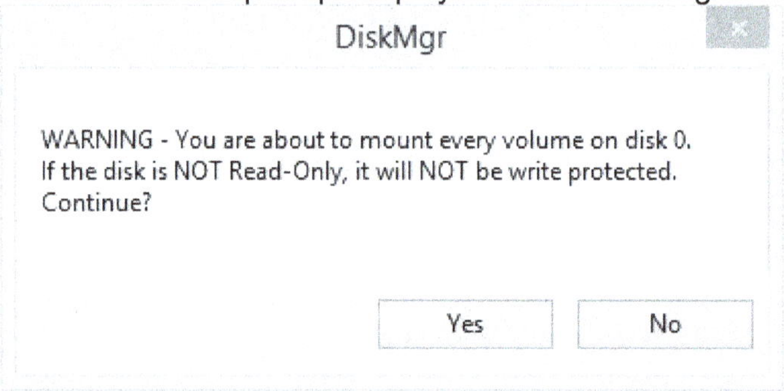

DiskMgr has been developed by *Erwan.L*. *Erwan* has kindly given consent for it to be distributed with *MistyPE*/*Mini-WinFE*. I would like to express my sincere gratitude to *Erwan* for spending his valuable time developing this program - thank you my friend.

WinFE Tests

Abstract

There are reports of Windows Forensic Environment (WinFE) performing disk writes in certain circumstances, with the write action performed during the boot process before disks are write protected or third party tools used to set disks as read-only. The reports of write action are linked to WinFE creating a four byte disk signature in LBA section 0 (the disk Master Boot Record (MBR)) at offset 0x1B8.

This research seeks to identify circumstances in which WinFE will write a disk signature to an internal storage device MBR.

The research will also explore whether internal disks are write protected when WinFE is running.

It expands on the results of a previous experiment completed in 2013, which pre-dates the release of Windows 10 based WinFE (see here).

Methodology

Tests to be completed in virtual systems utilising five disk images, with the common denominator between these disk images being the abscence of a disk signature at offset 0x1B8 to 0x1BB -

- Disk 1 - blank/empty disk image with all bytes set as 00. See *here* for a screenshot of the disk MBR.
- Disk 2 - offset 0x1FE set as 55 AA. All other bytes including the four byte disk signature at offset 0x1B8 to 0x1BB set as 00. This simulates an initialized disk due to the presence of the "magic number" 55 AA in the last two bytes of the MBR. See *here* for a screenshot of the disk MBR.
- Disk 3 - Windows 98SE boot disk used to create one primary partition spanning the disk. MSDOS FDISK does not write a disk signature at offset 0x1B8 to 0x1BB - the four bytes at this offset are set as 00. See *here* for a screenshot of the disk MBR.
- Disk 4 - copy of disk 3 with two bytes at offset 0x1FE to 0x1FF written as 00 00 (overwriting the "magic number" 55 AA in the last two bytes of the MBR). See *here* for a screenshot of the disk MBR.
- Disk 5 - copy of disk 1 with the addition of an entry in the partition table (offset 0x1BE to 0x1CD). All other bytes set as 00. See *here* for a screenshot of the disk MBR.

Tests to be completed on systems with the following firmware -

- UEFI - 64-bit (64-bit WinFE only)
- UEFI - 32-bit (32-bit WinFE only)
- BIOS (32 and 64-bit WinFE)

Four steps to be completed with each disk image and WinFE build, with duplicate tests on systems with BIOS and UEFI firmware.

1. Disk SHA1 checksum to be taken prior to booting WinFE.
2. Boot WinFE and check for the presence of a disk signature and any other changes to LBA sector 0 (using a disk editor).
3. Shutdown WinFE and recheck the SHA1 checksum.
4. Additional check to be completed to test whether the disk is write protected whilst WinFE is running (using a disk editor to attempt to write to LBA sector 0).

Test system setup

VMWare Workstation 16 Player (version 16.2.3 build-19376536). This virtual test environment supports BIOS and UEFI 64-bit and 32-bit firmware. UEFI 32-bit firmware supported with the addition of the following setting in the .vmx configuration file -

- firmware = "efi"

Test systems to be configured with one SATA disk.

WinFE based on boot.wim extracted from Windows installation source files.
WinFE to be configured with SANPolicy 3 (supported across all WinFE versions) and NoAutoMount.

About the Windows Forensic Environment

The Windows Forensic Environment (a.k.a. *WinFE*) is a Windows based boot disk that can be used as a platform for digital forensic analysis and acquisition. Being Windows based it enables users to run a number of Windows programs that they might already be familiar with. It is an alternative <u>or</u> addition to a number of forensically focused Linux distributions.

WinFE is a software write blocker used to prevent writes to storage devices. Usage may include gathering evidence on systems where hardware cannot be removed, triage investigations, or as an alternative to potentially expensive hardware write blockers.

Troy Larson, Senior Forensic Examiner of MicrosoftÂ©, is credited with creating the Windows Forensic Environment. *WinFE* does not appear to be available as a commercial product from Microsoft. It is however relatively easy to create *WinFE* for personal use from freely available tools. *WinFE* is in essence a Windows Preinstallation Environment (*WinPE* - see *here*) with two minor registry edits that are applied to ensure that any hard disks are not automatically mounted during the *WinPE*/*WinFE* boot process - minimising the risk of the contamination of data/evidence. *WinFE* is a lightweight version of Windows that can be used for many tasks - it is a complete, standalone operating system and will work independently of any other operating systems already installed.

WinFE Versions

As WinFE is essentially a Windows Preinstallation Environment (WinPE) with two registry modifications, there are multiple builds/versions of WinFE - all available in both 32-bit and 64-bit processor architectures. The earlier versions of WinPE used the same codebase as Windows XP/2003 - these are usually referred to as *WinPE* 1.*.

Earlier versions of *WinPE* (prior to the introduction of version 2.0) were aimed at enterprise customers and were not available to the general public. As of version 2.0 it was possible for non-enterprise customers to create their own *WinPE* by using the freely available Windows Automated Installation Kit (WAIK). The WAIK has now been replaced with the Windows Assessment and Deployment Kit (ADK).

Windows Operating Systems use a numbering format for identification purposes - these numbers can be used to identify the codebase from which a particular *WinPE* was created. Windows builds use the numbering format â€˜MajorVersion.MinorVersion.Buildâ€™ - e.g. 6.1.7600. Unlike the product names associated with Windows Operating Systems (e.g. Windows 7) these numbers can refer to multiple products - version 6.1.7600 for example refers to both Windows 7 and Windows Server 2008.

WinFE versions include -

WinPE	Major.Minor.Build	Windows Operating System source
2.0	6.0.6000	Windows Vista
2.1	6.0.6001	Windows Vista (SP1) / Server 2008
3.0	6.1.7600	Windows 7 / Server 2008 R2
3.1	6.1.7601	Windows 7 (SP1) / Server 2008 R2 (SP1)
4.0	6.2.9200	Windows 8 / Server 2012
5.0	6.3.9600	Windows 8.1
5.1	6.3.9600	Windows 8.1 Update

Following the release of Windows 10, *WinPE*/*WinFE*versions are identifed by MajorVersion.MinorVersion.Build numbers that generally correspond with the Windows 10 build from which they are compiled. WinPE 10.0.16299 for example corresponds with Windows 10.0.16299 (aka Version 1709 / Fall Creators Update).

There are some exceptions to this rule as the *WinPE* included in Windows 10.0.18362 (May 2019 Update (1903)) and 10.0.18363 (November 2019 Update (1909)) sources are both based on *WinPE* 10.0.18362.

Another example of the same *WinPE* version being included in multiple Windows sources is *WinPE* 10.0.19041. The following Windows 10 sources all include/use *WinPE* 10.0.19041 -

- May 2020 Update (10.0.19041 / 2004)
- October 2020 Update (10.0.19042 / 20H2)
- May 2021 Update (10.0.19043 / 21H1)
- November 2021 Update (10.0.19044 / 21H2)

WinPE 10.* versions include -

WinPE Build	WinPE Version	Windows Operating System source
10.0.10240	1507	-
10.0.10586	1511	November Update
10.0.14393	1607	Anniversary Update
10.0.15063	1703	Creators Update
10.0.16299	1709	Fall Creators Update
10.0.17134	1803	April 2018 Update
10.0.17763	1809	October 2018 Update
10.0.18362	1903	May 2019 Update (Windows 10.0.18362 / 1903)

		November 2019 Update (10.0.18363 / 1909)
10.0.19041	2004	May 2020 Update (10.0.19041 / 2004) October 2020 Update (10.0.19042 / 20H2) May 2021 Update (10.0.19043 / 21H1) November 2021 Update (10.0.19044 / 21H2)

Registry Changes

The registry settings that are used to create WinFE are **NoAutoMount**....

Key	HKLM\System\ControlSet001\Services\MountMgr
Name	NoAutoMount
Type	DWORD
Data	1

...and **SANPolicy**....

Key	HKLM\System\ControlSet001\Services\partmgr\Parameters
Name	SANPolicy
Type	DWORD
Data	3 (or 4 in WinFE versions 4.0 or newer)

Earlier version of WinFE (versions 2.x/3.x) utilise SanPolicy 3. SANPolicy 4 can also be configured in WinFE versions 4.0 and newer (from here) -

- SAN policy **3** - Doesn't mount storage devices.
- SAN policy **4** - New for Windows 8. Makes internal disks offline. Note. All external disks and the boot disk are online.

It is possible to set the SANPolicy as 3 (or 4 in WinFE 4.0/5.x/10.x) without setting NoAutoMount. Some results with different combinations of these two registry keys are available here. Use caution as any Online disks will be allocated a drive letter if NoAutoMount is not set - potentially resulting in disk writes and evidence contamination. NoAutoMount adds a greater level of security, particularly if WinFE 2.x\3.x is used.

Disk Signatures

WinHex screenshot highlighting the location of a disk signature (offset 0x1B8 to 0x1BB) -

Offset	0	1	2	3	4	5	6	7	8	9	A	B	C	D	E	F
000001A0	00	00	00	00	00	00	00	00	00	00	00	00	00	00	00	00
000001B0	00	00	00	00	00	00	00	00	00	00	00	00	00	00	80	01
000001C0	01	00	0B	FE	7F	04	3F	00	00	00	86	FA	3F	00	00	00
000001D0	00	00	00	00	00	00	00	00	00	00	00	00	00	00	00	00
000001E0	00	00	00	00	00	00	00	00	00	00	00	00	00	00	00	00
000001F0	00	00	00	00	00	00	00	00	00	00	00	00	00	00	55	AA

The most common reports of WinFE writing to a hard disk are linked to a disk signature being written when the disk does not contain a valid disk signature. For more information about WinFE and disk signatures in Windows NT based systems refer to the WinFE Script Updated topic on the *reboot.pro* forum. More specifically post #15 (reboot.pro forum member *Wonko the Sane*) -

> *"...Rest assured that as soon as a Windows NT EITHER: finds the 4 bytes of the disk signature set as 00 00 00 00 OR: finds two disks with the SAME disk signature - the disk signature will be written at mount time."*

and also post #5 in the "Is WinFE Forensically Sound?" thread (by reboot.pro forum member *Wonko the Sane*) -

> *"...Any NT based system, as part of the "mounting" procedure for a volume (please read as "to assign a drive letter to it") needs to identify UNIVOCALLY the disk on which the volume resides AND the volume itself. This identification is made through TWO pieces of data:*
>
> 1. *the disk signature*
> 2. *the Volume PBR offset on that disk..."*

The following information from reboot.pro forum member *joakim* suggests that disk signature creation is linked to the Windows kernel -

> *"...I did some testing yesterday (not with WinFE, but with the 2 special registry entries), and it seems difficult to prevent Windows from writing this 4 byte signature when it's missing. I was tracing it into the kernel and suspect the relevant code is somewhere within IoCreateDisk (look for references to DeviceObject), but was unable to prevent the writing..."* (post #14)
> *...The disk-signature-writing-process is unrelated to any mounting, and will happen regardless of whether any volume on that physical disk is mounted. In the kernel it is referenced to as "UniqueDeviceObjectNumber"...."* (post #16)

Based on this information, disks previously mounted on Windows NT systems will contain an existing disk signature unless it has been manually removed or the MBR has become corrupted. Disks not exposed to Windows NT systems may also contain a disk signature - as an example the following screenshot shows a disk signature on a disk with ubuntu Linux installed (the operating system was installed in a virtual machine and has never been mounted on a Windows NT system) -

Offset	0	1	2	3	4	5	6	7	8	9	A	B	C	D	E	F
000000000	EB	63	90	10	8E	D0	BC	00	B0	B8	00	00	8E	D8	8E	C0
000000010	FB	BE	00	7C	BF	00	06	B9	00	02	F3	A4	EA	21	06	00
000000020	00	BE	BE	07	38	04	75	0B	83	C6	10	81	FE	FE	07	75
000000030	F3	EB	16	B4	02	B0	01	BB	00	7C	B2	80	8A	74	01	8B
000000040	4C	02	CD	13	EA	00	7C	00	00	EB	FE	00	00	00	00	00
000000050	00	00	00	00	00	00	00	00	00	00	00	80	01	00	00	00
000000060	00	00	00	00	FF	FA	90	90	F6	C2	80	74	05	F6	C2	70
000000070	74	02	B2	80	EA	79	7C	00	00	31	C0	8E	D8	8E	D0	BC
000000080	00	20	FB	A0	64	7C	3C	FF	74	02	88	C2	52	BB	17	04
000000090	F6	07	03	74	06	BE	88	7D	E8	17	01	BE	05	7C	B4	41
0000000A0	BB	AA	55	CD	13	5A	52	72	3D	81	FB	55	AA	75	37	83
0000000B0	E1	01	74	32	31	C0	89	44	04	40	88	44	FF	89	44	02
0000000C0	C7	04	10	00	66	8B	1E	5C	7C	66	89	5C	08	66	8B	1E
0000000D0	60	7C	66	89	5C	0C	C7	44	06	00	70	B4	42	CD	13	72
0000000E0	05	BB	00	70	EB	76	B4	08	CD	13	73	0D	5A	84	D2	0F
0000000F0	83	D0	00	BE	93	7D	E9	82	00	66	0F	B6	C6	88	64	FF
000000100	40	66	89	44	04	0F	B6	D1	C1	E2	02	88	E8	88	F4	40
000000110	89	44	08	0F	B6	C2	C0	E8	02	66	89	04	66	A1	60	7C
000000120	66	09	C0	75	4E	66	A1	5C	7C	66	31	D2	66	F7	34	88
000000130	D1	31	D2	66	F7	74	04	3B	44	08	7D	37	FE	C1	88	C5
000000140	30	C0	C1	E8	02	08	C1	88	D0	5A	88	C6	BB	00	70	8E
000000150	C3	31	DB	B8	01	02	CD	13	72	1E	8C	C3	60	1E	B9	00
000000160	01	8E	DB	31	F6	BF	00	80	8E	C6	FC	F3	A5	1F	61	FF
000000170	26	5A	7C	BE	8E	7D	EB	03	BE	9D	7D	E8	34	00	BE	A2
000000180	7D	E8	2E	00	CD	18	EB	FE	47	52	55	42	20	00	47	65
000000190	6F	6D	00	48	61	72	64	20	44	69	73	6B	00	52	65	61
0000001A0	64	00	20	45	72	72	6F	72	0D	0A	00	BB	01	00	B4	0E
0000001B0	CD	10	AC	3C	00	75	F4	C3	76	A1	B0	8D	00	00	80	20
0000001C0	21	00	83	FE	FF	FF	00	08	00	00	00	F0	3F	01	00	00
0000001D0	00	00	00	00	00	00	00	00	00	00	00	00	00	00	00	00
0000001E0	00	00	00	00	00	00	00	00	00	00	00	00	00	00	00	00
0000001F0	00	00	00	00	00	00	00	00	00	00	00	00	00	00	55	AA

Disk 1 test results

Disk 1 - blank/empty disk image with all bytes set as 00.

- SHA1 check - confirms that a SHA1 checksum of the diskimage was taken prior to booting WinFE.
- Disk signature check - LBA sector 0 checked for changes from the running WinFE (visual check of bytes at offset 0x1B8 to 0x1BB using a disk editor). ✗ denotes that a disk signature was written.
- SHA1 recheck - disk image SHA1 checksum tested after running WinFE. ✗ denotes that a disk write occurred.
- Read-only check - check to establish if the disk is write protected when WinFE is running (using a disk editor to attempt to write to LBA sector 0). ✗ denotes that the disk is not write protected.

64-bit WinFE

WinFE version	WinFE source	SHA1 check	Disk signature check	Read-only check	SHA1 recheck
2.1	Vista source 1	✓	✓	✗	✓
3.0 **BIOS**	7 source 2	✓	✓	✗	✓
3.0 **UEFI**	7 source 2	✓	✓	✓	✓
3.1	7 SP1 source 3	✓	✓	✗	✓
4.0	8.0 source 4	✓	✓	✓	✓
5.0	8.1 source 5	✓	✗	✓	✗
5.1	8.1 Update source 6	✓	✗	✓	✗
10.0.10240	1507 source 7	✓	✗	✓	✗
10.0.10586	1511 source 8	✓	✗	✓	✗
10.0.14393	1607 source 9	✓	✗	✓	✗
10.0.15063	1703 source 10	✓	✗	✓	✗
10.0.16299	1709 source 11	✓	✗	✓	✗
10.0.17134	1803 source 12	✓	✗	✓	✗
10.0.17763	1803 source 13	✓	✗	✓	✗
10.0.18362	1909 source 14	✓	✗	✓	✗
10.0.19041	21H2 source 15	✓	✗	✓	✗

32-bit WinFE

WinFE version	WinFE source	SHA1 check	Disk signature check	Read-only check	SHA1 recheck
3.1	7 SP1 source 16	✓	✓	✗	✓
4.0	8 source 17	✓	✓	✓	✓
5.1	8.1 Update source 18	✓	✗	✓	✗
10.0.19041	21H2 source 19	✓	✗	✓	✗

The tables above dispay results from WinFE running on systems with UEFI and BIOS firmware. The majority of the results are identical across BIOS and UEFI, with the exception of WinFE versions highlighted with a background.

Based on these results there is clear evidence that Windows 5.*/10.* versions of WinFE will write a disk signature if the disk MBR contains zero bytes. WinFE 4.0 does not write a disk signature and also write protects the disk. WinFE 2.0 and 3.* do not write a disk signature, however these versions do not write protect internal SATA disks. 64-bit WinFE 3.0 based on Windows 7 source appears to be an anomaly when running on UEFI firmware, as it also adds write protection.

Disk 2 test results

Disk 2 - offset 0x1FE set as 55 AA. All other bytes including the four byte disk signature at offset 0x1B8 to 0x1BB set as 00. This simulates an initialized disk due to the presence of the "magic number" 55 AA in the last two bytes of the MBR.

- SHA1 check - confirms that a SHA1 checksum of the diskimage was taken prior to booting WinFE.
- Disk signature check - LBA sector 0 checked for changes from the running WinFE (visual check of bytes at offset 0x1B8 to 0x1BB using a disk editor). ✗ denotes that a disk signature was written.
- SHA1 recheck - disk image SHA1 checksum tested after running WinFE. ✗ denotes that a disk write occurred.
- Read-only check - check to establish if the disk is write protected when WinFE is running (using a disk editor to attempt to write to LBA sector 0). ✗ denotes that the disk is not write protected.

64-bit WinFE

WinFE version	WinFE source	SHA1 check	Disk signature check	Read-only check	SHA1 recheck
2.1 **BIOS**	Vista source 1	✓	✗	✗	✗
2.1 **UEFI**	Vista source 1	✓	✓	✓	✓
3.0	7 source 2	✓	✗	✗	✗
3.1 **BIOS**	7 SP1 source 3	✓	✗	✗	✗
3.1 **UEFI**	7 SP1 source 3	✓	✓	✓	✓
4.0	8.0 source 4	✓	✓	✓	✓
5.0	8.1 source 5	✓	✓	✓	✓
5.1	8.1 Update source 6	✓	✓	✓	✓
10.0.10240	1507 source 7	✓	✓	✓	✓
10.0.10586	1511 source 8	✓	✓	✓	✓
10.0.14393	1607 source 9	✓	✓	✓	✓
10.0.15063	1703 source 10	✓	✓	✓	✓
10.0.16299	1709 source 11	✓	✓	✓	✓
10.0.17134	1803 source 12	✓	✓	✓	✓
10.0.17763	1803 source 13	✓	✓	✓	✓
10.0.18362	1909 source 14	✓	✓	✓	✓
10.0.19041	21H2 source 15	✓	✓	✓	✓

32-bit WinFE

WinFE version	WinFE source	SHA1 check	Disk signature check	Read-only check	SHA1 recheck
3.1	7 SP1 source 16	✓	✗	✗	✗
4.0	8 source 17	✓	✓	✓	✓
5.1	8.1 Update source 18	✓	✓	✓	✓
10.0.19041	21H2 source 19	✓	✓	✓	✓

The tables above dispay results from WinFE running on systems with UEFI and BIOS firmware. The majority of the results are identical across BIOS and UEFI, with the exception of WinFE versions highlighted with a background.

Based on these results there is clear evidence that WinFE 4.0/5.*/10.* versions of WinFE do not write a disk signature to internal SATA disks if the two bytes at offset 0x1FE to 0x1FF (the last two bytes of the MBR) contain the "magic number" 55 AA. These versions of WinFE also write-protect internal disks, reducing the risk of accidental disk writes in forensic applications.

WinFE 2.1 and 3.* will write a disk signature if the two bytes at offset 0x1FE to 0x1FF (the last two bytes of the MBR) contain the "magic number" 55 AA. These versions of WinFE do not write-protect media - with the possible exceptions of 64-bit WinFE 2.1 and 3.0 (based on Windows Vista and Windows 7 respectively) running on UEFI firmware.

Disk 3 test results

Disk 3 - Windows 98SE boot disk used to create one primary partition spanning the disk. MSDOS FDISK does not write a disk signature at offset 0x1B8 to 0x1BB - the four bytes at this offset are set as 00.

- SHA1 check - confirms that a SHA1 checksum of the diskimage was taken prior to booting WinFE.
- Disk signature check - LBA sector 0 checked for changes from the running WinFE (visual check of bytes at offset 0x1B8 to 0x1BB using a disk editor). ✗ denotes that a disk signature was written.
- SHA1 recheck - disk image SHA1 checksum tested after running WinFE. ✗ denotes that a disk write occurred.
- Read-only check - check to establish if the disk is write protected when WinFE is running (using a disk editor to attempt to write to LBA sector 0). ✗ denotes that the disk is not write protected.

64-bit WinFE

WinFE version	WinFE source	SHA1 check	Disk signature check	Read-only check	SHA1 recheck
2.1	Vista source 1	✓	✗	✗	✗
3.0	7 source 2	✓	✗	✗	✗
3.1	7 SP1 source 3	✓	✗	✗	✗
4.0	8.0 source 4	✓	✓	✓	✓
5.0	8.1 source 5	✓	✓	✓	✓
5.1	8.1 Update source 6	✓	✓	✓	✓
10.0.10240	1507 source 7	✓	✓	✓	✓
10.0.10586	1511 source 8	✓	✓	✓	✓
10.0.14393	1607 source 9	✓	✓	✓	✓
10.0.15063	1703 source 10	✓	✓	✓	✓
10.0.16299	1709 source 11	✓	✓	✓	✓
10.0.17134	1803 source 12	✓	✓	✓	✓
10.0.17763	1803 source 13	✓	✓	✓	✓
10.0.18362	1909 source 14	✓	✓	✓	✓
10.0.19041	21H2 source 15	✓	✓	✓	✓

32-bit WinFE

WinFE version	WinFE source	SHA1 check	Disk signature check	Read-only check	SHA1 recheck
3.1	7 SP1 source 16	✓	✗	✗	✗
4.0	8 source 17	✓	✓	✓	✓
5.1	8.1 Update source 18	✓	✓	✓	✓
10.0.19041	21H2 source 19	✓	✓	✓	✓

The tables above display results from WinFE running on systems with UEFI and BIOS firmware. The results are identical across BIOS and UEFI systems.

Based on these results there is clear evidence that WinFE 4.0/5.*/10.* versions of WinFE do not write a disk signature to internal SATA disks if MSDOS is already installed. These versions of WinFE also write-protect internal disks, reducing the risk of accidental disk writes in forensic applications.

WinFE 2.1 and 3.* will write a disk signature if MSDOS is installed and the disk does not already contain a disk signature. These versions of WinFE do not write-protect media.

Disk 4 test results

Disk 4 - copy of disk 3 with two bytes at offset 0x1FE to 0x1FF written as 00 00 (overwriting the "magic number" 55 AA in the last two bytes of the MBR)

- SHA1 check - confirms that a SHA1 checksum of the disk image was taken prior to booting WinFE.
- Disk signature check - LBA sector 0 checked for changes from the running WinFE (visual check of bytes at offset 0x1B8 to 0x1BB using a disk editor). ✗ denotes that a disk signature was written.
- SHA1 recheck - disk image SHA1 checksum tested after running WinFE. ✗ denotes that a disk write occurred.
- Read-only check - check to establish if the disk is write protected when WinFE is running (using a disk editor to attempt to write to LBA sector 0). ✗ denotes that the disk is not write protected.

64-bit WinFE

WinFE version	WinFE source	SHA1 check	Disk signature check	Read-only check	SHA1 recheck
2.1	Vista source 1	✓	✓	✗	✓
3.0 **UEFI**	7 source 2	✓	✓	✓	✓
3.0 **BIOS**	7 source 2	✓	✓	✗	✓
3.1	7 SP1 source 3	✓	✓	✗	✓
4.0	8.0 source 4	✓	✓	✓	✓
5.0	8.1 source 5	✓	✓	✓	✓
5.1	8.1 Update source 6	✓	✓	✓	✓
10.0.10240	1507 source 7	✓	✓	✓	✓
10.0.10586	1511 source 8	✓	✓	✓	✓
10.0.14393	1607 source 9	✓	✓	✓	✓
10.0.15063	1703 source 10	✓	✓	✓	✓
10.0.16299	1709 source 11	✓	✓	✓	✓
10.0.17134	1803 source 12	✓	✓	✓	✓
10.0.17763	1803 source 13	✓	✓	✓	✓
10.0.18362	1909 source 14	✓	✓	✓	✓
10.0.19041	21H2 source 15	✓	✓	✓	✓

32-bit WinFE

WinFE version	WinFE source	SHA1 check	Disk signature check	Read-only check	SHA1 recheck
3.1	7 SP1 source 16	✓	✓	✗	✓
4.0	8 source 17	✓	✓	✓	✓
5.1	8.1 Update source 18	✓	✓	✓	✓
10.0.19041	21H2 source 19	✓	✓	✓	✓

The tables above display results from WinFE running on systems with UEFI and BIOS firmware. The majority of the results are identical across BIOS and UEFI, with the exception of WinFE versions highlighted with a background.

Based on these results there is clear evidence that WinFE 2.1/3.*/4.0/5.*/10.* versions of WinFE do not write a disk signature to internal SATA disks if MSDOS is already installed and the two bytes at offset 0x1FE to 0x1FF (the last two bytes of the MBR) are set to 00 00 (overwriting the "magic number" (55 AA)))

WinFE 4.0/5.*/10.* will write-protect internal disks, reducing the risk of accidental disk writes in forensic applications. WinFE 2.1 and 3.* do not write-protect media - with the possible exception of 64-bit WinFE 3.0 (based on Windows 7) running on UEFI firmware.

Disk 5 test results

Disk 5 - copy of disk 1 with the addition of an entry in the partition table (offset 0x1BE to 0x1CD). All other bytes set as 00.

- SHA1 check - confirms that a SHA1 checksum of the disk image was taken prior to booting WinFE.
- Disk signature check - LBA sector 0 checked for changes from the running WinFE (visual check of bytes at offset 0x1B8 to 0x1BB using a disk editor). ✗ denotes that a disk signature was written.
- SHA1 recheck - disk image SHA1 checksum tested after running WinFE. ✗ denotes that a disk write occurred.
- Read-only check - check to establish if the disk is write protected when WinFE is running (using a disk editor to attempt to write to LBA sector 0). ✗ denotes that the disk is not write protected.

64-bit WinFE

WinFE version	WinFE source	SHA1 check	Disk signature check	Read-only check	SHA1 recheck
2.1	Vista source 1	✓	✓	✗	✓
3.0 **UEFI**	7 source 2	✓	✓	✓	✓
3.0 **BIOS**	7 source 2	✓	✓	✗	✓
3.1	7 SP1 source 3	✓	✓	✗	✓
4.0	8.0 source 4	✓	✓	✓	✓
5.0	8.1 source 5	✓	✓	✓	✓
5.1	8.1 Update source 6	✓	✓	✓	✓
10.0.10240	1507 source 7	✓	✓	✓	✓
10.0.10586	1511 source 8	✓	✓	✓	✓
10.0.14393	1607 source 9	✓	✓	✓	✓
10.0.15063	1703 source 10	✓	✓	✓	✓
10.0.16299	1709 source 11	✓	✓	✓	✓
10.0.17134	1803 source 12	✓	✓	✓	✓
10.0.17763	1803 source 13	✓	✓	✓	✓
10.0.18362	1909 source 14	✓	✓	✓	✓
10.0.19041	21H2 source 15	✓	✓	✓	✓

32-bit WinFE

WinFE version	WinFE source	SHA1 check	Disk signature check	Read-only check	SHA1 recheck
3.1	7 SP1 source 16	✓	✓	✗	✓
4.0	8 source 17	✓	✓	✓	✓
5.1	8.1 Update source 18	✓	✓	✓	✓
10.0.19041	21H2 source 19	✓	✓	✓	✓

The tables above display results from WinFE running on systems with UEFI and BIOS firmware. The majority of the results are identical across BIOS and UEFI, with the exception of WinFE versions highlighted with a background.

Based on these results there is clear evidence that WinFE 4.0/5.*/10.* versions of WinFE do not write a disk signature to internal SATA disks if it contains an existing entry in the partition table.

WinFE 2.1/3.* do not write a disk signature to internal SATA disks if it contains an existing entry in the partition table and the two bytes at offset 0x1FE to 0x1FF (the last two bytes of the MBR) are set to 00 00 (overwriting the "magic number" (55 AA))).

WinFE 4.0/5.*/10.* will write-protect internal disks, reducing the risk of accidental disk writes in forensic applications. WinFE 2.1 and 3.* do not write-protect media - with the possible exception of 64-bit WinFE 3.0 (based on Windows 7) running on UEFI firmware.

Analysis - WinFE 2.*\3.*

The results when running WinFE on disks 1-5 indicate that WinFE 2.*\3.* does not provide write-protection for internal SATA disks. There are some exceptions when running WinFE on systems with UEFI firmware, however these can potentially be interpreted as anomalies.

Although DiskPart documentation states that it can be used to set disk attributes as read-only, the command failed in practice. The following is output from running DiskPart in WinFE 3.1 and attempting to set disk attributes as read-only (adding write-protection) –

```
Microsoft DiskPart version 6.1.7601
Copyright (C) 1999-2008 Microsoft Corporation.
On computer: WinFE

DISKPART> list disk

  Disk ###  Status         Size     Free     Dyn  Gpt
  --------  -------------  -------  -------  ---  ---
  Disk 0    Online         2048 MB  2048 MB

DISKPART> sel disk 0

Disk 0 is now the selected disk.

DISKPART> detail disk


Disk ID: 00000000
Type   : SATA
Status : Online
Path   : 0
```

```
Target : 0
LUN ID : 0
Location Path : PCIROOT(0)#PCI(1101)#PCI(0300)#ATA(C00T00L00)
Current Read-only State : No
Read-only  : No
Boot Disk  : No
Pagefile Disk  : No
Hibernation File Disk  : No
Crashdump Disk  : No
Clustered Disk  : No

There are no volumes

DISKPART> attribute disk
Current Read-only State : No
Read-only  : No
Boot Disk  : No
Pagefile Disk  : No
Hibernation File Disk  : No
Crashdump Disk  : No
Clustered Disk  : No

DISKPART> attribute disk set readonly

DiskPart failed to set disk attributes.
```

It is possible to set the *READONLY* attribute using third party tools including *Colin Ramsden's write-protect* and *Erwan Labalec's DiskMgr*, however this cannot prevent the writing of a disk signature as this appears to occur earlier in the boot process.

The following screenshot shows output following an attempt to write to LBA sector 0 (using a disk editor) after using *DiskMgr* to change disk attributes, and demonstrates write protection having been applied –

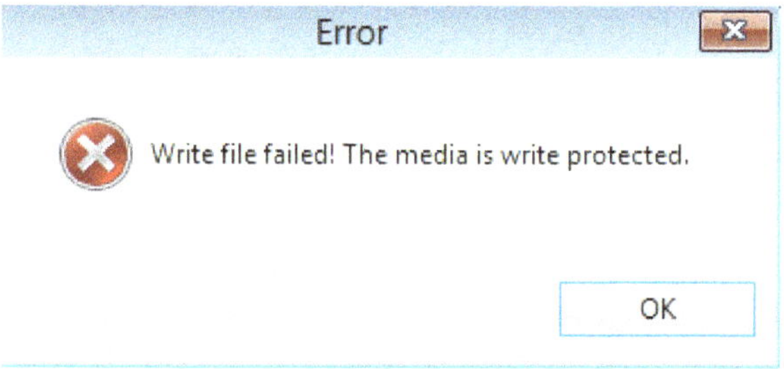

Output from using the command-line to attempt to write to the disk (with an existing volume mounted as C:\)

```
Microsoft Windows [Version 7.1.7601]

C:\>echo WinFE write protection test > WinFE_Test.txt
```

```
The media is write protected
```

Results from previous tests indicate that although it is not possible to use Diskpart to change the disk attributes to *READONLY*, it is possible to change volume attributes. It is well documented that changing volume attributes will perform a write to the disk.

Results from previous tests also indicate that mounting a drive and viewing its contents (e.g. in a file manager or at the command line using the dir command) resulted in the disk image files MD5 checksum changing - indicating that a write had been performed. This change occurred when navigating the directory structure, without attempting to carry out any writes to the disk. It is possible to prevent disk writes using third party tools to set disk attributes as read-only prior to running any applications.

To summarise, when using WinFE versions 2.*/3.* there is no way to prevent these versions of WinFE from writing to a disk if it does not already contain a disk signature. The abscence of the bytes 55 AA (the "magic number" at offset 0x1FE to 0x1FF in the last two bytes of the MBR) appears to mitigate against a disk signature being written in WinFE 2.1/3.*, however it is unlikely that these bytes will be missing on any disks containing a partition irrespective of the operating system used to prepare/partition the disk.

Analysis - WinFE 4.0

WinFE 4.0 is the only version of WinFE that passed all tests undertaken in this research. Results were consistent across 32-bit and 64-bit versions of WinFE, on systems using BIOS and UEFI firmware. Internal SATA disks were write protected early in the boot process and a disk signature was not written under any of the conditions likely to be encountered in normal operations, including -

- MBR containing 00 bytes
- Magic number (55 AA) present at offset 0x1FE to 0x1FF
- Absence of magic number (55 AA) at offset 0x1FE to 0x1FF
- Entry in MBR partition table

Analysis - 5.*\10.*

These versions of WinFE passed the majority of tests undertaken in this research. Results were consistent across 32-bit and 64-bit versions of WinFE, on systems using BIOS and UEFI firmware. Internal SATA disks were write protected early in the boot process and a disk signature was not written under any of the conditions likely to be encountered in normal operations, including -

- Magic number (55 AA) present at offset 0x1FE to 0x1FF
- Absence of magic number (55 AA) at offset 0x1FE to 0x1FF
- Entry in MBR partition table

The only instance in which a disk signature was written was during tests using disk 1, a disk with the MBR containing 00 bytes. It is unlikely that this condition will be encountered on any disks containing a partition irrespective of the operating system used to prepare/partition the disk.

Conclusion\Recommendations

Disks previously mounted on Windows NT systems will contain an existing disk signature unless it has been manually removed or the MBR has become corrupted. Other operating systems may also write a disk signature. Based on limited anecdotal evidence there appears to be some instances of WinFE writing to disks in Forensic applications, creating a disk signature if this information is missing. Assuming the disk writes are limited to disk signature creation, circumstances in which this will occur appear to be negligible.

Based on the results of the tests undertaken during this research, WinPE 4.0, 5.x or 10.x sources with **SanPolicy** set as **3** are recommended. Based on the results these versions appears to provide robust write protection, in particular against writes to bytes at offset 0x1B8 to 0x1BB (disk signature). As indicated by the results from the tests, WinFE 5.x and 10.x did write a disk signature when the MBR was empty. This condition is highly unlikely to be met in real use.

Use of earlier versions of WinPE (2.x/3.x) is discouraged. When using these versions there is no way to prevent writing a disk signature. The abscence of the bytes 55 AA (the "magic number" at offset 0x1FE to 0x1FF in the last two bytes of the MBR) appears to mitigate against a disk signature being written in WinFE 2.1/3.*, however it is unlikely that these bytes will be missing on any disks containing a partition irrespective of the operating system used to prepare/partition the disk. If WinFE 2.x/3.x is required, then the disk should be flagged as read-only as early as possible. Without adding write protection the act of mounting a drive and navigating the file\folder structure is likely to write to the disk.

Warning - it is possible with all versions of WinFE to manually override protection. Use caution.

Limitations

The tests were limited to a virtual environment and WinFE may function differently on physical hardware.

The majority of test were completed using 64-bit versions of WinFE. A much smaller subset of WinFE versions were used when testing 32-bit systems.

The WinFE versions used in tests were modified *boot.wim* files from Windows Installation Media with the WinFE registry settings applied. They were not created using the Windows Automated Installation Kit (WAIK) or the Windows Assessment and Deployment Kit (ADK). WAIK or ADK builds of WinFE can contain different combinations of optional *"Packages"* which *might* affect usage.

WinFE Source files

The tables below shows more detailed information about the sources used in the tests. The *Mini-WinFE* project was used to modify boot.wim from these source files, applying the registry edits documented in the *Registry Changes* section of this page.
64-bit sources -

Source	WinPE version	ISO name SHA1
source 1 Vista SP1	2.1	en_windows_vista_with_service_pack_1_x64_dvd_x14-29595.iso SHA1: bdadc46a263a7bf67eb38609770e4fdbd05247cb
source 2 Win 7	3.0	en_windows_7_home_premium_x64_dvd_x15-65733.iso SHA1: 336779ea6b65f63e11a609b4d021439c47ab315b
source 3 Win 7 SP1	3.1	en_windows_7_enterprise_with_sp1_x64_dvd_u_677651.iso SHA1: a491f985dccfb5863f31b728dddbedb2ff4df8d1
source 4 Win 8	5.0	en_windows_8_x64_dvd_915440.iso SHA1: 1ce53ad5f60419cf04a715cf3233f247e48beec4
source 5 Win 8.1	5.0	en_windows_8_1_x64_dvd_2707217.iso SHA1: bc2f7ff5c91c9f0f8676e39e703085c65072139b
source 6 8.1 Update	5.1	en_windows_8.1_enterprise_with_update_x64_dvd_6054382.iso SHA1: b7dd748446d89b9449a160cdc24bd282989bbd96
source 7 1507	10.0.10240	en-gb_windows_10_enterprise_2015_ltsb_x64_dvd_6848456.iso SHA1: 6476e33d7f50e66a53b347db7a3aa953516ac8a0
source 8 1511	10.0.10586	en_windows_10_multiple_editions_version_1511_updated_apr_2016_x64_dvd_8705583.iso SHA1: 1b247b5b348e78c9bc3afd3c1cbe10cee3d1b9d5
source 9 1607	10.0.14393	en_windows_10_enterprise_2016_ltsb_x64_dvd_9059483.iso SHA1: 031ed6acdc47b8f582c781b039f501d83997a1cf
source 10 1703	10.0.15063	en_windows_10_multiple_editions_version_1703_updated_march_2017_x64_dvd_10189288.iso SHA1:

		ce8005a659e8df7fe9b080352cb1c313c3e9adce
source 11 1709	10.0.16299	en_windows_10_multi-edition_vl_version_1709_updated_dec_2017_x64_dvd_100406172.iso SHA1: 1851a0007321fa084145ea24b8d30bf7a72bf1c6
source 12 1803	10.0.17134	en_windows_10_consumer_editions_version_1803_updated_march_2018_x64_dvd_12063379.iso SHA1: 08fbb24627fa768f869c09f44c5d6c1e53a57a6f
source 13 1809	10.0.17763	en_windows_10_enterprise_ltsc_2019_x64_dvd_be3c8ffb.iso SHA1: d5b2f95e3dd658517fe7c14df4f36de633ca4845
source 14 1909	10.0.18362	en_windows_10_business_editions_version_1909_updated_aug_2020_x64_dvd_f291e1db.iso SHA1: d2a857f5950f173f651334d6a5aae2e7f4a76b06
source 15 21H2	10.0.19041	us_windows_10_enterprise_ltsc_2021_x64_dvd_d289cf96.iso SHA1: 2fb2897373c4f71b06f4490943b3d564b0f0fd6d

32-bit sources -

Source	**WinPE version**	**ISO name SHA1**
source 16 Win 7 SP1	3.1	en_windows_7_enterprise_with_sp1_x86_dvd_u_677710.iso SHA1: 4e0450ac73ab6f9f755eb422990cd9c7a1f3509c
source 17 Win 8	4.0	en_windows_8_enterprise_x86_dvd_917587.iso SHA1: fefce3e64fb9ec1cc7977165328890ccc9a10656
source 18 8.1 Update	5.1	en_windows_8.1_enterprise_with_update_x86_dvd_6050710.iso SHA1: 584a9ad7e2bb3d7e189adcfba44a497cc9155937
source 19 21H2	10.0.19041	en-us_windows_10_enterprise_ltsc_2021_x86_dvd_9f4aa95f.iso SHA1: 3f7f38802043aa55ebe930655ee35be876213e4d

Download/Links

Mini-WinFE GitHub repositories -

- *main Branch* - forensic focus with a number of applications that could potentially perform disk writes removed.
- *WinFE Branch* - includes more applications and options - use with caution as it is possible to use settings that will **not** write protect disks.

Project *GitHub* page -

- **1** - *Branch* button - use to toggle between *main* or *WinPE* branches.
- **2** - *Code* button - use to download the selected branch.

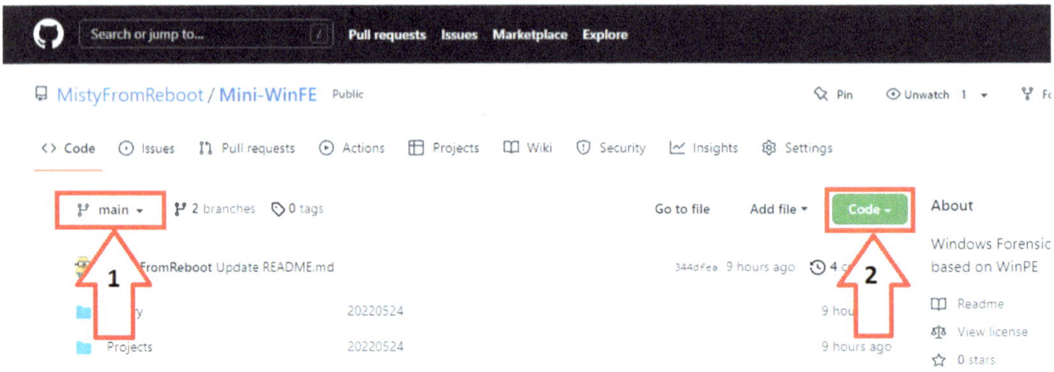

Detail when selecting the *Branch* button. Click on one of the listed branches (currently *main* or *WinPE*)-

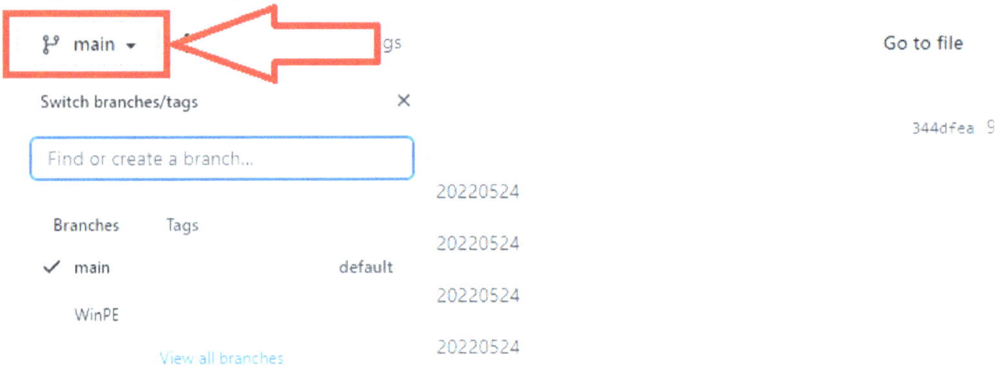

Detail when selecting the *Code* button. Click on *Download ZIP* to download the selected *Branch* -

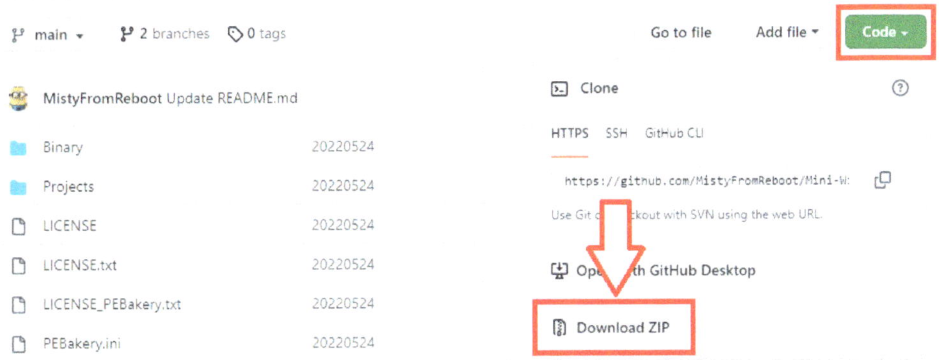

Alternative Download Link

The latest builds can be downloaded from the mistyprojects.co.uk site -

- *main* branch
- *WinPE* branch

Differences between Main and WinPE

The *WinPE* branch has some additions to the *main* branch. The following project scripts are included in *WinPE* -

- Project\WinFE\Applications\Diskmgmt.script
- Project\WinFE\Applications\JkDefrag.script
- Project\WinFE\Applications\sDelete.script
- Project\WinFE\Applications\Snapshot.script
- Project\WinFE\Applications\Tinyhexer.script
- Project\WinFE\FinaliseSubst.script

The following folders are included in the *WinPE* branch program cache (Projects\Cache\Programs\) -

- \Bootsect
- \Diskmgmt
- \JKDefrag
- \sDelete
- \Tinyhexer

Differences in Project\WinFE\Finalise\winfe.script, which effectively force the use of forensic settings in the *main* branch as *SANPolicy* can only be set as 3 or 4, *NoAutoMount* cannot be disabled and *DiskMgr/Protect.exe* running at startup cannot be disabled -

WinPE branch (lines 24-32)

```
24 pScrollBox3=1,1,4,20,140,80,20,1,3,4
25 pTextLabel3="2] SAN Policy",1,1,213,140,90,18,8,Bold
26 pButton3=HELP,1,8,430,140,70,20,HELP.3,0,True,_HELP.3_,True
27 pBevel4=,1,12,10,190,500,40
28 pScrollBox4=,1,4,20,200,80,20,,ENABLED
29 pTextLabel4="3] NoAutoMount",1,1,205,200,117,21,8,Bold
30 pButton4=HELP,1,8,430,200,70,20,HELP.4,0,True,_HELP.4_,True
31 pBevel5=,1,12,10,250,500,40
32 pScrollBox5=NO,1,4,20,260,80,20,YES,NO
```

main branch (lines 24-32)

```
24 pScrollBox3=3,1,4,20,140,80,20,3,4
25 pTextLabel3="2] SAN Policy",1,1,213,140,90,18,8,Bold
```

```
pButton3=HELP,1,8,430,140,70,20,HELP.3,0,True,_HELP.3_,True
pBevel4=,1,12,10,190,500,40
pScrollBox4=ENABLED,1,4,20,200,80,20,ENABLED
pTextLabel4="3] NoAutoMount",1,1,205,200,117,21,8,Bold
pButton4=HELP,1,8,430,200,70,20,HELP.4,0,True,_HELP.4_,True
pBevel5=,1,12,10,250,500,40
pScrollBox5=YES,1,4,20,260,80,20,YES
```

Differences in Project\WinFE\Settings\Recommended.script, which removes BootSect from the *main* branch -

WinPE branch (lines 16-20)

```
16 pCheckBox1="1] BootSect",1,3,40,80,180,18,True
17 pCheckBox2="2] CMD Here",1,3,40,110,180,18,True
18 pCheckBox3="3] Keyboard Layout",1,3,40,140,180,18,True
19 pCheckBox4="4] ScreenRes",1,3,40,170,180,18,True
20 pButton1=?,1,8,10,80,18,18,?option1,0,True,_?option1_,True
```

main branch (lines 16-20)

```
16 //
17 pCheckBox2="2] CMD Here",1,3,40,110,180,18,True
18 pCheckBox3="3] Keyboard Layout",1,3,40,140,180,18,True
19 pCheckBox4="4] ScreenRes",1,3,40,170,180,18,True
20 //
```

Differences in Project\WinFE\Settings\wallpaper.script, which changes the default wallpaper -

WinPE branch (lines 25-27)

```
25 Filecopy,"%Cache%\Programs\Wallpaper\winpe.jpg","%TargetDir%\Programs\WinXShell\wallpaper.jpg"
26 End
27 Else,Filecopy,"%Cache%\Programs\Wallpaper\winpe.jpg","%Target_System32%\winpe.jpg"
```

main branch (lines 25-27)

```
25 Filecopy,"%Cache%\Programs\Wallpaper\winfe.jpg","%TargetDir%\Programs\WinXShell\wallpaper.jpg"
26 End
27 Else,Filecopy,"%Cache%\Programs\Wallpaper\winfe.jpg","%Target_System32%\winpe.jpg"
```

Acknowledgements

Many thanks to the following people, without whom this project would not have happened -

- **synchronicity** - *wimlib* developer. This project has been made possible by the release of this fantastic utility.
- **Erwan Labalec** - (aka *Erwan.l*) *offlinereg* and *DiskMgr* developer.
- **Peter Lerup** - author of *LaunchBar*. This utility is redistributed with his permission.
- **ChrisR** - contributor to the PESE projects. This project has been named after *ChrisR* in honour of the significant contribution he has made to the *WinPE* community.
- **JFX** - contributor to the PESE projects and developer of *GetWAIKTools*.
- **Nuno Brito** - creator of *WinBuilder* and all round nice guy. Board Administrator of the reboot.pro forum.
- **slore** - *WinXShell* developer.
- **Hajin Jang** (aka *ied206* and *joveler*) - creator of *PEBakery* build engine.
- Thanks also to the authors/developers behind all of the other utilities and programs used in this project. As their licences generously allow redistribution I have not had to contact them individually.

And a special thanks to the PEBakery Team members. This includes (in no particular order) - *Hajin Jang*, *Atari800XL*, *alacran (Taviruni)*, *homes32* and *Misty*.

Training Resources

WinFE was initially released only to law enforcement and a few persons outside of law enforcement in 2008. Since then, the only formal training available has generally been only available to law enforcement or law enforcement-related associations. This has not prevented examiners outside of law enforcement from self-learning or using WinFE, but it does present an issue of having a lack of documented training in WinFE.

Perhaps the most glaring issue in not having documented training in WinFE is when using WinFE as a qualification in job applications, resumes, or court testimony as there isn't anything to show for training (unless you have access to law enforcement-only WinFE training).

Colleges and universities have included introductions to WinFE, particularly when WinFE is noted in forensic textbooks like the *Guide to Computer Forensics and Investigations* by Bill Nelson (2009, 2014). Multiple bloggers have detailed creating various types of WinFE builds, mostly the early, command line builds.

For those with access to law enforcement training, providers include the Federal Law Enforcement Training Center (FLETC), SEARCH, International Association of Chiefs of Police (IACP), Internet Crimes Against Children (ICAC), and others. Several associations have provided presentations on WinFE, such as those from the High Tech Crime Investigators Association (HTCIA) and the Computer Technology Investigators Network (CTIN). I've been fortunate enough to have been a presenter on WinFE at several of these associations over the years.

One thing that I have noticed on more than a few occasions has been watching instruction via online videos and a conference, in which the WinFE was incorrectly built. The incorrect builds turned out to be a Win**PE**, not a Win**FE**, simply by inadvertently not making changes in the registry. Although in these instances it was clear the instructors weren't aware of the mistake, I don't know if everyone watching also didn't know. This is an important mistake that can affect many!

The importance of knowing the proper use of WinFE cannot be overstated, since WinFE collects the initial evidence! The entire chain of custody typically will start at collection and misusing a collection tool affects the entire validity of evidence. Having comprehensive training in WinFE lessens the risk of ineffectively collecting evidence.

Bibliography

Autopsy (Sleuthkit) . http://sleuthkit.org/index.php

Cowen, David, director. *Adding WinFE to XBoot. Adding WinFE to XBoot*, YouTube, 25 Feb. 2014, www.youtube.com/watch?v=Ce9eQ0OG2jA.

Cowen, David. *Computer Forensics: InfoSec Pro Guide*. McGraw-Hill, 2013.

"Forensic Incident Response." *Windows Forensic Environment*, 16 Aug. 2008, www.forensicir.blogspot.com/2008/08/windows-forensic-environment.html

"Forensics from the Sausage Factory." *Windows FE*, 4 Jul. 2008, www.forensicsfromthesausagefactory.blogspot.com/2008/07/windows-fe.html.

FTK Imager (Accessdata). http://www.accessdata.com

Muir, Brent. "WinFE: The (Almost) Perfect Triage Tool." *WinFE: The (Almost) Perfect Triage Tool*, 11 Aug. 2014, www.slideshare.net/bsmuir/winfe-the-almost-perfect-triage-tool.

"Mini-WinFE Boot CDs and USB Drives." *Guide to Computer Forensics and Investigations*, by Nelson Nelson and Steuart Enfinger, Cengage, 2009, pp. 96–96.

Misty. "WinFE" *Windows Forensic Environment*, http://www.mistyprojects.co.uk/documents/WinFE/winfe.htm#about.

"The Ultimate Collection Kit." *Integriography: A Journal of Broken Locks, Ethics, and Computer Forensics*, 2011, www.integriography.wordpress.com/2011/04/30/the-ultimate-collection-kit/.

Troy Larson. How to Build Windows FE (Forensic Environment) with the Windows Preinstallation Environment 2.1, 03-2008

"Windows Forensic Environment On-Scene Triage." *SEARCH*, www.search.org/get-help/training/high-tech-crime-investigations/instructor-led-training/windows-forensic-environment/.

"WinFE: Windows Bootable Forensic CD." *Dark Reading*, www.darkreading.com/risk/winfe-windows-bootable-forensic-cd/d/d-id/1130430.

"WinFE 10. *Colin Ramsden*, http://www.winfe.net

Valca, Claus. "Windows FE – Details Teased out of the Web." *Windows FE – Details Teased out of the Web*, 14 Feb. 2009, http://www.grandstreamdreams.blogspot.com/2009/02/windows-fe-details-teased-out-of-web.html.

X-Ways Forensics, http://www.x-ways.net

ABOUT THE AUTHOR

Brett Shavers has been in the digital forensics field since the early 2000s. First entering "computer" forensics as a law enforcement detective to eventually moving into the private sector as a consultant, speaker, trainer, and author.

Brett has authored *Placing the Suspect Behind the Keyboard, X-Ways Forensics Practitioner's Guide* (First and Second Editions), *Hiding Behind the Keyboard* (with John Bair), and *Ultimate DFIR Cheats! X-Ways Forensics.* Brett has trained hundreds of law enforcement officers, deputies, and special agents in criminal investigative methods, open source intelligence gathering, digital forensics, and police tactics on several continents.

www.ingramcontent.com/pod-product-compliance
Lightning Source LLC
LaVergne TN
LVHW081341050326
832903LV00024B/1253
* 9 7 9 8 3 9 8 6 2 4 2 6 7 *